BATEK NEGRITO RELIGION

Frontispiece. A Batek man holding a white-handed gibbon which he has killed with his blowpipe. The Negrito thunder-god is often pictured as looking like a gibbon, possibly because the booming cry of the gibbons recalls to mind the rumble of thunder.

BATEK NEGRITO RELIGION

THE WORLD-VIEW AND RITUALS OF A HUNTING AND GATHERING PEOPLE OF PENINSULAR MALAYSIA

KIRK ENDICOTT

CLARENDON PRESS · OXFORD

1979

Oxford University Press, Walton Street, Oxford OX2 6DP

OXFORD LONDON GLASGOW
NEW YORK TORONTO MELBOURNE WELLINGTON
IBADAN NAIROBI DAR ES SALAAM LUSAKA CAPE TOWN
KUALA LUMPUR SINGAPORE JAKARTA HONG KONG TOKYO
DELHI BOMBAY CALCUTTA MADRAS KARACHI

*Published in the United States
by Oxford University Press,
New York*

British Library Cataloguing in Publication Data

Endicott, Kirk Michael
  Batek Negrito religion.
    1. Batek (Malayan people) – Religion
  I. Title
  301.5′8   BL2082.M/   79–40385
  ISBN 0–19–823197–0

*Printed and bound in Great Britain by
Morrison & Gibb Ltd., London and Edinburgh*

To my daughter Britt
with love

PREFACE

The Batek Negritos of Peninsular Malaysia are one of the few remaining nomadic hunting-gathering peoples in South-East Asia. They have maintained their ancient way of life not by merely resisting the forces of change, but by adapting to them and sometimes even taking advantage of them to reinforce their traditional mode of existence. Their way of life is in some respects a difficult and hazardous one, but it preserves the independence and freedom of movement which they value far more than material possessions or physical comforts. The Batek face the difficulties of their life with optimism and irrepressible good humour. Hardly a day goes by in a camp without spontaneous outbursts of singing and laughing, and even the older men and women decorate themselves with flowers and sweet-smelling leaves as they go about their daily tasks. The ultimate source of their remarkable vitality and optimism can be found in their religion—their cultural beliefs about the world and their place in it. These beliefs give meaning and value to their lives and reassure them that the way they live is right for them and is in harmony with the forces of nature. This monograph is a description and analysis of the basic assumptions, ideas, and values that give shape to Batek culture.

I first became interested in the Malaysian Negritos in 1967 at the suggestion of Rodney Needham, my supervisor at Oxford, and Geoffrey Benjamin, who was then writing a doctoral thesis at Cambridge on the Temiar aborigines of Peninsular Malaysia. They thought (as Robert Dentan also wrote to me) that there was an especially urgent need for fieldwork to be done among the Negritos before they gave up their traditional way of life. No major research had been done on the Malaysian Negritos since that of I. H. N. Evans and Fr. Paul Schebesta in the 1920s. Geoffrey Benjamin suggested that the most promising group to study might well be the Batek of Kelantan. Not only were they a fairly large (by Negrito standards) and flourishing group, but they had never been subject to extended anthropological study. And while most of the other Negrito groups had become settled to a considerable extent, the Batek continued to be nomadic and to live by hunting and gathering. It seemed, then, that by going to the Batek I would help to fill a serious gap in the ethnographic record of the Malaysian Negritos and would also be able to study the workings of a Negrito religion in the context of their traditional economic and social systems. There has been a good deal of anthropological interest in hunting-gathering peoples in recent years, but most of it has centred on their economic and social adaptations to their environments (see e.g. Lee and DeVore (eds.), *Man the Hunter* (1968)). With a few exceptions (e.g. Turnbull on the Mbuti Pygmies 1961, 1965), the studies have paid little attention to the ideas, values, and attitudes which are broadly speaking religious and which mediate between the people and the perceived environment. There is a need, I think, for studying the religions of hunting-gathering peoples as a means of discovering the world-view in terms of which the economic choices and decisions are made, including the choice of that way of life in the first place. This was what I set out to do among the Batek, and the choice of that group proved to be a very fortunate one indeed.

A considerable amount of information about the Malaysian Negritos has been published over the years, ranging from the casual and often misleading reports of travellers, adventurers, and administrators to the sophisticated observations of Evans and Schebesta. Yet almost all of the previous research has been done on the western Negritos (called Semang in the older literature) and, of the small amount that concerns the eastern Negritos (the so-called Pangan), practically nothing of any value has appeared in print regarding the Batek of Kelantan. This neglect of the Kelantan Batek by anthropologists is somewhat surprising, for they were one of the earlier Negrito groups to be visited by European observers. Miklucho-Maclay, a Russian ethnographer-explorer, went into the upper Lebir and Aring Rivers (from the Tembeling River in Pahang) in 1875 on an expedition intended to survey the 'Melanesian tribes' of the Malay Peninsula. He collected a short vocabulary in Ulu Kelantan which is at least partially Batek Dè', the dialect of the group with which I spent most of my time (Miklucho-Maclay 1878: 44). Clifford collected two vocabularies on the upper Lebir in 1894, during an expedition to punish the 'Pahang rebels' (the Malays who resisted the British intervention in Pahang), which also appear to be Batek Dè' (see 'Kerbat' and 'Lebir' vocabularies in Skeat and Blagden 1906b: 509–764 *passim*). Unfortunately, neither of these writers recorded any other details about the people from whom the word-lists were obtained. In 1900, Skeat's 'Cambridge Expedition of 1899–1900' passed through the Lebir-Aring area and took down two more lists of Batek Dè' words (see 'Pang. K. Aring' and 'Pang. U. Aring' vocabularies in Skeat and Blagden 1906b: 509–764 *passim*). However, Skeat's ethnographic information on the people, as recorded in *Pagan Races of the Malay Peninsula* (1906a, 1906b), was exceedingly scanty. After a gap of fifty years, government contact was established with the Batek in the mid-1950s by the newly formed Department of Aboriginal Affairs (Jabatan Hal Ehwal Orang Asli; hereafter abbreviated as 'J.O.A.'). Not until 1970, however, when Geoffrey Benjamin made a brief visit to them, were the Batek subjected to serious study from an anthropological point of view. Dr. Benjamin's notes on the language and other aspects of Batek culture, including their religion, were kindly made available to me before I started my fieldwork in 1971, and they were of very great value.

My own fieldwork was carried out mostly between January 1971 and May 1972. A further month of research was done in April 1973 and five more months between September 1975 and June 1976. I spent a total of about seventeen months in the forest, all but three weeks of that being with the Batek Dè' and Batek Teh of the Lebir, Aring, and Relai Rivers in Kelantan. About a week each was spent with the Mendriq of the Nenggiri River, Kelantan, and the Batek 'Iga' and Batek Nòng in Pahang. My enquiries were made in a mixture of Malay, of which I had a rudimentary knowledge when I began, and Batek Dè', which I studied as I went along. By the end of my stay with the Batek Dè' I was able to converse mainly in their own language, though falling back at times on Malay, in which they are fluent. For the first two months of my fieldwork I stayed in a cabin at Post Lebir which was provided by the J.O.A. During most of the rest of the time, however, I lived in forest camps in a small tent. Although the Batek are nomadic, I was usually able, by keeping my equipment to a minimum and by employing Batek as bearers, to move with a group or to join another camp whenever a shift in location became necessary. I worked alone during my earlier fieldwork, but was joined in my most recent trip by my wife, Karen Lampell Endicott. I found the Batek to be extremely open and friendly, and they readily accepted me into their camps and shelters and treated me as a friend. I was never put in a position in which I had to pay for information, though I happily paid wages whenever anyone did any work for me, and I gave them tobacco and

occasionally small amounts of food as partial compensation for the
inconvenience of having me prying into their lives.

My initial fieldwork was made possible by a pre-doctoral fellow-
ship (no. 7F01 MH 33054–01A2) and research grant from the
National Institute of Mental Health, a division of the National
Institutes of Health (U.S.A.). Subsequent field trips were financed
by faculty research grants from the University of Malaya and The
Australian National University. I am extremely grateful to these
institutions and to the many individuals who supported my
applications for funds.

The original draft of this book was written as a D.Phil. thesis for
the University of Oxford under the supervision of Professor Rodney
Needham. Whatever merit the book may have is due largely to his
patient guidance and criticism. I am very grateful for this and for
the continuous moral support he has given me through the years,
without which I might never have done this study. I wish to thank
my other teachers as well, especially Evon Vogt and James Fox at
Harvard, for contributing greatly to my understanding of non-
western religions. I also thank my colleagues at The Australian
National University and my many other anthropologist friends who
helped me to understand my data. I have received many useful
comments on the original thesis from Godfrey Lienhardt, Stephen
Morris, Geoffrey Benjamin, Robert Barnes, and A. Thomas Kirsch,
as well as from Professor Needham; I am extremely grateful for their
time and trouble. I give special thanks to Dr. Benjamin who has
been a constant source of help, information, and ideas ever since we
first met in 1967.

I am indebted to a great number of individuals and agencies in
Malaysia, but can name only a few of them here. The research was
done with the kind permission and in many instances the direct
assistance of the Jabatan Hal Ehwal Orang Asli. I thank all the
members of the department and in particular Dr. Baharon Azhar
Raffie'i (the Director-General), Encik Jimin Idris (the Deputy
Director-General), Encik Mohd. Ruslan Abdullah, Encik Osman
Idris, Encik Ahmad Khamis, Encik Mohd. Tap Salleh, Encik Nik
Hassan, Encik Abd. Ghani Abdullah, Encik Mahmood Mohamed,
Dr. Malcolm Bolton, and Dr. Peter Schindler, all of whom went out
of their way to help me. Encik Shahrum Yub, the Director-General
of the National Museum, and his staff were unfailing in assistance
with my practical problems. Mr. Raymond Phillips and Dr. Ben-

jamin Stone and his colleagues at the Department of Botany, University of Malaya, made great efforts to identify the many plants used by the Batek. In Kelantan I had the help of Mr. Wong Chew Meow in finding supplies in Kuala Krai and of Encik Jaafar Abdul Rahman, the former school teacher at Post Lebir, in making my initial adjustment to life in the field. I am also grateful for the hospitality of Brian Lunn, Jack and Louise Shively, and Nordin Ariffin and Halimah Ab. Rahman in Kelantan; and Ken and Dalia Connell, Hood Mohd. Salleh and Maherani Mohd. Ishak, Ben and Michiko Stone, and Peter and Jan Schindler in Kuala Lumpur. Mr. Howard Biles, the former Protector of Aborigines in Pahang and Kelantan, was good enough to give me information on earlier conditions among the Batek of those two states.

I am extremely indebted to my wife Karen, who was a constant source of help and encouragement both in the field, while she was carrying out important research of her own, and in the writing up of the results of my studies. I also give my most heart-felt thanks to the Batek and Mendriq who so generously accepted me into their lives. I made especially heavy demands on Penghulu Selé', my chief informant on the religion of the Aring River Batek; Keladi, my assistant while with the Batek Teh; and Tanyong and Langsat, our close friends and 'guardians' on the upper Lebir. I could never repay the many kindnesses of the Batek, but I can only hope that this monograph, by faithfully recording the basic tenets of their religion, may be of some interest and value to future, educated generations of Batek.

CONTENTS

1. INTRODUCTION   1
   The People   1
   Environment   6
   Social Organization   9
   Economy   11
   A Typical Day in a Batek Forest Camp   15
   The Nature of Batek Religion   22
   The Present Study   26

2. COSMOS   33
   The Earth   33
   The Sky and Firmament   36
   The Sun   38
   The Moon   39
   The Stars   41
   Stone Pillars   42
   The Afterworld   49
   Orientation of the Cosmos   50
   Summary   51

3. MAN AND ENVIRONMENT   53
   Batek Attitudes toward the Forest   53
   The Forest as a Source of Food   54
   The Forest as a Source of Danger   67
   Conclusions   82

4. HUMAN BEINGS   83
   The Origin of Human Beings   83
   The Separation of the Races   86
   The Components of Human Beings   88
   Birth   98
   Disease and Curing   102
   Death and Burial   110

5. SUPERHUMAN BEINGS — 124
   Hala' 'Asal — 124
   Shamans — 128
   Communication with the Superhuman Beings — 141

6. DEITIES: DESCRIPTION — 161
   Deities of the Batek Dè' — 163
   Celestial Deities of Other Groups — 173
   Earth Deities of Other Groups — 184
   Tohan — 189
   Other Beings — 189

7. DEITIES: INTERPRETATION — 191
   Previous Researchers — 191
   Reinterpretation — 198
   Batek Dè' Deities in Perspective — 214

8. CONCLUSIONS — 216
   Batek Religion and the Batek World — 216
   Batek Religion and the Religion of Ancient Man — 220

   BIBLIOGRAPHY — 223
   INDEX — 227

   MAPS
1. The Batek Area — 4
2. Locations of Negrito Dialect Groups — 178

ORTHOGRAPHY

In the spelling system used here, each symbol represents a single phoneme except for 'ng' where the two letters together represent one phoneme. In the following list I give the approximate British English values of the vowels and a few of the consonants (the standard linguistic symbols are given in brackets).

a—[a]   pronounced like 'a' in 'hat'
e—[ə]   pronounced like 'a' in 'above'
é—[e]   pronounced like 'a' in 'way' (but without the i-offglide)
è—[ɛ]   pronounced like 'e' in 'desk'
i—[i]   pronounced like 'ea' in 'beat'
o—[o]   pronounced like 'o' in 'vote'
ò—[ɔ]   pronounced like 'o' in 'hot'
u—[u]   pronounced like 'oo' in 'boot'
ü—[ʉ]   pronounced like 'ü' in German 'Hütte'
c—[č]   pronounced like 'ch' in 'church' (but with the blade of the tongue)
ng—[ŋ] pronounced like 'ng' in 'singer' (but 'gn' in terminal position)
ñ—[ɲ]   pronounced like 'ny' in 'banyan'
'—[ʔ]   glottal stop, pronounced like 't' in Cockney 'battle'

A hook (,) under a vowel indicates phonemic nasality. Stress in Batek words falls on the final syllable, even in words borrowed from Malay.

Malay words are spelt according to the 'new orthography' (*ejaan baharu*), which was officially adopted by the governments of Malaysia and Indonesia in 1973, except in direct quotations from older sources.

I

INTRODUCTION

The People

The Malaysian Negritos[1] are members of an apparently ancient and once widespread race which is now represented in relatively pure form only in the Andaman Islands off the coast of Burma, in isolated pockets in the Philippines, in the northern half of the Malay Peninsula (Peninsular Malaysia), and in the extreme southern part of Thailand. They are characterized as 'Pygmies' by some writers and indeed they are smaller on the whole than the other peoples of these areas, though they are muscular and well-proportioned. Their most distinctive feature is their curly, sometimes woolly, hair, a type which is very rare among the Mongoloid populations of the region except for the neighbouring Temiar who have undoubtedly mixed with the Negritos in the past. Typically their skin is dark brown but not black, and their faces are roundish with broad, flat noses and rather receding chins.

The evolutionary history of the Asian Negritos is still somewhat uncertain. It was once thought, especially in the circle of Fr. Wilhelm Schmidt, the well-known student of primitive religion, that they were closely related to the African Pygmies (Schmidt 1910), but Fr. Paul Schebesta, who conducted fieldwork among both groups specifically to test that hypothesis, came to a negative conclusion (1952: 478–9; see also Garvan 1964: v). Perhaps a more likely possibility is that they are, as Cole contends, 'diminished survivors' of a Palaeo-Melanesian race that once passed through South-East Asia on its way to present-day Melanesia (1965: 48, 89). The oldest skeletal remains found in the Peninsula are thought to be

---

[1] I retain the term Negrito, which means 'little black' in Spanish, because it has gained general acceptance in the anthropological literature and because it has none of the pejorative connotations of the Malay terms for the people. The Negritos are called Semang in the western half of the Peninsula, which is roughly equivalent to the English term 'savage'. In Kelantan they are generally termed Pangan, which means, among other things, 'people who live like animals and eat their food raw'. The Negritos do not have a distinctive term for persons of their race; they call each aboriginal group by a dialect indicator and do not make broader distinctions by physical or cultural category.

of members of that hypothetical race (Trevor and Brothwell 1962: 10–11; Snell 1949: 24–5; Mijsberg 1940: 117). But the connection between those skeletons and the modern Negritos is highly tenuous. No recognizably Negrito bones have yet been found in the Malay Peninsula. For the moment, then, we can only say that the present-day Negritos seem to be the remnants of an ancient race that was once widespread in South-East Asia, but was later crowded out of many areas by more powerful groups that were expanding in population.

The languages of the Malaysian Negritos are in the Austroasiatic language family and thus are fundamentally different from Malay, which is an Austronesian language,[1a] although all the Negrito languages are infused to some extent with loan-words from various Malay dialects. The Negrito languages along with the related languages of the Senoi (Mongoloid aboriginals who are mostly slash-and-burn agriculturalists) have recently been grouped by linguists as a distinct branch of Mon-Khmer which has been termed 'Aslian', from the Malay expression 'Orang Asli' (literally 'original people'), the term adopted by the Malaysian government for the aboriginal peoples of the Peninsula (Benjamin 1976; Diffloth 1974). All the Negrito languages except Lanoh, which is a Senoi dialect, fall into the 'Northern Aslian' subdivision of that language family. Although the grammar of the Negrito languages fits the Mon-Khmer pattern and many Negrito words have Mon-Khmer cognates, there are a number of common Negrito words that cannot be traced to either a Mon-Khmer or Austronesian source (Skeat and Blagden 1906b: 462–3). Presumably these are the residue of a more ancient language which was somehow superseded by one or more Mon-Khmer languages. Why and from whom the Mon-Khmer language was adopted is difficult to know. According to Blagden there are two levels of Austroasiatic influence in the languages of the Malaysian aborigines: the ancient common basis of the languages and a more recent and superficial, specifically Mon-Khmer influence (Skeat and Blagden 1906b: 460). The former probably split off from the other Mon-Khmer languages some time before 1000 B.C. (Thomas and Headley 1970: 404), whereas the latter most probably came from Mon-Khmer traders and colonists who were in the

[1a] The Austroasiatic languages, which include Khmer and Vietnamese, are mostly found in mainland South-East Asia, while the Austronesian (or 'Malayo-Polynesian') languages are found mainly in the islands of South-East Asia and the Pacific. The Malay Peninsula is a meeting place of these two major language families.

Peninsula between A.D. 400 and 900 (Skeat and Blagden 1906b: 469). The present evidence seems to suggest that the Negritos took over, probably gradually, the language or languages of the Austroasiatic speaking Senoi who must have come into the Peninsula several thousand years ago. Subsequent micro-evolution from the proto-language, especially following the sedentarization of the Senoi, would have led to the present diversity of the Aslian language family (see Benjamin 1976). The connection between the languages of the Malaysian Negritos and those of the Andamans and Philippines is so ancient as to be virtually undemonstrable (see e.g. Radcliffe-Brown 1922: 495). This makes it all the more interesting, for purposes of this study, that the name for the thunder-god of the Negritos of the northern Camarines in the Philippines, 'Kayai' (Garvan 1964: 227), is cognate with the most common name given the thunder-god by the Malaysian Negritos, 'Karei'.

According to recent Department of Orang Asli Affairs figures, the Negritos of Peninsular Malaysia now number about 2,000 persons. These are divided, by Negrito reckoning, into a number of *bangsa*' (Malay *bangsa*, 'races') which are distinguished mainly by differences in dialect. Members of different *bangsa*' may now be found living together, especially at J.O.A. settlements such as the one at Post Lebir (see Map 1) and another near Baling in Kedah. But traditionally the different dialect groups were associated with different areas, though they would sometimes move out of them temporarily, and occasionally, due to some serious disruption, they would move for good. The traditional area is not a clearly bounded section of land among the Kelantan Batek, although Schebesta claims that it is for the western Negritos (1954: 229–30). The Batek associate a group with a river, rather than with the land itself, but there is never any question of trying to exclude other groups from that river or the land around it. The dialect group with which I deal most extensively is the Batek Dè' group of Kelantan (*batèk* means 'person of our group' and *dè*' means 'this'). The Batek Dè' number about 350 persons and are now centred on the Aring and upper Lebir Rivers, though they sometimes establish camps on the upper Relai and even the Chiku (see Map 1). A closely related group speaking an almost identical dialect is found on the Tahan and Kechau Rivers in Pahang. These people, numbering about sixty-five, are termed Batek 'Iga' by the Batek Dè', '*iga*' being a distinctive alternative term for the pronoun 'I'. Another major group with which I deal is the Batek Nòng (*nòng*

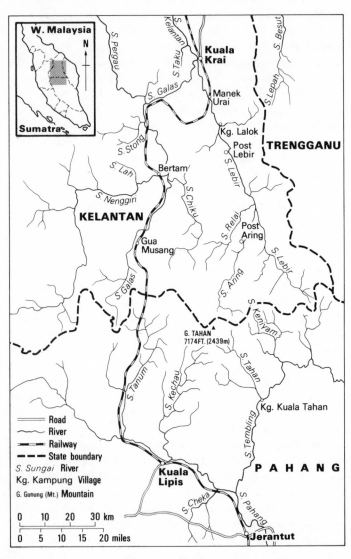

Map 1. The Batek Area

means 'do not' (imperative)) of the Cheka River in Pahang. This group, which includes about eighty-seven persons, is now cut off from other Negrito groups and shows a number of cultural differences from them. A fairly large but scattered Kelantan dialect group is the Mendriq (*menri'* means 'person of our group') which comprises about 118 persons. Mendriq are now found in two villages on the lower Nenggiri (one a short way up the Lah River), one village on the Taku River, below Kuala Krai, and there are a few families at Post Lebir. A small group of closely related people, calling themselves Batek Teh (*teh* means 'this'), are also found at Post Lebir. They number about twenty-two persons. The final group with which I had direct contact, though I got very little information of any interest, was the Batek Tẹ̀' (*tẹ̀'* means 'this'). This dialect group consists of thirteen persons at Post Lebir and about thirty on the Lepah River in the upper Besut district of Trengganu. The latter are probably the easternmost Negritos in the Peninsula.

The boundaries of Negrito dialect groups are not fixed or sharply demarcated. Marriages quite often take place outside one's own *bangsa'*, and a person may be gradually absorbed into the spouse's group if he or she habitually lives with it. Most individuals can speak more than one dialect and will identify with whichever dialect group they are living with at a given time. There have been mass as well as individual shifts in *bangsa'* affiliation within the last few generations in Kelantan. There is good evidence that the Batek Dè' and Batek 'Iga' were one group until about fifty years ago when the increase in the Malay population in the upper Aring drove some of them (the present Batek Dè') into the Relai and others (the present Batek 'Iga') across the Pahang border into the upper Tahan River. Also, before the Second World War there were quite a few Batek Teh living on the Chiku River, but they fled when the Japanese army came down the railway line from the Kelantan coast. Some of them went over to Pahang, others joined the Batek Teh already on the middle Lebir, but a substantial number joined the Batek Dè' then living on the Relai. Those people, who were born Batek Teh, inter-married with the Batek Dè', adopted their dialect and customs, and now make up a substantial proportion of the Batek Dè' population. One of my best informants on Batek religion, Penghulu Selé', is one of these 'immigrants', and he is undoubtedly influenced by the Batek Teh traditions of his childhood as well as the Batek Dè' traditions within which he is now immersed. But it would be pointless to dismiss his views because they are mixed or hybrid, for it is a fundamental characteristic of Negrito cultures that they are constantly changing under the impact of these individual and mass movements across *bangsa'* boundaries. These same forces have caused the Negrito dialects to remain in a mesh of interconnectedness while the dialects of the sedentary Senoi have diverged like the branches of a tree (Benjamin 1976: 74–6).

Environment

Most of the Malaysian Negritos today live in the foothills of the main mountain range, which runs north and south down the centre of the Peninsula, and in sparsely occupied up-river (Malay *ulu*) areas in Kelantan and Pahang. The higher elevations in the central mountain range are occupied by semi-sedentary swidden agri-culturalists, the Temiar and Semai. The Batek Dè' usually live in primary lowland tropical rain forest. There is some secondary forest along the rivers where Malays and occasionally Batek previously cleared to plant crops, but even this is relatively mature now, since most of the Malay farmers were removed from the area in the early 1950s (see below). The primary forest is dominated by tall, thin trees whose branches form an almost continuous canopy 140 to 160 feet above the ground. These trees are of many different species, but their general shape is the same. The trunks are mostly slender and straight, branching only near the top, and many of them have flange-like buttresses at the base. The bark is usually thin and smooth, and the large, leathery, dark green leaves are oval shaped, tapering to points at both ends (Richards 1952: 4–5). Because the soil contains few nutrients below the surface, the roots of the trees are very shallow. This makes them highly vulnerable to being blown over in wind-storms, and this fact has great importance in Batek religion. The trees support numerous species of epiphytes on their trunks, branches, and even their leaves. They are thickly festooned with vines and climbers, some as big round as a man's arm. The tops of the trees are so entangled with vines that often a tree that has been chopped through will not fall. Compared to the canopy, the floor of the primary rain forest is relatively open. This is because as much as 99 per cent of the sunlight falling on the forest is cut off before it reaches the ground (Poore 1964: 46). The undergrowth consists mainly of stemless palms, tree seedlings, and a few shade-tolerant herbs and ferns. Most of the low palms and the lower stems of the climbers are armed with thorns, making it hazardous to push through the undergrowth without a bush-knife. Along the edges of rivers and where trees have fallen, thus letting in the sunlight, the undergrowth is much denser, sometimes nearly impenetrable. The terrain is basically low, rolling hills, but it is cut through at close intervals by streams which often carve steep ravines in the soft laterite soil. Travelling is fairly easy between the streams, but getting across the streams is sometimes difficult, especially when the ground is wet and slippery. Sometimes the stream-beds are the best trails, and the Batek use them as such whenever they can.

Invertebrates, especially insects, make up the bulk of the animal life in the primary rain forest. The trees, earth, and air are alive with countless insects of numerous species. Many of them make their presence known by biting, stinging, or sucking one's blood. Land leeches are also plentiful, especially during the wetter parts of the year. Most of the vertebrates live in the forest canopy. The great majority of them are birds and bats which feed in the tree-tops on fruit, leaves, and insects. Squirrels and other arboreal rodents are quite plentiful, and monkeys and gibbons are not rare in the less disturbed areas. Arboreal predators, mostly civets of several species, are also fairly common. The vertebrate fauna of the forest floor is relatively impoverished because there is little food to be found there. Specialized feeders such as porcupines and scaly ant-eaters occur, but in small numbers and widely scattered. The most numerous of the larger mammals are the wild pigs, which feed mainly on roots and tubers. Browsing animals, such as deer, are scarce, because there are relatively few edible leaves near the ground. Wild elephants are common enough to be a serious nuisance whenever the Batek attempt to grow crops. Tigers and leopards are not as uncommon as one would hope, but they seldom come near Batek camps. There are quite a few snakes, many of which are highly poisonous, living in the trees and on the ground, but they are seldom seen. The rivers contain many fish of numerous species. Small numbers of turtles, water monitors, and otters also live in the streams.

The tropical rain forest is a rich environment for those who have the knowledge and skills needed to harvest its bounties. Adequate food supplies are available throughout the year, and at times, such as during the fruit season, there is more food than the Batek can possibly eat. The Batek know where and when to look for all the plants and animals they depend upon as food, and they have the skills necessary to obtain them. For example, much of the food in the rain forest, such as fruit and honey, can be harvested most efficiently by climbing trees. Both Batek men and women are extremely proficient climbers: they can literally walk up small trees, holding the trunk at arms' length, and they can scale even the largest trees using an intricate system of rattan 'rope-ladders'. The forest also provides all the materials for making shelters, fires, mats, baskets, rafts, and most other necessary implements within easy reach of any camp. The only necessities that must be obtained from outside sources are salt, and iron for tools. Travelling in the forest presents no great difficulty for the Batek, even when they are carrying heavy loads. They are extremely strong and fit, and have excellent body control. They move quickly over, under, and through obstacles, and they cut through anything they cannot avoid, usually with a single stroke of the bush-knife.

The rain forest is also a safe environment for those who know how to deal with its potential dangers. The Batek have a realistic appreciation of these dangers; they do not fear the forest, nor do they populate it with imaginary evil spirits as many agricultural peoples do. One source of danger in the forest is wild animals. Children learn early to avoid such things as snakes, scorpions, and poisonous centipedes. If tigers or elephants are thought to be nearby, the Batek simply form larger than normal work-groups on the generally correct assumption that there is safety in numbers. They may also take special care to keep their fires smouldering at night, knowing that wild animals avoid smoke and fire. In the past, when tigers were more numerous in the area, the Lebir Batek sometimes built their huts in trees, because tigers are known to be poor climbers. The Aring Batek, on the other hand, used to build fences or barricades around their camps (see Skeat and Blagden 1906a: 176). A person who happens to meet a tiger in the forest will usually just run away, but if there are several people together, they may scream at it and scare it off. Another source of danger in the rain forest is the strong winds that accompany thunderstorms. Enormous trees can often be heard crashing to the ground during thunderstorms, and if one were to fall on a Batek camp, it could easily kill most of the inhabitants. One precaution the Batek take before setting up a new camp is to study the trees near the chosen spot to determine whether any are rotten or over-large and thus unstable. Sometimes they cut down a dangerous tree before building their shelters. Such practical measures make living in the rain forest at least as safe as living in a city.

The Batek concepts, attitudes, and ritual practices concerning their natural environment form an important part of their religion. The practices intended to prevent and halt thunderstorms are especially significant. These matters will be discussed in detail in Chapter 3 and Chapter 5.

At present the social environment of the Batek Dè' is very simple, though it has not always been so. After 1890 or so, a large number of Malay swidden agriculturalists moved into the upper Lebir and Aring Rivers from Pahang. But during the early years of the Emergency (the communist insurrection that began in 1949), all the Malay farmers were resettled by the government in new villages on the lower Lebir, to remove them from possible communist guerrilla pressures. They left behind many fruit orchards which are now exploited by the Batek. Today the only outsiders who are often encountered by the Batek are a few Malay entrepreneurs who come up the main rivers by motor-boat to trade for forest products. They are also visited at varying intervals by field-staff of the Department of Orang Asli Affairs. The nearest Malay village of any size is about thirty miles downstream from where the Batek Dè' usually live. Communication with the outside world is still almost exclusively by river—by motor-boat, raft, and canoe—but logging roads are now being built which reach into Batek country. Although the Batek are affected by outside society in various ways, they are still very isolated. Their immediate social environment consists almost entirely of other Batek.

Social Organization

The social organization of the Batek Dè' is quite simple. The relationship terminology is bilateral, and kinship ties are established equally through both parents. The Batek Dè', unlike the western Negritos, allow marriage between first cousins, though not of course between closer relatives. Most of the Batek Dè' are related to each other, through known links, by descent, marriage, or both.

The most stable and well-defined group in Batek society is the conjugal family, though even that is not always very durable. Batek usually marry for the first time while in their teens. Marriage partners choose each other on the basis of personal attraction; parents have little influence in such matters. To be considered married it is sufficient for a couple to set up a shelter together, though it is usual also for the boy to give the girl and her parents some small gifts and for the girl to give him something in return. Often early marriages break up, and the youngsters may try several partners before finding one to whom they will 'stick', as the Batek say. Divorce is far less frequent after a couple has children. The conjugal family is the basic unit of production and consumption in Batek society. A couple co-operates to supply the family's needs. Usually the wife provides most of the tubers and fish, and the husband provides game and rice, which he obtains in trade for rattan, but often they work together as a team on a single project. The Batek do not consider resources to be owned until they have been collected, and then they are the property of the conjugal family, though any food beyond what the family needs is readily shared. Conjugal families are also politically independent units. Decisions on what activities to engage in and when and where to move are made separately by each couple, though there is usually some consultation with others.

There are no lineages, bands, or other corporate groups larger than the conjugal family in Batek society. However, there is a feeling that the Batek Dè' who normally live on the Aring and those associated with the Lebir are separate groups in some sense, even though they speak the same dialect and there is much visiting and intermarriage between them.

The characteristic residential unit of the Batek is the camp. Physically a camp consists of a cluster of lean-to shelters made of palm thatch attached to three sticks which are driven into the ground at a forty-five degree angle. There is one shelter for each conjugal family, and groups of adolescents of the same or different sexes often have separate shelters as well. The shelters are arranged more or less at random, though they more often face toward each other than toward the undisturbed forest. The area between shelters is not deliberately cleared, but it opens up gradually as the bushes get trampled and the saplings are cut for use in camp. Each shelter has its own cooking fire in front of it, and the family's possessions— a few clothes, cloths, sleeping mats, baskets, cooking-pots, blowpipes, knives, and other tools—are arranged inside, the smaller items being lodged in the thatch.

The composition of Batek camps is highly fluid. They fluctuate in size depending on the richness and concentration of the resources being exploited. For example, during the fruit season as many as twenty families may gather together in an abandoned fruit orchard, but once the fruit supply is exhausted the families will split up into several smaller camps to exploit the more scattered resources, such as wild yams. Also, the composition of a particular camp continually changes as individual families move in and out according to their changing interests. However, the movements of the various families are not entirely unco-ordinated. Each family tends to camp most often with certain other families, usually those of close friends or relatives, though there are no rigid rules of co-residence.

There is virtually no political power in Batek society. No adult is able to coerce any other adult Batek. Husbands have no authority over their wives, and even the authority of parents over their children is exceedingly weak. Some people have more influence than others because they are known to be knowledgeable and to make sound decisions, but whether others follow their lead is entirely up to those individuals. There are a few Batek who are called 'headmen' (Malay *penghulu*), but these titles have usually been bestowed upon them by outsiders, often by J.O.A. officials. These 'headmen' may act as spokesmen for the group in relation to outsiders, but they have no real authority inside Batek society.

Although a camp is made up of highly independent families and it has no formal leadership, it does have a moral unity. Batek ethics strongly emphasize the need for sharing and mutual aid among all the people living together. Food, especially meat, is always shared with as many people as possible, whether it is needed or not; so unless there is a severe shortage, no one in camp will go hungry. Batek social organization, then, allows great personal freedom, yet provides a cushion against starvation in case of old age, illness, or other misfortune.

Economy

The economy of the Batek Dè' is complex. It combines a number of different economic activities and is characterized by frequent shifting from one to another. Before explaining the dynamics of the system, I shall briefly describe the various activities that make it up.

The most reliable means of getting food is gathering, by which

I mean procuring wild food by methods other than hunting or fishing. Most but not all of the foods gathered are vegetables. The most important source of carbohydrates is wild yams (*Dioscorea* spp.), about ten species of which are eaten. They grow scattered throughout the lowland rain forest and are identified by their vines which climb into the treetops where their leaves can reach the sunlight. Batek women, and less often men, dig up the tubers with metal-bladed digging sticks. Usually a work-day of about six hours will yield a load of about fourteen pounds of tubers, enough to feed the average family for a day with some left over. Wild tubers can be obtained throughout the year. Another type of food that is gathered in large quantities is seasonal fruit. Both wild and domesticated varieties, which are found mostly in abandoned Malay orchards, are so numerous and prolific that the Batek are able to live virtually on fruit alone for two months of the year (July and August) and to supplement their diet with fruit for several more months. Some types of fruit fall when ripe and need only be picked up. Others are harvested by someone climbing the tree and cutting off the small limbs from which the fruit hangs. Usually young men do the climbing, and women and children collect the fruit as it falls. Large quantities of honey are also obtained during some months of the year (April to June). When the forest trees are in flower, the bees build large nests underneath the limbs of tall trees. Usually one man climbs the tree just after dark, when the bees have returned to the nest, and stuns the bees with a torch made of dry leaves. Then he cuts the nest loose, places it in a bark basket, and lowers it to the ground on a rattan line. Large amounts of honey are eaten by the Batek, but considerable amounts are also sold or traded to the Malay traders. Many other wild foods—such as palm-cabbage, mushrooms, and fern shoots—are collected as needed or as found. These are gathered by all Batek, including children and old people.

The most important method of getting protein is hunting. This is normally done by using bamboo blowpipes to shoot darts tipped with poison made from the sap of the *ipuh* tree (*Antiaris toxicaria*). This method of hunting is highly effective for killing game in the tree-tops, the usual victims being monkeys of various species, gibbons, civets, squirrels, and birds. Hunting is done mainly by men, either alone or in small groups. A good hunter can expect to make a kill perhaps once in every two hunting-trips. Ground-living animals, such as porcupines and scaly ant-eaters, are sometimes found and smoked out of their holes in the ground or in hollow trees. One frequent source of meat is the bamboo rats, which reach six pounds in weight, that live underneath clumps of bamboo where they feed on the roots. They are dug up with digging sticks and are obtained by women as well as by men.

Another source of protein is fish, which are plentiful in the undisturbed rivers and streams in Batek country. The most common method of fishing is with a shop-bought hook and line on a rod made from the rib of a palm frond, usually with worms for bait. This type of fishing is done mainly by women, and it brings in a small but steady supply of meat. A few Batek have cast-nets or gill-nets which they have obtained by trade. These are effective when new, but tend to deteriorate rapidly. Fish may also be caught by poisoning. The poison is extracted from several kinds of bark and roots and released into a small stream. Then the stunned fish are collected as they float to the surface.

Another important economic activity of the Batek is collecting and trading rattan cane. Rattan is the stem of various species of climbing palms. The Batek simply pull down the smaller diameter rattans, slice off the crowns, and cut them into measured sections or roll them into coils. To get the larger diameter rattans they must climb the tree that supports the rattan and cut the vine free from the crown. This work is done mainly by the younger men and a few of the young women. They trade the rattan to Malay traders with whom they make short-term 'contracts' to supply an agreed number of pieces. In return, the Batek get money, rice, salt, sugar, flour, swimming suits, sarongs, electric torches, batteries, and a few other things. The foods obtained in this way are a useful supplement to their normal diet of wild foods. Usually the Malays take the rattan down-river by raft and sell it to buyers in the towns and larger villages.

The Batek also know how to grow crops and have done small-scale farming off and on for many years. The traditional pattern was for a group to make a small clearing, burn it off, and then plant whatever seeds, tubers, and cuttings they had been able to obtain from the nearby Malay hill-farmers. The crops planted usually would include rice, maize, and cassava. After the crops were planted, the group would continue on its foraging round and then would come back to the clearing at about the time they thought the crops would be ripe. They would camp by the clearing for a few days or weeks and eat whatever portion of the crops had escaped the predations of wild pigs, birds, rodents, and monkeys. In recent years another pattern of agriculture has occasionally been followed by the Batek. The Department of Orang Asli Affairs, in a campaign to get the Batek to settle down, has tried giving them tools, seed, technical advice, and rations (mostly rice), which are supposed to support them until their crops are ripe. Each time this has been tried, the Batek have happily participated in the project, going through the motions of farming until the rations have run out, when they have immediately abandoned the clearings and gone back to hunting and gathering (see also Carey 1976: 118). It seems that the resource the Batek have been exploiting in these schemes is not their own plantations but the Department of Orang Asli Affairs!

At one time the Batek, like most other Malaysian Negritos, gained some income and food by working for outsiders. For example, they would help the Malay hill-farmers harvest their rice in return for a small share of the crop. But the opportunity to do this largely disappeared when the local Malays were moved out of the area. A few people still get temporary employment in Department of Orang Asli Affairs projects and working as guides for travellers coming into the area.

In most years the Batek can be expected to engage in all the economic activities described, with the possible exceptions of planting and working for outsiders, though it is impossible to predict when and where they will take up each pursuit. The relatively fixed points in the general state of flux are the flood season and the fruit season. During the floods (usually December and January) the Batek almost always live on wild foods alone, though occasionally they have some rice which they have saved from earlier planting, trading, or gifts from the J.O.A. During the fruit season (July and August) they invariably move to a place where they can get a lot of fruit, even if it means abandoning farming or some other useful activity (cf. Schebesta 1954: 90–1). While living on fruit, they may collect other foods, hunt, or trade a little rattan for rice to add variety to their diet, but they feel no compulsion to do so. They generally take life easy, sampling the different types of fruit and holding singing sessions in the evenings. During the rest of the year, the Batek will take up whatever economic activity offers the most advantages at the moment. Usually they will take any opportunity to trade rattan or work for outsiders because it enables them to get rice, which they prefer to wild tubers, and helps conserve the tubers for the flood season. But if there is no employer or buyer for rattan, they will normally revert to hunting and gathering, though they may bring in a little rattan for future trade. Agriculture is their last resort unless it is sweetened with free rations. The routine followed will vary from year to year depending upon changing opportunities. If a demand arises for a forest product other than rattan—such as wild rubber, resins, fragrant woods, or forest medicines—they may switch over to collecting that. If they get a chance to work for loggers, mineral prospectors, or some other such employer, they may decide to pursue that line of work for a while. In this way, the Batek participate in a foraging economy, a money or barter economy, and an agricultural economy, rarely confining themselves to one at a time.

A Typical Day in a Batek Forest Camp

A more vivid picture of the Batek way of life can be given by a brief description of a typical day in a Batek camp. The hypothetical day described below would be most characteristic of the periods between the floods and the honey and fruit seasons (February to April and September to November).

The camp begins to stir when the sun comes up, which occurs about 6.30 a.m. all the year round near the equator. As the drone of frogs and night insects fades, it is gradually replaced by the murmur of human voices. Soon people wrapped tightly from shoulders to knees in their cotton blankets or sarongs begin drifting into the bushes to relieve themselves and moving stiffly down to the stream to bathe and often to fetch water in bamboo tubes. Fires are stirred and built up to ward off the 'cold' (the temperature never falls below about 20° C.). Mothers search through the embers, containers, and cooking pots for bits of food left from the night before. Sometimes a small amount of tubers or rice is cooked. However little food there is in camp, parents try to give something to the children, though they themselves may go hungry. They say the children cannot 'hold out' against hunger, though they learn to as they grow older.

While preparing the morning meal, the adults begin to discuss what they will do that day. Several people who are tired or feeling ill decide to stay in camp and mind any children who may be left there. Three women agree to go and dig tubers together and fall into a discussion of where would be the best place to go. The men who were out hunting the previous day mention some promising tuber vines they saw, and others recall places where they have found tubers on previous stays in the area. Someone remembers a cluster of immature vines she found the year before and suggests that the tubers should be edible by now. After weighing the various possibilities, they decide to go across the stream and into the valley of a small side-stream where they have found tubers before and where they have not yet gone digging while at the present camp. Two of the men decide to go hunting. As the camp is only a few days old, they believe that they can still find monkeys quite nearby. They decide to go into the hills behind the camp where one of them got a leaf monkey the day before. They say they will try to find the family of the one that was killed. Four young men and two adolescent girls decide to go after Malacca cane ('awey manaw; Malay rotan manau), the large diameter rattan used in the frames of rattan furniture. Two men had cut about sixty pieces the day before, but had only been able to carry in half of them before dark. They decide they had better bring in the rest of those before looking for more. But they think there should be more rattan further along the same stream and advise the others to go there and have a look. They all agree to go together and then split up when they reach the place where the two men left their extra rattan. In this way the work groups for the day are formed. They may be entirely different groups from those of the previous day, for the Batek like variety both in their work and in their companions.

The people who have decided to go out to work then set about preparing their equipment. Some of the women sharpen the chisel-shaped metal blades of their digging sticks by rubbing them on a piece of dense sandstone. A few of the rattan hunters sharpen their bush-knives in the same way. The women finish by jabbing their digging-sticks smartly into a nearby tree to fix the blade firmly in the wooden handle. One of the hunters heats a bamboo spatula covered with hardened dart poison to soften it. He rolls the tips of some new darts in the poison and sets them on a bamboo rack to dry. He repeats this process four or five times and then slips the darts into his bamboo quiver. Another hunter slips the outer bamboo casing off his blowpipe and heats the inner tube over the fire. Then he sights down it and begins rubbing it firmly with a piece of cloth, removing the moisture the bamboo has absorbed from the air and straightening the tube at the same time. He then passes a bamboo cleaning rod through it several times, to polish the bore, and reassembles the blowpipe. A few people go around asking others for a little tobacco, as they have run out and do not want to be without it while out working. About 9.00 a.m. everyone is ready to go.

The women who are going digging take up their digging sticks, slip the straps of their carrying baskets over one shoulder, and the mothers with babies place them in cloth slings on their backs or chests. They move off in the direction of the stream and disappear down the bank. Some of the young children trail along behind their mothers. Suddenly one of the children who had stayed behind in camp, apparently playing happily, loses his nerve at the realization that his mother is gone and cries out miserably, 'oh mother, oh mother, oh mother'. In a few minutes she reappears in camp, and with a resigned grin, picks the child up and carries him off.

The women walk up the stream-bed for about half a mile and then climb up the bank when they reach the side-stream they are looking for. They work their way up the gully made by the small stream. It gradually broadens out as they move up the hillside, searching as they go for any signs of tubers. One woman finds a vine and stops to examine it. The vine and the leaves are bright green, however, indicating that the tuber is still too young to be eaten; so they continue up the ridge. Finally they spot a few pieces of dead *takop* stem (the most commonly found wild yam) among the debris on the forest floor. They stop and unload their burdens. One woman quickly digs down where she thinks the stem had been growing and soon brings up a small piece of the tuber, which is about three-quarters of an inch in diameter but as much as six feet long. She examines it, and, finding it to be mature, she begins to dig in earnest. The other women fan out along the hillside, and soon all of them have found promising vines and are hard at work. Although they are out of sight of each other in the undergrowth, they are within earshot. One woman places her baby on some large leaves beside her, but another woman's baby remains asleep in a cloth sling on her back. The older children settle down to playing— climbing trees, rushing around in the bushes, and cutting down saplings with their mothers' bush-knives.

The women dig down following a branch of the tuber as it twists and turns underground, chopping it out in pieces until they reach the end. Then they go back to where the stem had been and begin digging along another branch. *Takop* tubers usually have two or three branches on each stem. By the time she has got the whole tuber, a woman may be sitting in a hole four feet deep. The women dig about half an hour at a time and then stop for a short rest. They roll cigarettes and light them with flint and steel or with a smouldering ember they keep wrapped tightly in a piece of cloth in their baskets. Sometimes they stop for a few minutes to nurse their babies. When the first tubers are finished, the women move on looking for another. One woman who has found several promising stems calls the others over, and all three dig together for a while.

About 2.00 p.m. the children become hungry. They make a fire and roast a few pieces of tubers from their mothers' baskets. The women themselves keep on digging for another hour, until their baskets are nearly full. The children are becoming tired, and a distant roll of thunder announces a possible storm. The women stop digging. By now they have loads of tubers ranging from ten to twenty pounds. They gather up all their tools and children and set off for camp. They walk slowly so that the children can keep up. One child carries a baby on her back to free the mother to carry a basket of tubers. They arrive back in camp before 4.00 p.m.

The rattan party leaves camp about the same time as the tuber-digging group. They walk quickly along an established path, not bothering to search for food. They walk for about an hour and a half, going far into the hills away from the main stream. They stop when they reach the rattan pieces collected by two of the men the day before. They all have a smoke, and the two men tie up their rattan in bundles of ten to fifteen sticks each. The two men each hoist a bundle on to one shoulder and set off back toward camp. The remaining four people continue on up the valley, scanning the tree-tops for the characteristic feathery, pale green fronds of the Malacca cane palm. Soon someone spots one, and they all scramble up the slope to have a look at it. It is a long vine, and the crown is in the top of a very tall tree. The tree trunk is too big round at the base to climb; so one of the young men quickly climbs up a small tree nearby. When he gets near the top of the smaller tree, he sets it to swaying back and forth until he is able to catch hold of a limb of the larger tree. He then swings up on to the limb and proceeds to climb the large tree, hoisting himself from limb to limb. When he reaches the crown of the rattan, he cuts the stem loose with his bush-knife.

While the climber descends, the other three people cut through the vine at the bottom and pull it down to the ground. Then they slice off the thorny leaf-sheaths adhering to the stem and drag it down the hill to a level place. One man measures off a distance of nine feet on the ground, using his forearm as a gauge, and places small logs across the path at both ends of the measured space. Then they drag the vine across this measuring jig and cut it into nine-foot sections, the standard trade length for large diameter rattan. The first vine is a long one and yields nineteen good sections, which the work party piles beside the path.

The party continues on up the valley looking for more Malacca cane plants, as they usually have only one stem per root. After three more hours of work, they have dragged four additional stems back to the cutting place. They cut those into sections and begin tying them up into bundles. The two men who had taken a load down earlier have arrived back, and they are also given bundles. The size of the bundle varies according to the strength of the carrier. After a smoke they take up their loads and start back toward camp, stopping every half hour or so to rest. At one stop one of the men cuts down another type of rattan, the pith of which is used for the butt-cones of blowpipe darts, and inserts several sections of it in his bundle. A girl collects a few medicinal leaves and tucks them in the waistband of her loincloth. They arrive back in camp about 3.30 p.m.

The two hunters leave camp shortly after the other work parties. They walk quickly up the bed of a small stream behind the camp, then turn straight up the side of the hill. When they reach the top, they begin to walk quietly along the ridge, listening and scanning the tree-tops. They stop for a few minutes to investigate the tracks and diggings of a scaly ant-eater, but after searching around for a while, they conclude that it has gone up a tree. They move on toward the spot where the monkey was killed the day before. They stop every two or three minutes and listen. After about an hour they hear some leaf monkeys calling, down the slope to their left. They move quietly downhill and then split up. Suddenly with a great rustling of leaves, several leaf monkeys rush away through the tree-tops, jumping from branch to branch and sometimes falling many feet. The hunters continue on, as some of the monkeys have not fled. When one man sees a monkey high in a tree, he creeps along to the base of it and stops. He puts a dart in the blowpipe and shoots, almost vertically. The first dart hits the mark, and the monkey flinches, not knowing what has happened. The hunter quickly reloads and shoots five more darts, hitting the animal twice more. As darts are silent, the prey does not necessarily run off as it does when shot at with a gun. The monkey pulls out two of the darts, but the poisoned tips stay in its flesh. It scrambles for a short distance through the tree-tops and then stops. The hunter hears the other man whistle, a prearranged signal meaning 'come to me'. He finds the other hunter sitting on a log further down the hill. He too has hit a monkey, and now they must wait for them to die.

The two men sit together, talking quietly and smoking cigarettes. They do not pursue the wounded animals, as it would only make them run off. After about twenty minutes, one of the monkeys falls. One hunter moves off to get it. It is not yet dead, and it tries to run away when he comes upon it, but he finally catches it and kills it by hitting it on the head with a stick. By the time he gets back to his friend, the other monkey has also fallen. They both walk in the direction it was heard to fall and soon find it dead.

The hunters decide to cook the two monkeys, both mature males, in the forest. They make a fire and place the carcasses in it, one after the other, to singe the fur. Then they scrape it off with a stick. They cut open the abdomen and remove the innards. Then they impale the carcasses on crossed sticks and lean them over the fire. While the carcasses are roasting over the fire, they cook the livers separately and eat them. When the meat is done, they cut it into pieces and wrap each monkey up in a bundle made of leaves tied with vines. They place these bundles in lengths of cloth which they tie across the chest, forming a sort of rucksack on their backs. Then they head back to camp. They arrive just after 4.00 p.m.

The people who stay in camp occupy themselves with various chores and crafts. In the morning one man makes darts, and another just rests. Two women sit together on the ground making sleeping mats of pandanus, while their babies play together nearby. Another woman sits in her shelter and picks lice out of her children's hair. The young children play in camp, running around and chopping at trees and logs with bush-knives. Later they all go swimming for a couple of hours. The children play boisterously, but are seldom aggressive, and they have no competitive games. Two boys about ten years old go hunting just outside camp with their own miniature blowpipes. They climb high up in the trees to get better shots at the birds. Some adults in the camp shout at them to come down and play on the ground, but their admonitions are blithely ignored. The boys manage to kill two small birds which they proceed to cook and eat.

In the early afternoon, the two women who had been making mats decide to go fishing. They say they are tired of sitting around camp. They strip the leaves off two palm fronds and attach their fishing lines. Then, taking up their babies, they head off down the main stream. About an hour and a half later they return. They are carrying bundles of fresh pandanus leaves for making mats, and one woman has a small leaf bundle containing three tiny fish. She explains with a laugh that they were just playing around at fishing.

Soon after getting back to camp, the members of the various work groups go down and bathe in the stream. Then they collect some firewood and begin preparing the evening meal. A brief rain storm passes over, but there is no close thunder or strong wind. The adults sit out the shower in their shelters, while the children play in the rain. The hunters share out the meat, sending roughly equal amounts to each family. Some boys wash out the intestines and cook them over their own little fire. The women begin roasting and boiling tubers in front of their huts. Those who did not go digging are given some tubers by those who did. Each family eats in its own shelter, but the smaller children are sent scurrying from hut to hut carrying plates of cooked food to every other family, even though everyone has enough already. In this way the children learn the importance of sharing, and the camp maintains its sense of community.

After eating, everyone relaxes. People move from one fire to another, smoking, laughing, and gossiping into the evening. The cicadas begin to sing before dusk, and by the time it is dark they form a raucous chorus. A group of youngsters sitting in the centre of camp begin singing, and a few adults wander over and join them. Two women sit making mats by the light of a resin torch, and a man sits by another torch making blowpipe darts. Gradually people drift off to their shelters and go to sleep, but bursts of conversation or laughter may be heard well into the night.

The Nature of Batek Religion

A Malay I once met at Kuala Tembeling in Pahang told me that
the Batek he knew at Kuala Tahan (Batek 'Iga') had no religion,
for they had no prophets (Malay *nabi*) and no sacred scriptures
(Malay *kitab surat*). Certainly the Batek religion is not Islam or
anything closely analogous to it in form or content. But in anthropology it is normal to use a much broader definition of religion, to
include many types of shared metaphysical beliefs and ritualized
activities, and by that measure the Batek not only have a religion,
but it is of central importance in their thought and behaviour.

Skeat, writing in 1906, gives the following summary of the
characteristics of Negrito religion as they were then known:

The Semang religion, in spite of its recognition of a 'Thunder-god' (Kari)
and certain minor 'deities,' has very little indeed in the way of ceremonial,
and appears to consist mainly of mythology and legends. It shows remark-
ably few traces of demon-worship, very little fear of ghosts of the deceased,
and still less of any sort of animistic beliefs (Skeat and Blagden 1906b:
174-5).

This summary applies quite well to the Batek religion, though it
requires some qualification.

There is, as Skeat says, relatively little 'ceremonial' in Batek life.
The Batek appear at first glance to be eminently practical people.
They go about their daily lives with few signs of those 'irrational'
behaviours that cry out 'religion' to the anthropologist (cf. Sperber
1975: 2-4, 139). For example, they use very few magical means to
try to improve their luck in hunting, fishing, planting, and similar
endeavours. They seem to believe that they can succeed at such
projects if they just do them correctly and with proper care. Failure
is accepted as natural and to be expected in a certain proportion
of attempts. In addition, there are few 'rites of passage', and those
that occur are very simple. There are no initiation ceremonies
associated with growing up, and, as I mentioned above, there is
virtually no wedding ceremony. Only birth and death, of the so-
called life crises, are marked by what might be regarded as ritual,
though the Batek see their actions as purely practical and following
naturally from their ideas about life and death. Similarly, there is
no rite of initiation into the dialect group. As Schebesta says, 'when
a stranger has learnt the language and adapts himself to the customs
of the tribe, he becomes forthwith a member of it' (1928: 234). The

Batek are little concerned about spatial or conceptual boundaries in general, and therefore have little need for rites of passage or rites of boundary maintenance, though some of their prohibitions seem intended to maintain conceptual distinctions.

The few rituals the Bateks do have, such as the blood sacrifice and the singing and trancing sessions, do not follow rigidly fixed patterns. They contain a small core of standardized acts surrounded by a great mass of options and alternatives. As in most activities, the Batek assume that there is more than one way to achieve a given end. The Batek themselves do not make a sharp distinction between ritual, as a category of action, and other types of activity. They have no general term for ritual, and they normally designate particular rituals by ordinary terms describing the actions engaged in. For example, the blood sacrifice is called simply 'throwing blood'. But it is possible to distinguish categories of Batek behaviour according to the orientations of the activities. I think it is justifiable to regard as religious ritual all those actions that are directed toward the super-human beings, even though they may show few of the outward signs of behavioural patterning that are usually considered the mark of religious rites.

The absence of 'demon-worship' mentioned by Skeat also applies to Batek religion. The Batek do not generally believe, as the rural Malays do, that the environment is thickly populated with evil spirits (Malay *hantu*) which must be continuously avoided, combated, or propitiated. The absence of such a belief is one reason for the paucity of ritual in Batek life. But Skeat is misleading in saying that the Negritos do not fear the 'ghosts of the deceased'. This is refuted in general by the evidence of Evans (1937: 268) and Schebesta (1928: 105; 1957: 163, 170) and was even contradicted by at least one earlier writer (Annandale and Robinson 1903: 20). The Batek Dè' situation is somewhat complicated, as I shall show, but there is no doubt that at least some of the Batek fear some kind of ghost as well as the tiger which is supposed to come to eat the corpse. As for the absence of animism, Skeat is again rather misleading. If the term animism includes a belief in superhuman beings living in close contact with humans, then the Batek are certainly animists. But the remarkable thing about the superhuman beings of the Batek is that they are considered, with a few exceptions, to be thoroughly benevolent. One of the things I try to explain in this study is why these beings are pictured in this way.

Skeat is correct, however, in saying that Negrito religion consists in large part of 'mythology and legends', and, I would add, of mere explanations of how they see the world. Among the Batek, at least, there is no clear division between myths and explanations. There is no special ritual telling of myths or legends, and they are not preserved in a set form. The stories may be told on any occasion, as a whole or in fragments, and the episodes and incidents may occur in different orders and be described in different ways. The shared and traditional aspects of the stories are the general themes, some of the incidents and, to a lesser extent, the characters. Many of the explanations of the nature of the world come out in similar form, as standardized images and descriptions adjusted and organized to make a particular point or to answer a specific question. The content itself is often the same, as 'mythical' beings and their actions are cited as the causes of contemporary events. Both types of information are called *wayat* by the Batek (cf. Malay *riwayat*, 'story, account'), a term which would encompass roughly the Malay terms *cerita* ('story, tale') and *ilmu* ('knowledge, science'). Furthermore, there are no special words, symbols, metaphors, or levels of meaning in Batek 'myths' which do not also occur in ordinary explanation. I feel justified, therefore, in treating all types of statements made to me in roughly the same way: as direct information about the Batek world-view. There is one exception, however. The Batek know some Malay folk-tales, which they call *cerita'* (Malay *cerita*), such as the stories of Mr. Mousedeer ('Si-Pelandok') (see e.g. Skeat 1901). These are obviously borrowed intact, without adaptation, and are explicitly recognized as Malay stories by the Batek. They enjoy them, but say that are not *bed'ėt* ('good, beautiful, genuine') like their own stories (*wayat*). Usually I ignore these stories in the following study, as they are obviously completely alien to Batek conceptions, though the situation is apparently not so simple among the western Negritos, some of whose stories seem to combine Negrito and Malay themes and characters (see e.g. Evans 1937: 240–1). I do not, however, exclude any other Malay-derived elements from consideration because, where they exist, they have become integrated into the Batek religion in the same way as the myriad other elements that can be shown ultimately to be derived from external sources.

What this body of stories and explanations reveals is a complex theory of how the world is constituted, how it works, and the place of man within it. This world-view is also discernible, of course, in

Batek behaviour in general, though not everywhere so clearly or completely. The Batek world-view is a unified body of ideas. It would be arbitrary and unjustified to separate these ideas into 'sacred' and 'profane', 'supernatural' and 'natural', or 'irrational' and 'rational'. Batek explanations of a single phenomenon often weave together elements from both members of such pairs of categories. Similarly, it would only lead to confusion to separate those Batek concepts that are scientifically incorrect from those that happen to be 'true'. Both are arrived at, held, and used in the same way. For example, the Batek explanation of ordinary rain is scientifically correct, while their explanation of thunderstorms is not, but the two sets of ideas are closely connected, and neither can be fully understood without reference to the other. Thus, the Batek world-view encompasses what we call science as well as religion. Unlike religion in most modern western societies, Batek religion has not become separated from its world explaining role. This is not to claim that the Batek world-view *is* science in the western sense, but that it plays the role for them that modern science does for us, namely, to make the world intelligible.[2] Although the Batek world-view is a unified body of ideas, it would be impossible as a practical matter to describe all areas of Batek knowledge in a single study. Because I choose to concentrate on the more metaphysical concepts of the Batek, I consider it slightly more accurate to call this a study of their religion rather than their science.[3]

What I mean by Batek religion, then, is the world-view revealed by the Batek stories and explanations and the behaviours that are directly shaped by this world-view. As I have suggested, what I am calling Batek religion is not a separate compartment of Batek culture, but an all-encompassing framework of ideas and actions that makes the world intelligible and gives meaning and value to the whole of Batek life.

[2] For a detailed review of the similarities and differences between western science and primitive religion see Horton 1967a and 1967b.

[3] Of course all peoples have concepts with which to understand the world, but whether they are termed religious or something else is a matter of definition (see e.g. Lienhardt 1961: 170; Geertz 1975: 45–6, 363; Barth 1975: 123; Schneider 1976: 208).

The Present Study

Aims

My ethnographic aim in this study is to record as accurately and completely as possible the world-view and rites that make up the Batek Dè' religion. This may have some intrinsic interest for students of non-western religion, and it may also contribute to the understanding of the fast disappearing hunting and gathering way of life. In addition to describing the Batek religion, I want to see what the form and use of Batek religious concepts can tell us about the general process by which human beings understand the world they live in. From this perspective, the religion of the Batek ceases to be the object of study and becomes instead the means for a deeper investigation into the nature of cultural cognition.

The problem of variation in beliefs

One feature of Negrito religions in general that must be dealt with is the enormous amount of variation in beliefs between and even within dialect groups. One has the feeling that the more one knows of these beliefs, the less one understands them, for the patterns get lost as the variations mount up. Schebesta spends fifteen pages describing the deities (which he calls *orang hidop*, a Malay expression which means literally 'living persons') as conceived by seven Negrito groups and ends up with six lists containing over a hundred names (1957: 10–25, 28–9). As he rightly shows, many of these are just the same character with different names, but often there are slight differences in their attributes as well, and sometimes these differences are so great that one might say they are different characters with the same name. As with deities, most other features of belief and practice vary greatly from group to group and informant to informant. Such variation in belief is to be expected in societies which have no religious authorities, no formal training in religious precepts, and little public expression of one's personal understanding of those precepts either in words or in action. Moreover, the Negritos perfectly well realize that there are different *wayat* stories among different groups, because of the constant flow of individuals in and out of any dialect group, and they accept this variety as an interesting fact. Few of them worry about these alternative definitions of reality any more than Englishmen and Americans worry about the existence in their countries of different religious denominations with different theologies. There are, of course, a few native philosophers in any society who do think about and attempt to reconcile such differences, and the Batek are no exception. One of my best informants, Penghulu Selè', who was born a Batek Teh and is now a Batek Dè', is one such man.

In this study I attempt to describe and explain the religion of the Batek Dè' of Kelantan. One might well argue, however, that there is no such thing, the differences in belief between the individual Batek Dè' being of the same order and type as those between members of different dialect groups. One would be forced in the end to describe either the religion of a single individual or that of the Malaysian Negritos as a whole. There is some merit to such an argument, but I think it is possible to isolate a relatively distinctive combination of beliefs at least for groups such as the Batek Dè', who have been well established in a particular area for a long time, and the Batek Nòng, who have been cut off from other Negrito groups. One reason is that the members of each dialect group think of themselves as having different customs (Malay *adat*) from the members of other dialect groups, and they usually consider their own to be better. Each set of customs, like the dialect, is associated with a particular area rather than particular people. Thus, someone who moves into the Aring River valley, for example, would expect to take up the Batek Dè' customs, including religious ones, as well as that dialect. The distinctiveness of the religious beliefs of different dialect groups is marked and maintained in many cases by differences in the religious vocabularies. In some cases similar concepts are called by different terms, which have different local connotations. Alternatively, the words may be the same or cognate, but the meanings quite different. In this respect religious words merely follow a general tendency among Negrito languages for the same or similar words to have different meanings in different dialects. But this situation means that the medium in which religious matters are expressed and discussed is distinctive for each dialect group, and this would tend to act as a filter if not a barrier to the flow of ideas across dialect group boundaries. Because this study is in part a study of the Batek Dè' terms of religious expression, it can to that extent at least be considered a study of the religion of the Batek Dè' in particular.

This is not to imply that the religion of the Batek Dè' is unique or even uniquely Negrito. In fact all of the Orang Asli religions seem to draw their stories, concepts, and images out of a common store, and many of these 'elements' are not even confined to the Malay Peninsula. For example, Needham has shown how a highly complex association of beliefs, rites, and prohibitions is shared by the Malaysian Negritos and the Penan of Borneo (1967). Many other connections between Malaysian aborigines and native Borneans could be added. It is only as a matter of convenience that I limit my comparative considerations to the Negritos, for the work of Benjamin (1967) and Dentan (1968) shows clearly that the Temiar and Semai also participate in this common store of religious ideas, and a recent work of Benjamin's suggests that the folk-religion of the Malays is related to it as well (1974). In a sense the religions of the various Malaysian Negrito dialect groups are selections of elements from a great number of cultural traditions, but they are by no means random selections.

The problem of how to deal with such variation in beliefs can be resolved in various ways. One is simply to record all the statements received and let the reader worry about making sense of them. Although this would have a certain value, it would also be impractical and frustrating for the reader. Another approach would be to attempt to reduce the variations, by some principle of abstraction, to a more manageable number of elements. For example, in dealing with the deities of the western Negritos, Schebesta reduces the number of beings by ignoring some of the differences between them and equating some of the similar figures while distinguishing others (1957: 26–34), but on the whole it seems a rather arbitrary and unsatisfactory process. Yet there is always the temptation to produce a tidy and 'elegant' model even when it may seriously distort the facts. The approach I take is to preserve the variations as far as possible and to make use of them to gain a deeper understanding of how Batek religious concepts are used and how they work. I return to this point below.

Approach taken

My foremost concern is to describe the Batek religion as nearly as possible in terms of their own concepts. I claim that, properly understood, Batek ideas make sense in their own right.[4] I do not

---

[4] In the anthropological study of religion this analytical stance has been called the 'literalist' position (Horton 1962: 217; Ross 1971: 105; Skorupski 1976: 10–11, 236).

think the Batek need an anthropologist to tell them what their
beliefs 'really mean'. I take what the Batek say about things, the
expressed ideas and feelings evoked by them, to be the meaning of
the things for the people. I treat what the Batek say as a body of
'native exegesis', to borrow Victor Turner's phrase, but it is exegesis
not of a set of contrived ritual symbols but of the world in which
they live.[5] This is, of course, only the conscious and expressible level
of meaning. I do not deny that there may be other levels of meaning
in any body of beliefs, but I do think that this one should be
explored fully before other levels of meaning are examined. What is
most important for understanding a people's concepts in their own
terms is that the full range of relevant ideas should be presented.
I would contend that a large component of the meaning of any
element in a belief system is derived from its relationship with the
other elements in the system. Ideas that are enigmatic in isolation
become clear in context, as related ideas shed light on each other.
The broader patterns of ideas are also important features of belief
systems, and they cannot be seen when only a portion of the beliefs
making them up is presented. Previous writers on Malaysian
Negritos have not generally given enough information on the beliefs
of any particular group to enable the patterns and internal connections to be seen (see e.g. Schebesta 1928, 1957; Evans 1937).
Schebesta came closest to achieving the necessary density of
information in his description of Jahai beliefs. In this study I concentrate very closely on the concepts of the Batek Dè' in order to
show the details and patterns that make their world-view a meaning-
ful whole. I make comparisons with the beliefs of other groups only
when they shed light on those of the Batek Dè'.

   Although I try to stay as close as possible in my description to the
actual Batek concepts, I do not mean to imply that all Batek have
something like this book in their heads. For one thing, knowledge is
unevenly distributed in any society. The information I give is
compiled from the statement of many informants. Some Batek
probably know less and some far more than I have written. But I
think it is fair to say that everything I have recorded is present in

---

[5] Some anthropologists consider everything with meaning to be symbols (see
e.g. Geertz 1975: 91, 208n.), including natural features of the environment, but I
think this makes the notion of symbolism far too broad to be useful as an analytical
tool. As Spiro points out (1969: 211), this approach merely substitutes the term
'symbolic' for what was once called 'cultural'.

the Batek cultural tradition, even though it probably does not correspond exactly to what is known by any particular individual. Another difference between Batek knowledge and my description is in the order I have imposed on the material. I have arranged the exposition in a way that I hope will be easily comprehended by the reader. But this does not actually violate Batek conceptions because there is no 'correct' order for describing the Batek world-view. The Batek never describe it themselves except in bits and pieces, which is also the form in which they learn about it. Any wider integration of ideas seems to be done individually or at least largely independently. Although the order of my exposition is imposed, I have tried to arrange the description in accordance with some of the more important relationships actually found in the material, rather than by using a wholly alien scheme of presentation. Finally, I must stress that this study is a description of publicly expressed concepts and is not about the inner states of Batek minds. When I use the term 'belief', I mean what the Batek say is true; I am not concerned with the question of how expressed beliefs are held by the individuals who express them.[6] My impression, however, is that the Batek are not sceptical about their basic world-view. Its truth is taken for granted and is unquestioned, perhaps because the only competing world-view to which they have been exposed in recent years, that of the Muslim Malays, is rejected for social as well as philosophical reasons. Although Batek do not question the truth of their basic world-view, many of them seem to withhold judgement on various minor points. They know there are differences of opinion on some matters, and they assume that one view is correct, but they do not worry about which one it is.

My other aim, as I stated above, is to see what the form and use of Batek religious concepts can tell us about the general process by which human beings understand the world they live in. To do this it is necessary to take another perspective, to step back from the data and ask not what *are* the Batek beliefs but *why* are certain concepts used in certain places instead of others? The best clues in this endeavour are the variations in beliefs that I discussed above. These provide an opening through which the analyst can see more clearly the relationships among concepts and those between concepts

[6] Needham (1972) has cautioned strongly against attributing 'beliefs' to others and has argued persuasively that one can never know the nature of the subjective experience associated with expressed ideas.

and the phenomena they are meant to explain. I assume that where a concept is generally accepted and agreed upon, it does not seriously conflict with other relevant concepts, and it provides an adequate understanding of the phenomenon to which it is attached. I assume further that where there are variations in belief, there is some kind of problem, some reason why no single concept will suffice. Sometimes the various concepts may simply be inadequate individually to explain the phenomenon fully. In such instances, the variant beliefs will each cast light on the phenomenon from a different angle, and thus each will provide a partial basis for understanding it. But there will be some conflict between the different beliefs that prevent their being represented by a single composite model. In other instances the alternative concepts may be different ways of resolving a contradiction or ambiguity in the belief system or in its relation to reality. I suggest, for example, that variations will cluster round areas of inherent ambiguity in the commonly held structure of ideas, as some groups and individuals resolve the ambiguity by emphasizing one aspect or interpretation and others another. Looked at in this way, variations in belief can help to show how the Batek, and by extension human beings in general, form, transform, and manipulate concepts in an attempt to understand their world. I must stress that these manipulations are performed by people, not by culture itself, but they are performed on cultural materials, concepts that are learned and shared, and at least partially according to culturally defined modes of reasoning.

Thus the description and analysis of Batek Dè' religion carried out in this book are distinct but complementary processes. I do not sharply separate the two, but I try to make clear to the reader when I am presenting the Batek ideas and when I am offering my own reflections on the data.

My procedure in this study will be to begin with the religion of the Batek Dè' as a point of departure and then move to as wide a frame of comparison as is necessary to reveal the significance of the Batek Dè' beliefs and practices. Often the meaning of the Batek Dè' idea is plain, and it would be pointless to list all the comparable ideas of other groups. Sometimes a comparison between the Lebir and Aring branches of the Batek Dè' dialect group is sufficient to establish the basic pattern. In still other instances, I find it necessary to consider the beliefs of many Negrito groups in order to arrive at a full understanding of the particular ideas of the Batek Dè'. Such a procedure, it might be argued, is not very systematic, but neither is it arbitrary. It aims always to elucidate the Batek Dè' beliefs by reference to general patterns in the religions of the Malaysian Negritos.

2

COSMOS

I begin this study of Batek religion with a description and discussion of their cosmology. This provides the broad framework within which other religious ideas are set, and it reveals some of the general principles of Batek religious thought.

The Earth

The Batek Dè' story of the origin of the earth (*té'*)[1] is rather simple, in spite of occurring in a number of different versions. I present here a combined version of the creation story and then discuss a few of the themes that appear in it.

In the beginning, it is said, there was only sea (*lawet*) where the land is now. This sea was surrounded by a narrow ring of solid matter (*besi' 'asal*, literally 'original iron') which extended under the water to form a container like a cooking-pot. The rim of this container, which is merely called 'the other side' (*gèl 'un*) of the sea, came only to the level of the surface of the water, where it was met by the firmament (*gelar ketò'*) which formed a flattened dome over the sea. Both the sun (*mềt keto'*) and the moon (*bulan*) were in existence, though the sun was not yet as hot as it is now. A number of *hala'*, superhuman beings, were living on top of the firmament, beneath the sea, on the moon, and on the (then cool) sun. Some of the *hala'* had the form of humans and others the form of various animals.

The formation of the earth began when a huge turtle (*labi'*) or snake (*naga'*) rose to the surface of the water at the centre of the sea. According to some versions this turtle-snake[2] just floated there while other beings built up the earth on its back, but in other versions the

---

[1] The term *té'* means both 'the land', as distinguished from 'the sea', and 'soil', the material of which the land is formed.

[2] Informants who know several versions of the story explicitly equate the *labi'* with the *naga'*. Descriptions of it make it seem a fabulous cross between the two: it is long like a snake but with a broad back like a turtle, huge horns like those of a water buffalo, and it speaks like a Batek.

turtle-snake takes an active role in forming the land. Some versions state that the first bit of earth, which was about the size of a plate, fell from the firmament and landed on the back of the turtle-snake. This original earth is variously described as ordinary earth, excrement ('*èc*) from heavenly (*hala'*) worms, and an umbrella (*payong*) which turned into earth. Another version states that the first lump of earth came out of the foam (*buwèh*) at the centre of the sea. This small lump of earth was then spun round by the turtle-snake or, as some say, a sandpiper bird (*kawaw kedidi'*) which came down from the firmament. The spinning created a whirling mass of foam out of which the turtle-snake or sandpiper extracted more earth to add on to the original lump. The process by which the earth was built up was compared by one informant to the way flour which is boiled in a pot of water gradually thickens into a ball as it is stirred. In another version the size of the original lump of earth was increased by the sandpiper defecating on it.[3] In any case the earth gradually expanded in size until it became a large island which stretched from Kuala Perak, on the west coast of the Malay Peninsula, to Kuala Trengganu on the east coast. Underneath the earth there is still sea, but the earth rests firmly on the back of the original turtle-snake. While the earth was still soft, the sandpiper stamped it down and moulded the mountains and valleys. After this, the sun became red-hot, producing a long drought. The intense heat caused the earth to become hard, and the roots of the grass that then sprouted bound it together. Then the *hala'* above the firmament dropped the first trees to earth. These were *cemcòm* (*Calamus castaneus*), the palm most commonly used for thatch; *gül* (Malay *tualang*; any of a number of species of large trees), the 'bee-tree'; *tekèl* (*Shorea sericea*), a large tree whose bark can be removed in thick sheets; and *cinhèr* (species unknown), a large tree with red bark and beautiful flowers. These were dropped because they are the plants necessary for building the large huts (*hayą' tebew*) used for the singing sessions which are engaged in by the *hala'* as well as the Batek. The floor is made from *tekèl* bark, the roof from *cemòm*, and the *gül* and *cinhèr* trees supply the good-smelling flowers used to decorate the hut and the performers. The *tekèl* tree also supplies the wood for the log-drum

[3] This, like the reference to the excrement of worms, recalls the dung-beetle which is said by several of the western Negrito groups to have brought up the original earth from the bed of the primordial sea (Evans 1937: 159; Schebesta 1957: 322). The difference, of course, is that the sandpiper supplied its own dung.

that accompanies the singing. All other trees were children of these original four. There were no food plants or animals on earth in the beginning because it was only occupied by *hala'*, who do not need to eat.

One interesting feature of this story is that the major creator beings are all semi-aquatic animals.[4] Their ambiguous nature, which they have in common, seems to express statically the process of creation which is essentially a transition from water to land. Yet they differ in that one of them, the turtle-snake, is associated more closely with the underworld, and the other, the sandpiper, with the upper world. In all versions it is the turtle-snake that provides the foundation for the earth and the sandpiper that gives the upper surface of the earth its shape. Much of the variation among different versions of the story concerns the relative amounts of work done by the turtle-snake and the sandpiper, and the relative amount of earth material derived from the water and the sky. Most versions agree, however, that both the upper and lower worlds, and their representative animals, make some contribution to the establishment of the earth. One of the basic themes in Batek religion is that the continued existence of the earth depends on the forces of the upper world and the underworld remaining under control or else they could 'undo' the earth's creation.

One important part of the process of creation is the separation of earth, solid matter, from water. It is commonly said that the turtle-snake or sandpiper 'sifted' or 'sieved' (*'ayak*) earth out of the foam or murky water (*tòm be'ak*) and stuck it on (*lekèt*) to the original lump of earth. This is similar to the Jahai story of the dung-beetle lifting 'the earth out of the ooze' (Schebesta 1957: 35). Even the defecation of the sandpiper can be seen as a process of separating more or less solid matter from the mixture of water and food which the bird ingests. The maintenance of the separation of earth from water is precarious, however, and depends on the turtle-snake making a continuous effort to hold the earth together, to prevent it from dissolving. The *naga'* (or three *naga'* in one version) upon which the earth rests cannot turn or rotate its body without causing the destruction of the earth. It can, however, move short distances

---

[4] One witty young man claimed that the creator of the earth was a frog (*cangkay*), and he insisted that I record (on tape) the song about the original frog. This song turned out to be the term for frog repeated many times, followed by gales of laughter.

forward and backward, some say, as this will only cause floods.[5] The notion that the earth would be utterly destroyed, the soil dissolved in the primordial sea, without the continued co-operation of the turtle-snake is of fundamental importance in the Batek religion.

The earth is pictured by the Batek as a roughly round disc of land resting in the sea which underlies it and forms a ring around it. The earth is conventionally described as having seven layers, following the Malay expressions *tujuh lapis dunia* and *tujuh petala bumi*, but these layers are not differentiated by the Batek. As the origin story reveals, this disc of earth is supposed to extend outward equally in all directions from a point (the axis upon which the original mass was rotated) which is at the centre of the original sea. Thus the earth, sea, and the rim of the sea form a series of concentric circles.

The Sky and Firmament

The sky, the area above the earth but below the firmament, is termed *ketò'* in Batek Dè'.[6] It is conceived as an open space within which the clouds float, the sun and moon move, the rain falls, and the wind blows.

Above the sky is the firmament. This is called *gelar keto'* (literally 'split bamboo of the sky')[7] by the Batek Dè' of the upper Lebir. They describe it as a stationary layer of solid blue clouds which are entirely different from the ordinary black and white clouds (*kabut*)

---

[5] There is apparently some confusion here between the *naga'* which holds up the earth and those which are thought to live in the rivers. There are said to be many *naga'* under the earth, in the rivers, and even in pools on certain mountains. The Batek usually speak as if it were a single enormous *naga'* holding up the earth, however, and this is probably the same one through which, according to some informants, the sun passes when it goes under the earth.

[6] The term *ketò'* is very seldom used alone (it occurs mainly in compound expressions such as *mèt ketò'*, 'sun'), and there is some difficulty in establishing its meaning. It is given by Blagden as being the word for 'day' in a number of Negrito dialects (Skeat and Blagden 1906b: 573), and this may once have been one meaning of it for the Batek Dè', though they now use the Malay-derived term *hari'* for 'day'. The Batek today claim not to know what *ketò'* alone means, but when it is occasionally heard, it seems to refer to the sky or atmosphere (e.g. *ketò' jebéc* means 'threatening sky'). Schebesta became convinced that Kĕto' was a deity of the Batek Nòng who had the sun and moon for eyes (1928: 276; 1957: 25), but they told me it meant 'sky' (Malay *langit*).

[7] The term *gelār* is undoubtedly related to Malay *galar*, 'crushed bamboo floor mat'. Planks made by splitting bamboo are called *gelegar* in Batek Dè'. Skeat records the term *gĕlāl* (or *glarl*) for 'sky' in one Batek Dè' wordlist ('Lebir') (Skeat and Blagden 1906b: 737).

that bring rain. The Aring Batek, on the other hand, call the firmament *batu cara'* (probably 'visible stone'; cf. Malay *batu carak*). It is said to be a layer of stone as thick as the 'skin of the earth' (*kete' té'*). One knowledgeable Lebir woman reconciled the two views by saying that the actual firmament is stone and should be called *batu cara'*, while *gelar ketò'* is a layer of clouds immediately below the firmament. The variation in the conceptualization of the firmament seems to be due to the inherent difficulty of finding a suitable image for a layer of solid matter located in the sky. Although clouds are suited to the location, ordinary clouds are considered too soft to support an upper world. Stone has the required hardness and strength, but it is not so appropriate to the location, and it raises the problem of how shamans' souls and superhuman beings can get through the firmament to get to and from earth. Thus, each view partially answers the conceptual requirement, but neither is totally adequate. This probably accounts for the readiness of one of my more perceptive informants to accept both conceptions at once, with certain adjustments.

According to both views, the firmament is shaped like a flattened dome. It comes down like the roof of a lean-to and meets the rim of the world at the horizon (*can ketò'*, literally 'foot of the sky'). Some say it has a point which pierces the ground at the western horizon. Normally the firmament is described as if it were a single layer, but in some contexts it is said to have several levels, though informants do not always agree on the exact number.[8] In discussing the fate of the souls of the dead, the Lebir Batek mention a lower level where the newly dead are converted into superhuman beings, an intermediate level where most of the superhuman beings live, and an upper level where the *hala'* that guard the ropes that support the earth are located (see below). Also, the Malay expression 'seven layers of sky' (*tujuh lapis langit*) occasionally occurs in Batek Dè' songs, but, like the 'seven layers of earth', they are not actually differentiated.

It is generally agreed that the land on top of the firmament is covered with dry sand in which grass and low bushes grow. Some say the original trees are also represented there, though others insist that they were all sent to earth. It is cool on the firmament because the sun is beneath it (the implication being that the heat of the sun

[8] Skeat claims that both the Negritos and Jakun (Aboriginal Malays) conceive of the sky as being 'built in three tiers' (Skeat and Blagden 1906b: 186–7).

only radiates downward). It is light there but not bright (*pihey*) like it is on earth. It is as though the land above the firmament was bathed in strong moonlight. There is no wind because that also is below the firmament. Although there are few if any trees on the firmament, there are great quantities of flowers. These are the blossoms that the *hala'* send to earthly fruit trees in the proper season. In this respect the Batek Dè' conception of the firmament is like the Batek Nòng notion of a 'fruit island' (*polaw kebü'*) in the sky. This is supposed to be made of clouds and inhabited by certain *hala'* fairies, whom the Batek Nòng call *cemròy*,[9] and it is guarded by a deity known as Jawéc.[10] The main difference between the 'fruit island' and the Batek Dè' firmament is that the latter extends as an unbroken fabric down to the horizon on all sides. This is important because it means that the *hala'* who travel freely over the firmament, can be said to be above the firmament and at the eastern or western horizon at the same time.

The Sun

The sun is called *mẹt ketò'* ('eye of the sky')[11] or, less commonly, *kit ketò'* ('anus of the sky').[12] It is considered to be a hot, glowing disc like a crucible (*kosè'*; Malay *kui*) but not to be actually on fire. Its light is compared to the radiance (*bayang*; also means 'shadow') of an electric torch. The sun is supposed to have a bad smell (*pel'èng*, 'the smell of raw meat') because, when it goes down at the western horizon, it passes very near the spot where the corpses of humans

---

[9] No doubt these are the '*cenoi*' of the western Negritos (see e.g. Evans 1937: 142–305 *passim*; Schebesta 1957: 130–2).

[10] Skeat terms the idea of an 'island of fruit trees' a 'Malayan' belief (Skeat and Blagden 1906b: 239n.), presumably from the Aboriginal Malays (cf. Evans 1923: 40), though it is certainly found among at least one Negrito group besides the Batek Nòng, namely, the Kensiu of Kedah (Skeat and Blagden 1906b: 207).

[11] This expression is superficially like the Malay expression for 'sun', *mata hari*, which means 'eye of the day'. It may be that one reason *ketò'* was often recorded as meaning 'day' was because the investigator directly equated the Negrito expression *mẹt kèto'* with the Malay *mata hari*. Although *mẹt* does mean 'eye' in Batek Dè', it has a number of other meanings as well. Perhaps the most revealing comparison in this case is with the expression *mẹt 'òs*, which means 'the glowing tip of a firebrand'.

[12] Skeat and Blagden list this term for several Negrito groups including the Batek Dè' ('Pang. U. Aring' and 'Kerbat') (1906b: 573). Schebesta suggests that it might refer specifically to the declining sun of the afternoon (1957: 62). The Batek Dè' use *mẹt ketò'* and *kit ketò'* interchangeably, however. They say the expression 'anus of the sky' refers to the fact that human beings live underneath the sun.

and animals from previous eras (Malay *jaman dulu*) lie rotting. The sun travels across the sky, below the firmament but above most of the ordinary clouds. It descends into the sea near the western horizon in the afternoon and travels under the earth to rise in the morning near the eastern horizon. When it is under the earth it is daylight (*kelpah*) down there. Some informants say it enters the mouth of the (earth-supporting) *naga'* in the west and emerges from its navel or anus in the east.[13] According to the Batek, the sun does not have a solid path; it merely 'makes it way' through the clouds. However, it is surrounded by a halo of cloud which is called its *gelong*.[14] This *gelong* moves with the sun and, some say, actually carries it along. The *gelong* is hot like the sun itself. Although the sun (with the *gelong*) is said to move by itself, my informants assured me that it has no engine (*'ènjin*), and it is not alive, for it has no breath.

The Moon

The moon is called *bulan* (Malay *bulan*). It is considered to be a disc of a smooth, hard material which is variously described as being like metal, glass, or polished stone. The moon and the light that radiates from it are cool; therefore *hala'* can sit on the moon, though they can no longer sit on the sun. Unlike the sun, the moon has a good smell like that of flowers. The path of the moon is separate from and slightly higher than the path of the sun. Some informants say the moon only goes down into the sea at dawn and then rises up again the next evening, but most people consider it to travel under the earth during the day much as the sun does at night. Like the sun,

[13] This recalls the Lanoh tradition that a dragon (*rahu'*) causes eclipses of the sun and moon by climbing up to the firmament in the west and devouring them, later letting them out of its tail (Schebesta 1957: 64–5). Rahu, in Hindu mythology, is the name of the 'demon that causes eclipses of the sun and moon' (Schebesta 1957: 66n.). The Batek, however, know nothing of solar or lunar eclipses, which is not surprising since they live in the forest and seldom have an unobscured view of either the sun or the moon.

[14] According to Schebesta (1957: 12, 62–77 *passim*), the western Negritos believe there is a system of planks or beams, called *galog'n*, running through the sky. The sun travels along one of these, and the superhuman beings sometimes play on them. Evans points out that there seems to be some confusion in the minds of the Negritos over whether the paths of the heavenly bodies are like 'planks' (Malay *galang*) or like 'multiple loops of rattan' (Malay *gelong*) (1937: 165n.). The Batek De' explicitly compare the *gelong* to a coil of rattan, but it is a halo around the sun rather than the path along which it moves. This apparently is a case where a term has diffused but has been interpreted in quite different ways by the various groups that have adopted it.

the moon is surrounded by a halo (*gelong*), but the *gelong* of the moon is cool like mist. The moon is said to run from the sun because it is afraid of getting heat stroke (*perèñ panas*), and it dislikes the foul smell of the sun. That is why the moon normally goes down when the sun comes up, and vice versa.

There are a number of ways of speaking about the moon which seem to suggest that it is considered to be animate. Not only does it run from the sun out of 'fear' of its heat and smell, but the phases of the moon are described as its growing old (*bakès*) and becoming young (*kèn*) again. In addition there is a story that the moon, who was male, was once married to a large female star, *jong* (probably the Pole Star). And yet the Batek Dè' explicitly deny that the moon is alive, for it has no breath, and they say that its growing old and young again is merely a figure of speech.[15] Most informants claim not to know why the moon goes through its phases, though some say that it is merely obscured by clouds at times. The story of the moon being married to a star is considered a *cerita*' ('folk-tale'); it is probably borrowed from the Malays as is the term *jong* itself. On the whole the Batek picture the moon in far less animate terms than the western Negritos who have many stories of the celestial objects as living beings (e.g. Schebesta 1957: 62–6). This may be because these stories, like the story of the eclipse-causing monster Rahu, are borrowed from outside, especially Hindu, sources. The western Negritos are much closer than the Batek to the ancient centres of Hindu culture in the Peninsula, which clustered mainly on the Kedah coast (Rajah 1974, Stargardt 1973). In any case, personified and naturalistic conceptions of the heavenly bodies are not mutually exclusive in Negrito thought any more than they are in our own. For us to describe the features of the lunar surface in terms of the 'man in the moon' does not preclude our knowing about its geological composition. We simply hold these two sets of ideas in different ways, the one as folk-tale and the other as science.

The differential evaluation of the sun and moon by the Batek Dè' points to a fundamental distinction in Batek thought and values. This is the contrast between hot and cold.[16] The sun seems to

[15] The Batek Nòng bluntly state that both the sun and the moon are 'cauldrons' (Malay *kawah*).

[16] This refers to actual temperature and is not related to the Chinese and Malay concepts of 'heating' and 'cooling' foods. For the Batek it is not the nature of the foods that makes them hot or cold but whether they are cooked or not.

epitomize excessive heat, which the Batek are at pains to avoid. They blame heat, the sources of heat (e.g. fires and the sun), and heated things (e.g. cooked food) for many types of disease, and their dislike of the sun's heat is one of the basic reasons they resist taking up agriculture. The moon, on the other hand, epitomizes coolness, which the Batek highly value. Coolness is associated with comfort, good health, and the highly admired *hala'* who live, among other places, on the moon. To the Batek it is perfectly understandable that the cool moon should run from the hot sun. The distinction between hot and cold has far-reaching ramifications in the Batek Dè' world-view.

The Stars

The Batek Dè' term for stars is *bintang* (Malay *bintang*), although some *hala'* are said to call them *lip*, which may be an older Negrito word. They are considered to be small chunks of smooth stone about the size of a cauldron (Malay *kawah*), although they and the light they give off are cool. They hang on stems from the underside of the firmament. They stay in one place, but simply cannot be seen during daylight. The Batek Dè' do not seem to be aware of the movement of the stars, perhaps because, living in the deep forest, they seldom have an unobstructed view of the sky. One especially large star, or cluster of stars (probably the Pleiades),[17] is supposed to hang from a shoot which juts out of Batu Keñam, a tall stone pillar in Pahang (see below). This is sometimes called the 'original star' (*bintang 'asal*) or 'mother star' (*bintang na'*), and the ordinary stars are described as its 'coolies' (*kuliy*). This is the star that shamans usually visit; it is the only one that can move, but if it is seen to do so during the day, this portends a disastrous storm. Although there is an element of personification in these descriptions, the stars, like the moon, are unequivocally stated to be inanimate stones. The stars are evaluated much like the moon because they too are considered cool. Some of the western Negritos make the connection between the moon and stars even stronger in a series of stories which portray the stars as the children of the moon (Evans 1937: 167; Schebesta 1957: 62–4). I heard a similar story among the Batek Teh but never among the Batek Dè'.

[17] It was called *bintang ketika'* by one informant, which in Malay refers to the Pleiades, the stars used to judge the proper time to plant rice.

Stone Pillars

The Batek Dè' say there are two stone pillars in existence which reach from the earth to the firmament. There is some disagreement between the Aring and Lebir groups, however, regarding what is found at each pillar. Some of the features that one group places at one pillar are placed by the other group at the other pillar. I begin, therefore, by describing those features of the two pillars on which the Aring and Lebir people agree; then I go on to describe those features about whose location the two groups disagree.

One of the stone pillars, called Batu Keñam,[18] is located on the Keniyam River (*tòm keñam*) which is just across the Pahang border to the south of the headwaters of the Aring and Lebir Rivers (see Map 1). It is probably one of the large limestone outcroppings which occur in that area. It can be seen for many miles, even from some points in Kelantan. Supposedly it can be approached on foot, but no ordinary human can climb it, and even aeroplanes cannot fly over it. One of the features of Batu Keñam on which both the Aring and Lebir groups agree is that it is one of the places where bees and the flowers of fruit trees come from. The story of the origin of Batu Keñam is full of incongruities and *non sequiturs*, but I have heard very similar versions of it from a number of people, so it must be considered a well-established episode in the Batek Dè' oral tradition. The following is a brief summary of that story.

Once two young women, *hala'* sisters, made camp on the Keniyam River. They built a lean-to and then kept adding on more sticks and thatch until it reached the firmament. This huge hut contained many things, including stars which hung from the thatch. When the lean-to reached the firmament, it became the eastern 'foot of the sky', and the sea shifted westward until it covered the headwaters of the Aring and Lebir Rivers. A *hala'* 'spider-hunter' bird (*kawaw setsèt; Arachnothera longirostra*), who had been living nearby, became angry at them for moving the sea. One day, when the two sisters were bathing, the bird flew to the top of the hut and landed on the uppermost supporting stick. This caused the hut to turn into a stone pillar, Batu Keñam, which reached to the firmament. Then the horizon returned to the east and the waves that had been sea became hills. The sisters were angry and prepared to leave. Various versions of the story have them moving to the western horizon, the eastern horizon, and the firmament directly above

---

[18] The term *batu* means 'stone, rock' in Malay and Batek Dè'. This stone is called Batu Kenlim by some of the Aring Batek. I do not know any meaning for the term *kenlim*, so I choose to follow the majority of the Batek in referring to this stone pillar as Batu Keñam, which at least has the merit of recalling its location.

the stone pillar. Before they left, the sisters summoned the thunder-god (Gobar), who was then living on earth in human form, and ordered him to guard the hut-stone. He ascended (or was pulled by the sisters) half-way up the stone where he then made his home in a cave. After that he took charge of the thunderstorms, which he controlled from his cave.

The story seems to deal with an unsuccessful attempt to alter the structure of the world. The lean-to is intended to take the place of the original eastern slope of the firmament which it resembles even to the extent of being furnished with stars. The spider-hunter bird resents the sisters' action, perhaps because he is not a sea or shore bird[19] and thus does not appreciate having his home turned to water. By foiling the sisters' scheme, the bird reaffirms the original order of the world. The connection of the thunder-god with Batu Keñam seems an afterthought, and that part of the story is occasionally left out. Yet all Batek Dè' agree that the thunder-god lived on Batu Keñam at least at one time, and this episode provides a mythical justification for this association.

The other stone pillar, Batu Balok,[20] is located on the Palah River, a tributary of the upper Relai River (see Map 1). It is probably also a limestone outcropping, as a number of them are found in that area. This stone pillar is considered to be the centre of the world (*posat deña*; Malay *pusat dunia*) by most Batek Dè'. It is as old as the earth itself, being the central core round which the rest of the earth was formed. It was moulded into its present shape by the sandpiper bird. The most distinctive feature of Batu Balok is that there are many tigers living in caves round its base, and it is the home of Raja Yạh, the king of the tigers. The name Balok shows a connection between this stone pillar and the Malay *kandang balok*, the 'mythical home of tigers'. This so-called tigers' fold is described in detail by Skeat (1901: 37–8). It is supposed to be a place deep in the forest (Skeat's informants placed it in Ulu Setiu in Trengganu) where tiger-men live in a village of their own under the rule of a tiger-chief. 'It is this Chief whom men call by the name of the "Tiger Devil" or "Tiger Demon" and who enters the bodies of sorcerers when they invoke the Tiger Spirit' (Skeat 1901: 37). All these beings

[19] The spider-hunters are forest living birds which are similar in size, shape, colouring, and habits to the American humming-birds (Tweedie 1970: 56–9). In another story, the *hala'* spider-hunter bird teaches the Batek which fruits of the forest can be safely eaten.

[20] It is also called Batu Baley by some of the Batek Dè' and Batu Hala' by the Batek Teh.

have the form of tigers while in their village, except for the chief who is always in the form of a man. But the ordinary tiger-beings change into human form whenever they leave the 'tiger's fold' by swimming through a special pond, and they regain their tiger shape on return by swimming through another, similar pond. In another version of the story, the tiger-people have human form in their own village, but change to tiger form whenever they leave it (Rentse 1933: 246–9).

Although the Malay and Batek ideas are obviously connected, the actual nature of the tigers involved differs. The Malay tiger-chief and very probably the rest of the tigers are *hantu*, spirits which can take the form of tigers. I have argued elsewhere (1970: 17, 21) that these Malay tiger spirits are probably the ghosts of dead shamans, and, like all Malay free spirits, are incorporeal. The tigers at Batu Balok, on the other hand, are *hala'*-tigers (*yạh hala'*); they have animal bodies which are vulnerable to death, but have the shadow-souls of dead human shamans. Inside the caves the same shadow-souls may assume equally substantial human-form bodies. The *hala'*-tigers act as helpers and teachers to their shaman descendants and as guardians to the Batek, more like the Malay 'sacred tigers' (*rimau keramat*) (Skeat 1900: 70–1) than the 'tiger-spirit' (*hantu belian*). Nevertheless, the Batek say they are afraid to go near Batu Balok because there are ordinary tigers there as well.

Above the tigers' caves at Batu Balok are large quantities of seasonal fruit blossoms and also bees which rest in small caves 'like goods on a shop shelf' when it is not the proper season for them to be in the forest making honey. According to some informants, some of the superhuman beings who send the fruit blossoms to earth at the beginning of the fruit season also live on Batu Balok.

The disagreement between the Aring and Lebir Batek Dè' is over which of these stone pillars is the present home of the thunder-god (Gobar) and the origin of the components of the thunderstorm: thunder, lightning, and rain. The Lebir people say that Gobar still lives on Batu Keñam, which he ascended soon after it came into existence. Some of the Aring Batek claim, however, that he later moved to Batu Balok. Still other Aring people say that Gobar, who is considered by all Batek Dè' to be two beings in some contexts,[21] has left both pillars and now resides at the foot of the sky at the

[21] The structural ambiguity of the thunder-god is discussed in detail in Chapters 6 and 7.

eastern and western horizons. Although the Lebir people also associate the two persons who make up the thunder-god with east and west, they say it is only their voices that go out in these two directions while their bodies remain on Batu Keñam. All Batek Dè' agree that the wind and rain of the thunderstorms come from the place of Gobar, but these elements are conceived in several different ways. One notion that is held widely by both Aring and Lebir people is that there are 'ropes' (*tali'*) of wind, rain, and lightning which stretch from the upper part of Batu Keñam to the horizon (in all directions). There are seven ropes of each kind. The various components of the storms are sent down these ropes, from which they scatter in all directions. Those Aring people who place Gobar at the eastern and western horizons merely reverse the direction of the storm, saying that it travels from the periphery of the world toward the centre. The ropes are guarded by the *hala'* who live above the firmament to prevent them from breaking. This would result in the utter destruction of the world, the celestial counterpart to the turtle-snake's turning and allowing the earth to dissolve. That these ropes, which support the world, should be attached to Batu Keñam seems to imply a central position for that stone pillar, but even those Batek who hold this conception of the components of storms place the centre of the world at Batu Balok.[22] An alternative conception which is held by some of the Aring people is that wind and rain are stored in two caves in Batu Balok. The caves have doors which Gobar opens, allowing these elements to burst out, whenever he wants to cause a storm. A similar conception is held about Batu Keñam by some Lebir Batek. A further complication is that wind and rain are sometimes personified. They are then seen as human-form *hala'* who live near Gobar and send out the forces of the storm following his orders. This personification of the wind and rain can occur with both the 'rope' and 'cave' theories of storms. In spite of these variations and differences of opinion, the Batek Dè' are all agreed that the forces of the thunderstorm come from Gobar, and they are usually associated with one or the other of the stone pillars.

[22] One Aring man, who has been trained as a medical dresser at the J.O.A. hospital near Kuala Lumpur, claims that Gunung Tahan, rather than either of the stone pillars, is the centre of the world, the point from which the ropes of wind, rain, and lightning extend, and the home of the *hala'*-tigers. This seems to be a reconciliation of Batek traditions with a knowledge, probably acquired outside the forest, that Gunung Tahan is the highest mountain in the Malay Peninsula.

The meaning and significance of the Batek Dè' notions of stone pillars can be better understood by comparison with the related ideas of the other Negritos. Most of the Malaysian Negrito dialect groups have such ideas, though they are elaborated in different ways. The western Negritos generally speak of a single stone pillar which is called Batu Rib'm or some close equivalent (Schebesta 1957: 38). This stone pillar is regarded as the centre of the world (Evans 1937: 185; Schebesta 1928: 217; 1957: 40). The question of where the centre of the world is cannot be easily answered, however. Schebesta thought all the Negrito groups agreed that Batu Rib'm was at the headwaters of the Tadoh River in the extreme north-west corner of Kelantan (apparently near the village of Batu Melintang) (1957: 38). He even believed that he had seen it when he was taken by some Malays to a limestone outcropping near there which contained two caves that were considered *keramat* ('sacred places') by the local Malays (1928: 163; 1954: 38). To establish this consistency, he dismisses (1957: 38) the assertion by one of Evans' informants that Batu Rib'm (Evans writes Batu 'Rem) is at Jinerih in Kedah (Evans 1937: 188), and he even interprets his own informant's report that it is in the head-waters of the Perak River as indicating the Tadoh (1957: 38), in spite of the Tadoh's being on the opposite side of the central mountain range. Evans is probably closer to the mark when he says that 'possibly two, or more, limestone mountains may have the same story attached to them' (1937: 188).

The western Negritos seem to especially emphasize the fruit-source aspect of Batu Rib'm. It is conceived as a vertical stone column with a tree-trunk on top which supports a *rankel*,[23] a revolving disc from which hang clusters of fruit-tree flower buds (1957: 40). As this rotates over the earth, the different types of fruit come into season below. A similar device was termed a *lambong* by Evans' informants (1937: 189). Some of the groups Schebesta visited said that the tree-trunk which connected the *rankel* with the top of Batu Rib'm had rotted away, but the *rankel* was now supported by a *hala'* who holds it up with a length of rattan (1957: 41). This view was also expressed by a Jahai informant during Schebesta's second trip to the Peninsula in 1939. He said that, although the trunk of the tree was now gone,

---

[23] The term *rankel* may be related to Malay *rangkai*, a 'cluster' or 'chain' of things, e.g. *bunga serangkai*, 'a bunch of flowers'. The Temiar call the town of Kuala Krai 'Kerèèl', showing the same postulated sound shift in one Aslian language.

'the upper part extends through all of heaven to the very top' (Schebesta 1957: 43). Schebesta explicitly mentions that on the later trip 'nothing was said about a revolving disc and fruit umbels' (1957: 44). In addition to being the source of fruit, some of the Jahai make it the abode of the souls of the dead, the *hala'*-tigers (as do the Kintaq (Schebesta 1957: 153)), and the 'flower fairies' (*ćenoi*) (Schebesta 1957: 40). Another of his Jahai informants denied that the souls of the dead were at Batu Rib'm, though he agreed on the other points (Schebesta 1957: 40).

The Batek Nòng do not seem to have the idea of a stone pillar, but they have a story that there was once a giant tree at Kuala Pahang[24] which was called Jehọ' Mahang, the 'Mahang Tree' (Malay *mahang*, 'a generic name for soft-wood trees, *Macaranga* spp., *Mallotus* spp.'). It was so large it took a person three years to walk around the base. Tohan (God) said this was the original tree (*jehọ' 'asal*). Once some Malays tried to chop it down, but found they could not do it. They called a Batek *hala'* named Sang Kelmai who succeeded in cutting it down within a year. When it fell, water burst from the stump and became the Pahang River. This recalls a story of the Kintaq Negritos of Kedah and Perak which runs as follows. Once a *hala'* named Chong passed by Batu Rib'm and heard a mysterious murmuring inside. 'He drew his bow and shot an arrow into the mountain. Immediately water gushed out. That is how people obtained water' (Schebesta 1957: 40). The parallels between Batu Rib'm and the Batek Nòng Mahang Tree are so close that it is not unreasonable to compare the chopping down of the tree with the rotting away of the trunk of the *rankel* as reported elsewhere. This suggests that the branches of the Mahang Tree stayed aloft after the trunk was chopped down, forming the 'fruit island' mentioned above (unfortunately I have no explicit information on this point). Thus the 'fruit island' of the Batek Nòng can be seen to be equivalent to the Jahai *rankel* after its trunk had rotted away.

The Batek Dè' place most of the fruit-tree blossoms on top of the firmament, and they explicitly deny that the firmament is like the branches of a tree. Yet they also say that there are other flowers on Batu Keñam and Batu Balok. Like the Jahai, some of the Aring Batek place the *hala'* tigers and the fairies at the same stone pillar,

---

[24] This probably indicates the place where the small stream called Sungai Pahang joins the Jelai to form the main Pahang River, rather than whe˘ the Pahang River empties into the sea.

but none of the Batek Dè' see the souls of the dead as going to either of the stone pillars.

To some extent these variations in stone pillar ideas can be understood in terms of the Indian concept of the 'world-tree'. Stated very briefly, this is the idea that the world is centred around an enormous tree, whose roots form the underworld and whose branches form the upper world. The world-tree contains, among many other things, the sources of food and the souls of the dead and the yet unborn. This notion is widespread and highly developed in the Indian-influenced parts of South-East Asia and Indonesia (see e.g. Tobing 1956). The Malaysian Negrito stone pillars all seem to contain traces of the world-tree, but these are strongest among the western Negritos who would have been most directly exposed to the influence of the Indianized settlements on the Kedah coast. As one moves eastward, the unity of the world-tree breaks down and some of its features drop out. The Batu Rib'm of the western Negritos is unitary and central like the world-tree, but for the Batek Dè' it has split in two. Still, the shifting of some features from one to the other of the two pillars and the suggestions of centrality for both reveal a certain strain inherent in this division. Also as one moves eastward, the production of fruit blossoms becomes somewhat detached from the stone pillar. The Batek Nòng place the flowers on a fruit island in the sky, though this island, I have argued, may once have been the branches of a world-tree. The Batek Dè' consider both stone pillars to contain fruit blossoms, but the main source of them is the firmament which they explicitly say is not like the branches of a tree, though one could argue that there is a genetic connection which is no longer recognized. The connection of the stone pillar with the souls of the dead is apparently only weakly developed even in the west, though traces of it appear at least among the Jahai, as Schebesta reports (1957: 40). Most of the western Negritos, however, say there is a large tree in the afterworld which contains all kinds of food and also flowers which represent the souls of the living and the dead (Schebesta 1957: 178–9, 182). The soul-bearing aspect (and part of the food-producing function) has obviously been split off from the stone pillar to conform to the usual placement of the land of the dead at the western horizon.

The Afterworld

The afterworld is generally called just the 'place of the dead' (*tempèt batèk halòt*), but one Aring man said its name is *cemampeng*.[25] The Aring and Lebir people disagree on the location of the afterworld. The Aring Batek say it is in the west at the foot of the sky. Usually it is placed on the rim of the world, beyond the sea, though occasionally it is said to be on an island near where the sun goes down. In placing the land of the dead at the western horizon, the Aring Batek conform to the views of the great majority of Negrito groups, including the Batek Nòng and Batek Teh (see e.g. Schebesta 1957: 177–85).

The Lebir Batek, on the other hand, claim that the afterworld of their race is on top of the firmament, in the land of the original superhuman beings (*hala' 'asal*). (They say that the souls of Malays go into the ground.) The necessity for the soul to fly upward after death is explicitly given as the reason for their custom of tree-burial. Though the souls of the dead generally reside directly above the earth, they can travel down the firmament to the horizon in any direction whenever they wish. This allows some accommodation with the more general view, of which they are well aware, that the afterworld is in the west. Thus, they explain the custom of placing the head of the corpse toward the west by saying that, although the soul goes upward, it goes toward the west (at first) as well. Another type of accommodation may be seen in the idea that the place of the corpses of animals and men from previous eras, which contaminates the sun with an unpleasant smell, is in the west where the sun goes down. This afterworld is clearly distinguished, however, from that of the present-day Batek. The Lebir Batek idea that the afterworld is above the firmament, in the land of *hala'*, may be the last living example of an ancient Negrito belief. As Schebesta says, the placement of the realm of the dead in the west is probably an adaptation to foreign religious elements (it is a very widespread view among the peoples of South-East Asia), and he speculates that it may once have been located in the heavens (1957: 185). There are traditions of tree-burial, usually for shamans, among a number of Negrito groups (see e.g. Skeat and Blagden 1906b: 91; Schebesta 1957: 151, 157) and one quite clear case, among the Negritos of Chong in southern Thailand, in which the afterworld is described as a region in the sky

---

[25] Schebesta records that the Mendriq call the land of the dead *éepeg'n* (1957: 178).

(Evans 1927: 13). The Jahai reference to souls of the dead living on Batu Rib'm may also be a trace of a heavenly afterworld. Again the relative isolation of the Batek from outside influences may account for their retaining, on the Lebir at least, a belief that has been replaced elsewhere.

Although the Aring and Lebir Batek place the afterworld in different locations, they attribute similar characteristics to it. It is a flat, open place with few or no trees. It is cool and relatively dry, and it is not subject to thunderstorms. There are many flowers there, though there are no fruit-trees or fruit. There are no animals and no fire. This may seem a rather bleak and monotonous landscape, but it is a very desirable environment according to Batek values, especially because of its lack of heat. The absence of food is no problem, for the souls of the dead are free of the burden, as the Batek see it, of having to eat.

Orientation of the Cosmos

The main axes of orientation in the Batek universe are east-west and up-down. The east-west axis is based upon the movement of the sun. The ordinary term for east is *mệt ketò' ceweh*, 'sun rises'. The equivalent term for west is *mệt ketò' berey*, 'sun goes down' or, as the Batek Nòng say, 'sun dies'.[26] In the language of the *hala'*, east is *penlow*[27] and west *kenirèm*. These terms are not normally used, however, and many people do not know them or do not apply them correctly. The terms used for north and south clearly reflect the subordinate status of that axis of orientation. The Lebir people say *lenintang mệt ketò'*, 'across the sun', for both north and south.[28] The Aring Batek merely use the words for 'right side' (*tim*) and 'left side' (*wệ'*)[29] for north and

[26] The term *berey* seems only to be used for the sun. Many of the Negritos use the more general term *beles*, 'to fall, slip down', i.e. *mệt ketò' beles* (Skeat and Blagden 1906b: 573–4). The latter expression is readily recognized by the Batek Dè', as they use the term *beles* in other contexts.

[27] Evans records that *penlau* means 'the period when it is just becoming light in the morning' in the Kintak language (1937: 164n.).

[28] A similar expression, *lintang kit-kĕtok*, was recorded by Skeat for the Batek Dè' ('Pang. U. Aring') in 1900 (Skeat and Blagden 1906b: 574). The Batek Nòng also use a similar expression, *lentang ketò'*, for north and south. All these terms are probably derived from Malay *lintang*, 'position or barrier across'.

[29] The terms *tim* and *wệ'*, which have many cognates in other Negrito and Senoi languages (Skeat and Blagden 1906b: 646, 698), have been almost completely replaced by the Malay terms *kanan* and *kiri* among most of the Batek Dè', though a few of the older people still know the earlier terms.

south, the assessment being made from the point of view of a person (or the sun) facing west. The north-south axis has almost no significance in the Batek Dè' cosmology.

Time is also ordered by the passage of the sun. Many of the terms for different times of day refer directly to the position of the sun in the sky (cf. Evans 1937: 164n.). Thus, the terms for early morning (*mẹt ketò' ceweh*) and late afternoon (*berey*), like the English terms 'sunrise' and 'sunset', have a double reference: they indicate both a time and a place.

The up-down axis in the Batek cosmos is represented by the stone pillars, especially Batu Balok which is the centre of the earth. There is a systematic symmetry between the upper and lower worlds as well. The movement of the sun and moon ties together the vertical and horizontal (east-west) axes of orientation, however, by circling directly over and under the centre of the earth.

The east-west and up-down axes of orientation are differentially emphasized and elaborated by different Negrito groups. This is especially evident in relation to the locations of deities (see Chapter 6). One example that has already been mentioned is the disagreement between different groups of Batek Dè' over whether the thunder-god lives high up on a stone pillar or at ground level at the eastern and western horizons. The difference between the Lebir and the Aring Batek in the placement of the afterworld can also be seen in this light. The Lebir people tend in general to emphasize the vertical dimension slightly more than the horizontal and the Aring people the reverse. The de-emphasis of the north-south axis by all the Negrito groups gives their cosmologies a markedly two-dimensional quality.

Summary

The Batek Dè' conception of the world can be described briefly as follows. The earth is a flat disc of land which is surrounded and underlain by sea. The sea is contained by a 'bowl' of solid material which forms a narrow rim round the further side of the sea. This is met at the horizon by the firmament, a flattened dome of hard blue clouds which cover the earth and sea. The stars are attached to the underside of the firmament, and the sun and moon circle round the earth, moving across the sky (below the firmament) and through the underground sea. There is a vertical axis connecting earth and firmament in the form of one or more stone pillars, and the basic horizontal axis of orientation is established by the passage of the sun through the sky from east to west. This cosmology is fundamentally similar to those of the other Malayan Negrito groups, although there are a number of differences in detail (see e.g. Evans 1937: 159–69, 185–9, 256–65; Schebesta 1957: 35–48, 62–6, 177–85). This scheme, of course, is not confined to the Malaysian Negritos and is, in fact, widespread among the peoples of Malaysia and Indonesia. There may well be a pre-Muslim Malay influence involved, as Skeat seems to suspect (Skeat and Blagden 1906b: 179–80), with the ancient cosmology being preserved by the Negritos after Islamic conceptions took hold among the Malays. But many of the elaborations and emphases are distinctively Negrito, and whatever the ultimate origin of various features of the cosmology, it stands as the world-view of the Negritos today, and it is thus the proper context within which to examine the other features of their religion.

3

MAN AND ENVIRONMENT

Like all peoples, the Batek are strongly affected in the way they behave by their conceptions of the world in which they live. In this chapter I examine Batek views of their forest environment, as a source of subsistence and a source of danger, and show how they regulate their behaviour in terms of those views.

Batek Attitudes toward the Forest

The Batek identify closely with their rain forest environment. They sometimes call themselves 'forest people' (*batèk hep*) (cf. Carey 1976: 31). They regard the forest as their true home; whenever they camp in or near clearings, they say they are only 'lodging' (*tompang*) there. The Batek consider their living in the forest to be part of the natural order of things as established by the superhuman beings. Although individual Batek may leave the forest for varying lengths of time, it is generally believed that if all the Batek moved out of the forest, the superhuman beings would destroy the world. The Batek are not afraid of the forest and do not build symbolic defences against it. Their easy intimacy with the forest is clearly expressed in the layout of their camps. The huts at a campsite are scattered here and there, facing in various directions. No deliberate effort is made to remove the undergrowth from the space between the huts or to set off the area of the camp from the surrounding forest. When the thatch of the huts is still green, a Batek camp blends into its surroundings so well that only the sound of voices and the smoke of fires betray its presence to an observer a few feet away. Thus, the Batek, unlike most forest-dwelling agricultural peoples, do not attempt to carve out an island of culture in the sea of nature.

The main reason the Batek give for preferring to live in the forest rather than in clearings is that the forest is cool. It is not only more comfortable because of this, but also, according to their theories, more healthy. Heat is thought to cause or contribute to many types of illnesses. If anyone becomes seriously ill while living in a clearing, the whole group will immediately move back into the forest. Another reason the Batek like living in the forest is that it is avoided by most other ethnic groups. Only the Malay rattan traders go into their part of the forest regularly, and they do so only during the daytime. They always camp beside the larger rivers on sand and gravel bars. Thus, as long as the Batek live in the rain forest, they are assured of a certain amount of privacy and freedom from outside interference.

The Forest as a Source of Food

According to Batek stories, when the first human beings were created, many superhuman beings (*hala'*) still lived on earth in human and animal forms. Although the *hala'* themselves do not eat, it was they who created food for human beings. The Batek believe that most, if not all, of the plants and animals they eat were created specifically as food for them. Thus, when they exploit their forest environment, they are following an ancient plan laid down for them by the superhuman beings. Not only did the *hala'* originally create the Batek foods, but they also play a continuing role in the production of many important food resources, even though they no longer live on the surface of the earth. Consequently, the foraging Batek see their food-getting activities as placing them in a relationship with the superhuman beings as well as with the physical environment. In this section I describe some of the Batek beliefs about their major foods and show some of the ways these ideas affect their behaviour.

Wild tubers

The staff of life of the nomadic Batek is wild yams (*Dioscorea* spp.). There is no Batek name for the wild yams as a group except *bab*, the general term for 'food'. (They are usually called by separate 'species' names.) Supposedly, the wild tubers were once superhuman beings. After man had been created, some of the original superhuman beings (*hala' 'asal*) noticed that there was nothing for humans to eat. So they ordered some of their 'coolies' (*kuliy*), who were also *hala'*, to become tubers. These coolies sent their shadow-souls into the earth, leaving their human-form bodies behind, and they formed tuberous bodies for themselves. But after a while, the *hala'* who had become tubers missed their relatives, who by then were living on top of the firmament, and they began to cry. So they sent their shadow-souls up to the sky. But the tubers continued to live in the earth, and they now reproduce themselves without any intervention from the super-human beings. There is a separate story that explains how the Batek learned to process *gadong* (*Dioscorea hispida*), an important food source which is poisonous in its natural state. A human-form *hala'*, Pa' 'Angkòl, caused the *gadong* to become poisonous in order to poison a wicked old woman called Ya' Kedat (some say she was a Malay *hantu*, 'evil spirit') who had killed and eaten his younger sisters. Afterward he taught the Batek how to leach the poison out of the tubers so they could continue to eat them.

Although the wild yams were man's first food, they are now taken more or less for granted, perhaps because they are a relatively plentiful and reliable source of nourishment. There are no cere-monies, prohibitions, or magical practices connected with them. They are simply dug up and eaten as required.

Fruit

The Batek environment supplies them with an abundance of seasonal fruit (*kebü' tahun* or merely *tahun*; cf. Malay *tahun*, 'year'), which, along with honey, is the most prized of the wild foods. Some of the seasonal fruits are domesticated species which remain in the now overgrown orchards abandoned by the Malays. But according to Batek ideas, the true *tahun* are the wild species, which are supposedly produced and maintained only by the superhuman beings. Seasonal fruits are valued for their good flavour and also because many of them can be eaten raw. The Batek believe that raw food, being cool, is less likely to carry diseases than cooked food.

The origin of fruit is similar to that of tubers. It is said simply that some of the *hala'* were ordered by other *hala'* (or some say by Tohan, a deity) to become fruit for man to eat. Sometimes there is a suggestion that certain species of fruit preceded and were ancestral to others. The Mendriq told me that the *lop* (Batek Dè' *bangkong*; *Artocarpus integer*) was the original fruit from which all others descended. It is notable for the large size of the fruit (up to 60 lb. each (Burkill 1966: 251)) and its long fruiting season. The Batek generally say that the *tawès*, a large wild fruit (probably *Artocarpus* sp.), was the first fruit, though the other wild species were indepen-dently created by the transformation of other *hala'*. After the creation of the various species of fruit, human beings were still afraid to eat fruit because they did not know which species would make them sick or dizzy. This information was revealed, according to both Batek and Mendriq stories, by *hala'* in the form of birds. In the Batek Dè' account it is the spider-hunter bird, who also figures in the creation of Batu Keñam, that shows man which fruits can be eaten raw, which must be cooked, and, for some of the unpalatable or poisonous types, how they can be processed to make them edible.

Unlike tubers, fruit is not always available in the forest. There is no trace of fruit during the floods (December and January) or during the relatively dry period that follows the floods (February and March), and there are only fruit blossoms in April and the early part of May. The Batek explain this by saying that when there is no fruit on earth, it is in the heavens: above the firmament and on the stone pillars. Usually the fruit is pictured as taking the form of flowers while in the sky. In Kelantan, during February and March, one often hears thunder rumbling in the distance, but only rarely do thunderstorms pass over the Batek area. This distant rumbling is supposed to be the thunder-god, Gobar, signalling the superhuman beings to drop the fruit blossoms on to the earthly fruit-trees. The sound 'startles' or 'frightens' the *hala'* above. A common variant of this theory says that the seasonal fruits actually become human-form *hala'* while in the heavens. These beings are called *hala' tahun*, 'seasonal fruit superhumans', or just *tahun*, 'seasonal fruit'. When Gobar rumbles, they send their shadow-souls to earth where they enter the limbs of fruit-trees and cause flower buds to burst out. Then the shadow-souls return to the heavens, leaving the fruit to develop naturally. This version reconciles the notion that *hala'* produce the fruit with the knowledge that flowers actually develop on trees. It implies that fruits today, like the original fruits, are actually the bodies of superhuman beings. Occasionally the *hala' tahun* are pictured as storing the fruit blossoms or the shadow-souls that produce them inside their chests. When they hear the distant thunder, they burst open, scattering the flowers or souls far and wide, to all the earthly fruit-trees. The Batek are not clear about how many *hala' tahun* there are. Sometimes they speak as if there were many, perhaps one for each species of fruit or even one for each fruit that appears on earth. But I have also been told that there is a single being, called Tahun, who produces all the flowers of all the fruit species. This view might be described as a belief in a 'fruit deity'. I return to the question of whether Tahun can be considered a deity in Chapter 6.

The variant forms of the Batek theory of fruit production have slightly different imagery and emphases. But the Batek do not see the different versions as incompatible. The same informant may give all of them on different occasions. Although the details of the various versions differ, they agree on certain basic points. They all explain the periodic appearance of fruit by its movement, in some form, between the upper world and the earth. And they all affirm the crucial importance of the superhuman beings and the thunder-god in the production of fruit.

The Batek hold one or more singing sessions immediately following the floods each year to ensure that there will be an abundant crop of fruit. In fact, many Batek believe there would be no fruit at all if they did not sing. These sessions are held in a giant lean-to shelter (*haya' tebew*) if it is still wet or on an uncovered bark platform if the weather is dry (see Chapter 5). Songs for all the different species of fruit are sung, the singing being led by whoever knows each song best. The songs are intended to induce the *hala'* who control the fruit to be generous in sending flowers or the shadow-souls that produce flowers. According to the latter interpretation, singing for fruit is singing to the fruit beings in an attempt to entice them to return to earth and take up their edible form once again.

Fruit songs nearly all follow the same general pattern: each line begins with the name of the species followed by a phrase describing or praising it. The lines can be repeated any number of times. The following song for the *tawès* fruit, the first fruit to be created, is typical.

Haka' Tawès

Tawès tawès tawès tawès, teberengül tasek 'o',
Tawès tawès, terepel yòh 'o',
Tawès tawès, beregèl batang 'o',
Tawès tawès, 'o' cak cemeraw,
Tawès tawès, berengül nèm 'o',
Tawes tawès, berengül mẹt 'o',
Tawès tawès, tegehét laluh,
Tawès tawès, 'om yèm lẹt senguh,
Tawès tawès, 'om yèm ci' mẹt 'o',
Tawès tawès, tebed'èt batang 'o',
Tawès tawès, telpeng yòh 'o',
Tawès tawès, serajam yòh 'o',

Tawès tawès, tekeranèt hali' 'o',
Tawès tawès, tekeranèt jeli' 'o',
Tawès tawès, terenèk jeli' 'o',
Tawès tawès, kuning séc 'o',
Tawès tawès, yè' sayèng,
Yè' sayèng senguh benèr papa' bed'èt laluh,
Laluh laluh, 'om way, 'om ci' bab yè',
'Adeh 'adeh 'adeh 'adeh,
Yè' sayèng laluh tawès.

Tawès Song

Tawès tawès tawès tawès, very red when it is ripe,
Tawès tawès, very splayed are its branches,
Tawès tawès, striped horizontally is its trunk,
Tawès tawès, it sheds its fuzz,
Tawès tawès, red is its waistband,[1]
Tawès tawès, red is its seed,[2]
Tawès tawès, exceedingly sweet,
Tawès tawès, I really want to swallow it,
Tawès tawès, I really want to eat its seeds,
Tawès tawès, very beautiful is its trunk,
Tawès tawès, dense are its branches,
Tawès tawès, hanging down are its branches,
Tawès tawès, very small are its leaves,
Tawès tawès, very small are its thorns,
Tawès tawès, very fine are its thorns,
Tawès tawès, yellow is its flesh,
Tawès tawès, I love it,
I love it truly because it is exceedingly good,
Exceedingly exceedingly, want to open, want to eat my food,
Oh oh oh oh,
I love *tawès* very much.

If there is a fruit shaman in the group, the singing session will be climaxed by his going into trance and sending his shadow-soul to the

---

[1] This refers to the plaited waistband worn by the *tawès* when it is in human form above the firmament.

[2] Literally its 'eye'. The seeds of some fruits are edible, though usually they must be cooked. The skins of most wild fruits are thrown away.

thunder-god (Gobar) to steal some extra flowers (see Chapter 5). This is considered very hazardous because Gobar does not willingly give up his fruit blossoms, and he would kidnap the shaman's shadow-soul if he realized what was intended. This would cause the death of the shaman back on earth. The shaman deposits the flowers he steals in the appropriate fruit-trees. He does not produce them for the audience to see.

While the fruit is ripening, it is forbidden to cut branches off the trees, cut open the unripe fruit, or throw them up in the air. Any of these acts would cause the *hala'* to take the fruit back.

The Batek also perform a simple ceremony when they collect the first fruits of the year from the major wild species of seasonal fruit. This is not done for any of the domesticated species, however, whether or not the particular tree was planted by man. The ceremony consists of burning a bit of incense (*kemeyèn*) under the tree and singing a song, such as that given above, in honour of that species of fruit-tree. The Batek Teh say they recite a spell (*jampi'*) instead of singing a song. The smell of the smoke and the sound of the song are supposed to reach the top of the firmament and the stone pillars and thus to inform Gobar and the *hala'* that the Batek are thankful for the fruit. If this is not done, a *hala'*-tiger will come and kill the offender, or Gobar will kill him with a thunderstorm. Some say the offender will fall out of a tree while harvesting fruit.

Honey

Honey (*lèng*) is an important and highly valued source of food for the Batek. Their ideas about bees and honey are closely related to those about seasonal fruit. The first bees were *hala'* who lived by eating flowers. Even today, according to the Lebir Batek, the bees are actually *hala'* who take human form when they are absent from the earth. They normally live on the stone pillars and on top of the firmament. After the floods each year, they fly to earth in the form of bees. The fruit blossoms (or the shadow-souls that produce them) follow the bees to earth. The bees build their nests hanging from the branches of tall trees. They live off the dew (*mun*) they suck out of flowers, and honey is their urine (*kenom*). When the flowers disappear, they return to the sky and resume their human-like form. The Aring Batek say that bees nowadays remain in the form of bees even when they are in the sky. They are said to sit in special caves in the stone pillars like 'goods on a shop shelf'. The superhuman beings send them to earth just as they send fruit blossoms. Thus bees, like fruit blossoms, are sometimes seen as being manifestations of *hala'* and sometimes as mere instruments of the *hala'*.

The Batek sing 'bee songs' in an attempt to attract large numbers of bees to earth. These songs are also sung if a person wants to 'attack' a bees' nest during the daytime. This is supposed to prevent the bees from stinging. The songs used are similar in form to the fruit songs, and they are sung along with fruit songs in the same singing sessions. The following is a typical 'bee song'.

Haka' Lewéy

> *Layuh layuh layuh, wòng lewéy,*
> *Layuh layuh, lèng lewéy,*
> *Layuh layuh, wòng lewéy,*
> *Layuh layuh, kesar lewéy,*
> *Layuh layuh, 'o' còk ke-yè',*
> *Layuh layuh, 'o' còk bejuros,*
> *Layuh layuh, senangen jadiy,*
> *Layuh layuh, 'angin jadiy,*
> *Layuh layuh, jarum lewéy,*
> *Layuh layuh, senangen lewéy,*
> *Layuh layuh, seniring jadiy,*
> *Layuh layuh, senayuh benang,*
> *Layuh layuh, benang kisar.*

Bee Song

> Faded faded faded,[3] the larvae of the bees,
> Faded faded, the honey of the bees,
> Faded faded, the larvae of the bees,
> Faded faded, the stings of the bees,
> Faded faded, he stings me,
> Faded faded, he stings successfully,
> Faded faded, wings appear,
> Faded faded, wind appears,[4]
> Faded faded, the needles of the bees,

[3] This refers to the dry leaves of the torch used to stun the bees when getting honey.
[4] Wind is supposed to carry the bees to earth.

Faded faded, the wings of the bees,
Faded faded, a procession appears,
Faded faded, a thread fading in the distance,
Faded faded, a shifting thread.

This song expresses the singer's hope that the bees will come to earth in an unending procession. I have never heard of a shaman trying to steal bees from Gobar as he does with flowers. It would obviously be a hazardous bit of work.

It is forbidden to eat honey with *takop*, the most frequently obtained wild yam. If this is done, the bees will return to the sky and leave only empty nests behind. Honey can be eaten with rice and other kinds of tubers, however.

As with the first fruits of certain species, the first honey is greeted by the burning of incense and the singing of an appropriate song. The penalty for neglecting this rite is the same as for neglecting the first fruits ceremony, namely injury or death caused by a *hala'*-tiger, a thunderstorm, or falling out of a tree.

Agricultural products

Occasionally the Batek Dè' grow a few crops (*tanaman*), though more often they obtain such things as rice and sweet potatoes from Malay farmers and rattan traders in exchange for forest products. They do not have any indigenous agricultural rituals, and those of the Malays have not been adopted to any extent, probably because they are based on concepts such as that of evil spirits, that are incompatible with Batek beliefs. In spite of the small importance of agriculture to the Batek Dè', they do have a story of the origin of the cultivated plants.

Once two *hala'* brothers lived together on earth. Their names are unknown. One day they got hungry,[5] but they had no food. They lay down to sleep, and the younger brother dreamt that they should clear a field.[6] The next day they began cutting the trees and shrubs. After they had made a large clearing, they let the downed vegetation dry, and then they burned it. But

[5] They do not explain why *hala'*, who do not eat, should become hungry. When they are living on earth, the superhuman beings are usually described as more like humans than when they live in the sky.

[6] Apparently he received some instruction in the dream from other *hala'* who were not on earth. In stories, younger brothers are usually pictured as being more clever than elder brothers, but this stereotype is not held to be true for ordinary human beings, as far as I know.

they had no seeds. They went to sleep again and after a long time the younger brother suddenly awoke. He asked his elder brother, 'Are you brave? If you are brave, you must cut open my stomach'. The elder brother said he was brave enough to do it. So they took seven sleeping mats and placed them in the centre of the clearing, one on top of the other. The younger brother lay down on the mats, and the elder brother took a knife and cut open his brother's abdomen. He then put some white blood from his brother's heart in one container and some red blood from his body in another container.[7] Then he called to his brother, and the younger brother came back to life. The younger brother said they must sprinkle the blood on the ground. They stood in the centre of the field and sprinkled the white blood on one side and the red blood on the other. After a while the white blood sprouted as rice and the red blood sprouted as wheat.[8] In some versions of the story, they scattered the blood in a circle around them, and it gave rise to all the cultivated plants.

After that, the Batek lived on their crops until the Malays set fire to the grass around their fields and drove the Batek into the forest, where they have lived ever since (see Chapter 4). Stories of this type are found among many of the indigenous agricultural peoples of Malaysia and are especially common in Borneo. What is unusual is that one should be found among a people who do not normally practice agriculture. Perhaps by deriving rice from the *hala'*, this story helps reconcile the great liking the Batek have for rice with the knowledge that it now comes mainly from the Malays.

Game and fish

The main source of protein for the nomadic Batek is game and fish. The following story described the origin of most if not all animals.

Once two *hala'* brothers[9] came upon a huge bearcat (*cepük; Arctictis binturong*).[10] Its body was three times as large as an elephant's, and it was several hundred feet long. They blowpiped it and managed to kill it. Then they butchered it. They threw pieces of meat in different directions and, as they did, they called out the names of various edible plants[11] and animals.

[7] 'White' (colourless) blood is a characteristic of *hala'*. Perhaps having both white and red blood is meant to suggest that the heroes were semi-human when living on earth.

[8] Malay *gandum*. The Batek know of wheat because the J.O.A. gave them regular supplies of surplus American cracked wheat for a few years in an unsuccessful attempt to get them to settle down.

[9] One informant said they were sisters, but they are more often spoken of as males.

[10] In one man's version it was a *tòng*, probably a masked palm civet (*Paguma larvata*).

[11] The edible tubers are mentioned by some, making this an alternative to the story of the origin of tubers given above.

The meat became the things named. The blood became wheat,[12] the bones became iron, and the hair became the chaff of the rice. The veins and tendons ('*orèt*) were merely discarded (*pangka'*). For that reason, the animals that came from the '*orèt*—such as leeches, snakes, and millipedes—cannot be eaten. Those animals cannot be laughed at either; to do so would be *lawac*, punishable by the thunder-god (Gobar) and the earth-snake (*naga'*).

This type of story is common in the Malaysian region (see e.g. Jensen 1974: 75) and is obviously from the same mould as the story of the origin of the agricultural products given above. Yet the Batek story reveals certain peculiarly Batek concerns and ideas. The division between the edible and inedible animals (which are *lawac*)[13] is a basic feature of the Batek world-view, and it is neatly explained by this story. In fact the *lawac* species by no means all resemble veins or tendons, but a number of them do. Leeches are vein-like even to the extent of being containers of blood. The close connection between species and their names in Batek thought is also revealed. The story shows that the naming of the various plants and animals is an integral part of their creation. I was told that they could not have come into existence if the *hala'* had not called out their names. Why the bearcat should have been singled out as the source of all other animals is difficult to say, for it does not otherwise hold a special place in the Batek imagination. The notion that its bones became the first iron may be related to its ability to jump to the ground from high in the trees without breaking any limbs. The Mendriq make a medicine to heal broken bones from the bones of the bearcat and the serow, a sort of mountain goat (*Capricornia sumatraensis*). Perhaps a story of the origin of iron was merely expanded to include the origin of other things as well. In one respect the bearcat is an appropriate source of both edible and inedible food. The strong flavour and odour of its flesh nauseates many Batek; so, while it is edible to some Batek, it is inedible to others.

The animals that are supposed to have come from the veins and tendons of the original bearcat are mostly insects, worms, and reptiles. It is generally considered *lawac* to eat these animals as well as to laugh at them, though independent reasons for not eating them are given as well. They are usually said to be poisonous or physically dirty and therefore likely to make one sick. For the same

[12] Here the story overlaps that of the origin of agricultural products given above.

[13] The term *lawac* is used as an adjective to refer to any acts that are punished by Gobar with a thunderstorm and by the *naga'* with an up-welling flood. It is also used to indicate the animals that are protected from those acts.

reasons, most other insects and worms are also rejected as food.

Another category of animals that the Batek do not eat, though it is not explicitly prohibited, is the animals that can kill humans. These may be called collectively *pangan*, though the term refers more specifically to the tiger. They include the tiger, elephant, rhinoceros, and large snakes. The Batek say they would be afraid to eat these animals because they might be the bodies of *hala'* who, in new bodies, would take revenge upon them. Some types of pets are not eaten either. Monkeys and gibbons are occasionally captured as babies when their mothers are blowpiped. They may be nursed by Batek women, and, if they die, they are given a tree-burial as if they were human. If they live to maturity, they are normally turned loose. The Batek consider them to be like their own children once they have 'raised' them (*perigòs*; literally 'to cause life'). Theoretically dogs and cats are also inedible pets, and it is *lawac* to laugh at them. However, I have never known the Batek Dè' to keep either dogs or cats, though the more sedentary Batek Teh keep both. The reluctance of the Batek Dè' to eat pet monkeys does not extend to other kinds of pets. The most common pets are baby bamboo-rats which are often captured when their parents are killed. These are considered 'playthings' (*'ŏt*) just like toys and the flowers and leaves used for bodily decorations. The children feed them and play with them until they get fairly large and begin to bite. Then they are killed and eaten. Thus, pets are not an inedible category of animals for the Batek as they are for many peoples.

Batek ideas about most of the animal species they eat are basically rational and well-founded. They have detailed knowledge of the anatomy of these animals, although, as in the case of humans, they do not correctly understand the functions of some of the internal organs. Their knowledge of the living habits of the different species is astonishingly extensive and accurate. Most of the animals that can be eaten are regarded dispassionately as meat 'on the hoof'. They are captured and killed without any apparent concern for them as sentient beings. The monkeys and apes, however, pose a kind of dilemma for the Batek. They are recognized as being much more like human beings than are the other animals, and yet they are regularly eaten. This dilemma can be resolved in two ways. As mentioned above, the baby monkeys that are raised as pets are not eaten even if they die of natural causes. In other words, they are assimilated to the category of human being. The other way, which contradicts the first, is symbolically to deny the similarity between monkeys and human beings. For example, it is considered *lawac*, and is therefore prohibited, to bathe a pet monkey in a stream as one does a human baby. The pig-tailed macaque (*bawac; Macacus nemestrinus*) is one of the few animals that can be eaten but cannot be laughed at. It is particularly offensive, as the following story shows, to dress the monkey like a person and to cause it to act human.

Once some Malays persuaded a Batek shaman to bring a *bawac* he had killed back to life. He pulled out the darts and sucked out the poison. Then he blew some incense smoke on the animal, and it suddenly got up and looked around. This caused the Malays and the other Batek to laugh uproariously. The Malays then dressed the monkey up in Malay-style clothing, complete with a dagger (*keris*), and they made him dance. This caused everyone except the shaman to laugh even more. The shaman quietly slipped off to the top of a nearby hill. Suddenly the sky went dark, and a torrent of water burst out of the ground and destroyed the camp and all the people who had laughed at the *bawac*.[14]

The Batek say the main offence committed by the people in this story was laughing at the monkey, which is *lawac*, but it is also implied that the Malays were wrong to dress the monkey up and make it dance. Thus, one meaning of the story for the Batek seems to be that it is wrong to exaggerate or draw attention to the similarity between monkeys and men. The Batek consider the thought of eating humans abhorrent, so any confusion between the categories of men and monkeys, which are eaten regularly, would be deeply unsettling. This anxiety is expressed in a belief that there are pig-tailed macaques as big as cows (*bawac zay*) living in the mountains that kill and eat human beings.

Some gibbons (*keboñ; Hylobates* spp.) and banded leaf monkeys (*kaldüs; Presbytis melalophos*) are thought to be *hala'* and to behave in some ways like human shamans. I have heard vague claims that the gibbons, like tubers and fruit, were once *hala'* who were transformed into apes so that they could be eaten by man. Supposedly some

[14] This story is almost identical to one recorded by Evans among the Sungkai Senoi (Semai) of southern Perak (1923: 202–4). He adds that a very similar story occurs among the Orang Dusun of Borneo (1923: 204n.). In a story of the Kelantan Malays, some dogs and cats were made to fight at a festival, for the amusement of the assembled people. This caused a flood to come out of the mountains and submerge the whole area, turning it into sea (Skeat 1901: 65). Although these stories are obviously related, the meanings attributed to them no doubt differ for the different groups, depending on their individual concerns and views of the world.

gibbons are still *hala'*. If people kill too many gibbons, the *hala'* gibbons will come down to the ground and take human form, apparently to prevent themselves from being killed off. They can also take the form of leopards (*'ayǫ' kanèt*; literally 'small tigers') that live in the trees. The *hala'* banded leaf monkeys look and live like ordinary monkeys. But sometimes they decorate themselves with sweet-smelling leaves and sing their own *hala'* songs. Though humans could once hear these songs, they no longer can. If a hunter happens to shoot at a *hala'* leaf monkey, the monkey will snatch the dart out of the air before it reaches him. It can also take the form of a leopard and frighten the hunter off.

The Batek depend almost entirely on their skills and knowledge of animal habits to ensure their success in the hunt. The few 'magical' aids they employ are based on logical reasoning, though some of the premises are slightly faulty. Some Batek hunters use bones of gibbons or *siamang* (*bateyoh; Hylobates syndactylus*) as clasps for their dart-quiver cords. The odour of the bone is supposed to attract the apes, thus bringing them within range of the blowpipe. This practice is apparently based on the knowledge that gibbons are curious and will seek out a hunter who skilfully imitates their cries. It merely overestimates the power of smell of the apes, a natural mistake for a people who routinely use odours as communicators between the earth and the firmament (see Chapter 5). Monkeys, on the other hand, are thought to be afraid of the odour of their bones, and they do not respond to imitations of their cries. It is said in general that the reason Batek do not wear animal skins or feathers is that the odour would frighten away game. This may well be true for those species, such as pigs, which depend on their noses to warn them of danger. The attraction of animals to their food is also made use of. Some of the designs the Batek scratch on their dart quivers are supposed to represent plants that are eaten by monkeys, and occasionally informants claim that the monkeys are attracted by the designs. Such claims are rather whimsical, however, and there seems to be no special preference for those designs over designs representing inedible things. One general rule applies to all animals that have been killed with a blowpipe. Those animals must be cooked alone, not mixed with any other food or any seasoning except salt. If this rule is ignored, the hunter's dart poison is supposed to lose its power to kill. This idea may be based on the knowledge that the poison itself is stronger if it is not adulterated with other substances,[15] and the Batek merely extend this reasoning to include the meat of the victim as well as the poison that killed it. These few practices are, as far as I know, the total repertoire of magical hunting aids used by the Batek.

The Batek derive their subsistence from the forest by using, for the most part, straightforward, practical means. They have extensive knowledge of the foods available and all the skills necessary for obtaining them, regularly and in sufficient quantities, the whole year round. But to the Batek the environment is not just a collection of material resources, devoid of any other significance. They believe that their major foods were created expressly for them by the *hala'*. They assume that in harvesting and living off those foods they are living as they were meant to do. They acknowledge their debt to the *hala'* by observing a first fruits ceremony, and they take an active part in some of the processes of food production by singing for the fruit blossoms and the honey bees. In obtaining their subsistence from the forest, they feel they are being brought closer to the *hala'*. The ultimate expression of their identification with the *hala'*, which is seen also in their singing and bodily decorations, is that in eating the seasonal fruit, they believe they are eating the very bodies of the *hala'*.

The Forest as a Source of Danger

The forest environment provides the Batek with most of the necessities of life, but it contains certain hazards as well. The two things the Batek fear most are thunderstorms and tigers. In fact, many more deaths result from disease than from tigers and thunderstorms together, but diseases are not so fear inspiring because they do not normally strike so suddenly and violently. I have already mentioned the more practical measures taken to reduce the danger of thunderstorms and wild animals (see Chapter 1), and I discuss some of the precautions taken against disease below (Chapter 4). In this section I describe the major religious prohibitions that are meant to protect people from such environmental hazards and attempt to explain why particular acts are prohibited.

[15] The Kelantan Batek, like the other Negritos who use the sap of the *ipuh* tree (*Antiaris toxicaria*) as dart poison, do not mix it with other substances (see Schebesta 1954: 120–1). The Batek Nòng, who make their dart poison from a liana, *Strychnos tieute*, sometimes add other substances.

Prohibitions to prevent thunderstorms and flash-floods

Thunderstorms are common in Kelantan during most of the year. They are absent only during the floods, in December and January, and during the relatively dry period that follows, in February and March. The usual pattern is for a thunderstorm, which lasts about an hour, to blow up in the late afternoon or early evening. These thunderstorms are a real source of danger to the Batek. The heavy downpour of rain can loosen the roots of the shallow-rooted rainforest trees, and the sudden gusts of wind can blow down large branches and can topple even the largest of trees. During thunderstorms, the Batek stand nervously at the fronts of their shelters, holding their children and their most prized possessions, watching the trees. If it is dark, they have only the lightning and the beams of a few electric torches to let them know if a limb or a whole tree is starting to fall. With each gust of wind, the trees groan and crack. The air is filled with shouts of warning, and families rush from one shelter to another. It is against this background that an outsider can understand the great lengths to which the Batek go, even including the blood sacrifice, to protect themselves from the storm.

According to Batek Dè' theories, thunderstorms[16] are quite separate from ordinary rain (*'ujan banjil*; literally, 'flood rain'). Normal rain is said to come from the clouds that drift along below the firmament. After it falls, the rain-water sinks into the ground and then comes to the surface in streams. In the morning, clouds rise up from the streams and carry the water back to the sky. This cycle repeats itself without any intervention from the *hala'*.[17] Seasonal floods (*banjil*) are simply the result of the clouds releasing too much of their water. The rain that accompanies the thunderstorm, on the other hand, is sent out by Gobar, or by the *hala'* called 'Rain'

[16] The Batek Dè' do not now have a special term for the thunderstorm, though they may once have had one. Skeat records the expression *ketok si'* as meaning 'the day (or sky) is stormy' among the Aring Batek (Skeat and Blagden 1906b: 726), but the Batek do not now recognize the term *si'*. Normally they indicate the thunderstorm by reference to one of its components: thunder (*gobar*), strong wind (*'angin hali' kayu'*; literally 'tree leaf wind'), or heavy rain (*'ujan bew*; literally 'big rain').

[17] The Batek Nòng say the spray from the waves in the sea is carried aloft by the wind, and this becomes the clouds and rain. The Benua, an Aboriginal Malay people of Johore, have an almost identical explanation for the origin of rain (Skeat and Blagden 1906b: 348).

(Ujan) who acts on Gobar's orders, along with the wind, thunder, and lightning that make up the thunderstorm. Gobar is pictured by some as releasing the wind and rain from special caves in the stone pillar. Other informants picture Gobar as sending the wind and rain down the ropes of wind and rain which stretch from the stone pillar to the horizon. They travel part of the way down the ropes and then scatter over the land. The thunder and lightning are sent down separate 'ropes of lightning' (*tali' kilat*). Those few people who place Gobar at the eastern and western horizons merely claim that he sends the elements of the storm part of the way *up* the ropes, toward the stone pillar, before they descend to earth.

All thunderstorms are in theory punitive acts deliberately created by Gobar and directed at persons who have broken *lawac* prohibitions (see below). Not all thunder is associated by the Batek with thunderstorms, however. The mere rumbling of thunder in the distance is said to be Gobar just 'being annoying' (*'onar*) or, in the proper season, signalling the *hala'* to send down fruit blossoms. Such thunder is generally ignored. Many acknowledged thunderstorms are ignored as well. The Batek do not trouble themselves about thunderstorms which pass by some miles away. If they offer any explanation at all of such storms, it is that someone in another area must have committed a *lawac* act and is being punished for it. Even when thunderstorms pass overhead, they are not considered truly dangerous unless someone in camp has broken a *lawac* prohibition. When such a break has occurred, someone, preferably the offender, must perform the blood sacrifice (see Chapter 5), or else he and possibly others will be killed. Thus, most thunderstorms are taken for granted by the Batek, like many other repetitive phenomena in their environment. Yet their frequent occurrence seems to act as a reminder of what punishment awaits anyone who breaks a *lawac* prohibition.

The Batek also fear sudden, up-welling floods (*talañ*) which are somehow associated with thunderstorms. This notion is probably based on the flash-floods and accompanying landslides or earth subsidences that sometimes occur in mountainous areas during heavy storms. The Batek believe that they come from underground and are caused by the earth-snake (*naga'*) moving and letting the underground sea erupt through the skin of the earth. Such floods are clearly distinguished from ordinary floods which are attributed to too much rain. Up-welling floods are thought to be deliberately caused by the earth-snake (who is also pictured as an old woman) to punish people for breaking *lawac* prohibitions. The flood that swallowed up the people who laughed at the dancing macaque in the story given above is an example of such a punitive flood. The image of water spurting out of the ground seems further to associate the up-welling flood with the storm rain gushing out of a cave on the stone pillar in a punitive thunderstorm.

All acts that are thought to be punished by thunderstorms or up-welling floods or both are called *lawac*. The term *lawac* may be related to an old Negrito word for 'lightning' (see Skeat and Blagden 1906b: 648), though that word has now been replaced by the Malay-derived term *kilat* among the Batek Dè'. The prohibited acts include laughing at certain animals, cooking certain combinations of food over a single fire, pouring certain kinds of blood into streams, improper sexual behaviour, and a number of others. On the surface, the prohibited acts seem to have little in common. Perhaps it is not necessary to seek out a unitary explanation for such a varied set of regulations. In a sense *lawac* is like our term 'illegal', which covers numerous acts, from murder to parking violations. Yet I think there is an underlying unity to the *lawac* prohibitions, namely, that they all serve, in their very different ways, to affirm the order of the world as the Batek conceive it. In order to show the general significance of the *lawac* prohibitions, I discuss, very briefly, the full range of prohibitions observed.

Laughing lawac. The prohibition on 'laughing *lawac*' (*lawac pilngal*)[18] forbids laughing at certain animals or their names. The term *pilngal*[19] is the general term for laughing in Batek Dè' (equivalent to Malay *tertawa*), but it always implies that the laughing is directed *at* something, even when no direct object is given. It might best be glossed 'to laugh at' (i.e. to 'mock' or 'ridicule') rather than just 'to laugh'. For example, the Batek say *yè' pilngal pacat*, 'I laugh

[18] The names given to the different types of *lawac* are not standardized. Usually category distinctions are not made; an act is merely called *lawac*. The descriptive names I use are common but are not invariably the terms in which the category would be specified. Cross-cutting classifications of *lawac* in terms of severity ('big' and 'little' *lawac*) and the type of disaster caused (flood or thunderstorm) are also sometimes heard.

[19] The derivation of this term is difficult to discover. No cognates of the term *pilngal* have yet been recorded for other Orang Asli dialect groups (see Skeat and Blagden 1906b: 644; Benjamin 1976). Possibly it consists of a causative prefix, *pi(l)*-, attached to a root, *ngal*, but the Batek do not now attach any meaning to *ngal* alone or in other constructions.

at leech'. There is no need for a preposition (i.e. a word meaning 'at') to be inserted between *pilngal* and *pacat*.

The number and identity of the species protected from laughing vary slightly from group to group. The Batek Dè' list includes the following: (1) pig-tailed macaques, (2) long-tailed macaques, (3) land leeches, (4) water leeches, (5) dogs, (6) cats, (7) snakes, (8) millipedes (three types), (9) butterflies and moths, (10) centipedes, (11) scorpions, (12) spiders, (13) fireflies, (14) caterpillars, (15) beetles (two types), (16) lice, (17) grass lizards, (18) flying lizards, and (19) giant sowbugs. A number of others, mostly insects, might be added, but there is no general agreement among informants regarding them. Similar lists could be made for other groups. The shortest list I collected was from the Batek Nòng. It includes only the first seven animals on the Batek Dè' list above and no others.[20] The other groups I visited (Batek Teh, Batek 'Iga', and Mendriq) had lists comparable in length to that of the Batek Dè'. They coincide with the Batek Dè' list up to item 9, and there is partial correspondence beyond that, though much idiosyncratic variation as well. The first seven animals on the Batek Dè' list may be said to form the 'core' of a class with rather indefinite boundaries. Not only are they mentioned by all the groups I met, but they are also the animals mentioned most frequently by the members of each group. It seems that this core group of animals is known to be *lawac* by everyone and is taken as typifying the class. For most other animals, the informant must make a decision, and the criteria by which the decision should be made are not normally articulated or agreed upon. In those cases, informants show some uncertainty, and there is little agreement among them.

The Batek say that as a general rule one can laugh at any animal one can eat and cannot laugh at any animal one cannot eat. The *lawac* species supposedly cannot be eaten because they come from the veins and tendons of the original bearcat, which were thrown away by the *hala'* who created the animals. (Occasionally butterflies and moths are said to have come from the skin of the bearcat, which was also thrown away.) Yet the correlation between edibility and laughability is not exact. There are a number of animals, such as

[20] Possibly my informants overlooked some. Evans records that they forbid laughing at or playing with ants (1927: 18), and Schebesta gives a species of turtle as one of their 'tabooed animals' (1957: 99), though this may refer to a prohibition on letting the blood of the turtle flow into a stream, such as exists among the Batek Dè'.

ants and toads, which are not eaten, but can be laughed at. The Batek explain that eating such animals is not prohibited, but it would be foolish. They claim that none of them are good to eat, and many of them are actually poisonous. The two types of macaques, on the other hand, cannot be laughed at, but they are eaten as often as they can be killed. Some informants say the reason it is prohibited to laugh at them is that they eat *lawac* insects. This seems to imply that to laugh at them would be to risk laughing at the insects in their stomachs. The macaques can be safely eaten, however, because the contents of the stomach and intestines are always thrown away. Other informants say that in fact people can laugh at the macaques, but only a little bit. For a few animals, additional reasons are given for the prohibition on eating and laughing at them. For example, snakes are said to be protected because they are friends or relatives of the great snake (*naga'*) under the earth. The Batek do not attempt to explain why people should not laugh at the animals that cannot be eaten except to say that it is *lawac* and will lead to a punitive thunderstorm or flood.

The Batek explanations of laughing *lawac* are consistent and sound as far as they go. But they leave unanswered the underlying question of why laughing at some, but not all, animals should be prohibited on pain of a cosmic disaster. One is tempted to say, as Schebesta does in his early book (1928: 190), that the rules are intended to prevent abuse of captive animals. Yet the Batek say the rules apply to animals that are free as well. And, as Fürer-Haimendorf says (1967: 33), this interpretation does not explain why only some animals are protected. In fact it is only laughing at the animals that is prohibited. They can be and are abused and killed without any trace of empathy or compassion. For example, one type of large beetle (*kalpeng*) is regularly made into a toy, in spite of its being *lawac* to laugh at it. The children tie a fine strand of rattan to the beetle and use it as a flying buzzer until it gets battered to death. I think Schebesta's later interpretation, that the prohibitions are in reality 'based on world-view and superstitious considerations' (1957: 98), is actually closer to the mark.

One of the main themes of the Batek origin stories is that the plants and animals they eat were created especially for them by the *hala'*. Yet there are also animals in existence that are useless to man and many that are definite nuisances. Presumably these too were created by the *hala'*, though the reason they were created is unclear.

I think the reason the Batek are afraid to laugh at these animals is that by laughing at the apparently useless creations of the *hala'*, they would seem to be ridiculing the *hala'* themselves. It is not just the animal that cannot be laughed at, but also its name, the device by which its identity was established by the *hala'* at the creation. What is prohibited, then, is laughing at the very existence of the animal, at the order of things as established by the *hala'*. There are a number of animals, however, that are useless to man but are not protected from being laughed at. Some of them, such as tigers and elephants, would not be laughed at anyway because, as the Batek say, people would be afraid to laugh at them. Presumably, even if they were *hala'* animals, they would not take kindly to being ridiculed. There are also useless animals that do not inspire fear which nevertheless can be laughed at. But I think the most conspicuous and obnoxious of the useless animals are protected. It is worth noting that many of the *lawac* animals, especially the snakes and insects, cause involuntary reactions of revulsion (*geli'*; cf. Malay *geli geleman*) in many Batek. Even some of the bravest men admit that snakes give them the shivers. The large millipede (*talung*) is said to have a rank odour and is believed to have the disgusting habit of crawling across the faces of sleeping persons and urinating in their eyes, causing an intense burning sensation. Small children sometimes complain about leeches if they are unusually abundant in a place. The casual disregard of leeches seen among adults is apparently learned. Whether the squeamishness causes the prohibition or vice versa one cannot say, but I suspect that there is an innate component in the Batek's dislike for these animals. The macaques are, as the Batek acknowledge, a special case. The prohibition on laughing at them, even though they can be eaten, is apparently based on their uncanny resemblance to human beings, as I suggested above.

Fire lawac. 'Fire *lawac*' (*lawac 'òs*) is the cooking of certain incompatible combinations of food over a single fire, either at the same or different times. With a few exceptions, vegetables (*sayor*), such as palm cabbage and wild banana flowers, can be cooked on the same fire as starch food (*bab*), such as rice and tubers. Animals (*'ay*) can be cooked with *bab*[21] but not with *sayor*, except for small quantities of onions or wild ginger used for seasoning. Of course meat shot

---

[21] Some informants say the animals with strong-smelling flesh, such as the two types of macaques, cannot be cooked on the same fire as starch food. These are the animals that are subject to the 'blood *lawac*' prohibitions (see below).

with a blowpipe may be cooked only with salt, or the dart poison will lose its power. Most of the specific fire *lawac* prohibitions apply to various combinations of meat. One type of animal that cannot be 'cooked' over the same fire as any type of food is the leech. Though the Batek permit the killing of leeches by fire (cf. Needham 1967), they must not be burned on a cooking-fire. Usually a piece of firewood with glowing embers is taken out of the cooking-fire, placed on the ground a few feet away, and the leech is placed on the embers. It is generally said that birds can be cooked with any other meat, while fish can be cooked with no other meat except birds and other species of fish. In regard to the other animals eaten by the Batek, there is a great deal of disagreement from group to group and person to person over whether specific combinations of meat can be cooked together or not. In order to understand why this is so, it is necessary to consider the rationale behind the system of fire *lawac*.

According to the Batek, fire *lawac* occurs when foods with different odours (*meni' pɔ̀w*) are cooked together. It is the mixture of odours that is offensive to Gobar and the *naga'*, not the odours of the foods individually. Supposedly every species of animal has a different odour because each species has a distinctive diet. Thus, in theory, all species of animals should be cooked separately. But it is generally agreed that the odours of some species are so similar that their mixing would not be offensive. Unfortunately, there is no general agreement as to which animal odours are similar and which are different. With one exception (see below), there are no categories of animal odours that encompass more than one species; the only names that exist for animal odours are the names of the species from which they come, e.g. *meni' gaw*, 'pig odour'. Furthermore, the major edible animals, with the exception of the birds (*kawaw*) and the fish (*'ikan*), are known only by their species names. There is no classi-fication grouping them into larger categories which could guide the Batek in deciding whether the odours of particular species were compatible or not. Thus, in order to determine whether the odours of certain species are compatible, the Batek consider a number of other criteria of similarity between the species. The criteria most often mentioned are the following: (1) anatomical similarity (especially in the number and nature of the appendages), (2) similarity of habitat (the usual divisions being tree-dwelling, ground-dwelling, underground-dwelling, and water-dwelling), (3) similarity of body covering (the main types being fur, feathers, and scales), and (4) similarity in colour of skin or body covering. There would be no difficulty in applying these criteria, except that the Batek do not agree on the order in which they should be applied, and even the same informant may change the order from one case to another. For example, one man said that the land and water monitors could be cooked together, in spite of having different habitats, because their bodies are similar in shape; but he also said that squirrels and gibbons could be cooked together because they both live in trees, regardless of their differences in anatomy. The lack of consensus regarding what criteria are to be applied in what order has two major results. First, there is a great deal of disagreement over whether particular combinations of meat can be cooked together. The more common combinations (e.g. dusky leaf monkey and bamboo rat) are fairly consistently dealt with by individual families, but may vary from family to family. A rare combination (e.g. mousedeer and porcupine) may only be decided upon after a full-scale discussion involving everyone in camp. If no agreement is reached in a particular case, most people prefer to play it safe. I once saw a woman cooking two minnows, three tiny crabs, and two small shrimps over three separate fires. Secondly, there are no clear-cut, discrete categories of animals that can be cooked together. The classification of animals by dwelling place is cross-cut by the classification by skin colour and so on. For example, according to one informant the two types of macaques can be cooked together, and all species of frogs can be cooked together, but only one species of frog can be cooked with one species of macaque because they have the same skin colour. Instead of discrete categories, the whole set of edible animals (except fish) forms a single polythetic grouping (see Needham 1975) in which each species is associated with every other species by some, but not all, of the criteria which the Batek take into account. It seems to be unimportant, from the Batek point of view, that there is no clear-cut classification of edible animals by odour. What is important is the principle that foods with different odours should not be cooked together. The principle is perfectly clear even if the application of it is not.

The basic idea behind fire *lawac* seems to be that the identities of the different species of plants and animals used as food should not be confused when they are cooked (see Needham 1967: 283; cf. Dentan 1968: 36–7). The special concern with odours is not because they are the most basic defining features of the food-species, but because they are the features most prone to intermixing, even when the substances of the food-species are kept apart. Also, odours are the most communicable features of species, those which are capable of reaching the *hala'*. Mixed odours, then, would betray any person who confuses categories of food which were established as separate by the *hala'*.

Blood lawac. It is 'blood *lawac*' (*lawac yɔp*) to let certain types of blood flow into streams. Among the Batek Dè', the prohibition on blood *lawac* applies to the blood of the pig-tailed macaque, long-tailed macaque, one type of turtle (*kòh*), one type of land-tortoise (*hawang; Testudo* sp.) and, according to a few people, land monitors (*bagèn* and *kabuk; Varanus* spp.). The Mendriq and Batek Teh add the gibbons, *siamang*, and bearcats.[22] The effect of the prohibitions is that one cannot wash the carcasses of these animals in a stream or wash one's hands after butchering one of them, except in water that has been taken away from the stream. The Mendriq and Batek Teh even prohibit bathing for a day after a person has eaten an animal of one of these species. For the Mendriq, Batek Teh, and some Batek Dè' who are closely related to them, it is also blood *lawac* to let human menstrual blood or blood resulting from childbirth flow into a stream. Thus, a woman cannot bathe in a stream during her period or for a week or so after giving birth. She may bathe in water that has been removed from the stream, however.

The usual rationale given for the prohibition on blood *lawac* is that the thunder-god and the *naga'* do not like the odour of the prohibited types of blood. The Batek say the animals affected by the prohibition are those whose flesh and blood have a strong *pel'èng* odour, i.e. a strong odour of raw meat. The blood of these animals, like menstrual blood, is considered to smell bad (*jebèc*). The bad smell is a property of the blood, not a result of its being mixed with water, which has no odour itself. The reason these kinds of blood cannot be put in a stream, though they can be mixed with water elsewhere, is that the stream somehow carries the bad odour to the deities. This is easy to understand in the case of the *naga'*, for streams are commonly pictured in shaman songs as the entrance to the underworld where the *naga'* lives. The odour is also supposed to rise like smoke and thus to reach the thunder-god above. Why it should only rise from streams is not clear; I was told explicitly that

---

[22] The Mendriq alone include several species of birds, notably the hornbills, in the prohibition, and they also forbid letting salt into streams.

this process is not connected with the rising of the mist that creates rain clouds. A Mendriq informant said the *naga'* sends the blood aloft to the thunder-god (called Karei in their dialect) on a rope of wind. The Batek say the thunder-god does not like being sent blood except when he demands it by causing a thunderstorm. This suggests that the basic offence involved in blood *lawac* is that it is a sort of parody of the blood sacrifice (see Chapter 5). It is the sending of especially bad-smelling blood when it is not wanted, as against the sending of ordinary blood (from a person's leg) when it is wanted. The prohibition would serve to remind people that communication between man and deity by means of blood (mixed with water) is a serious matter and should not be done incorrectly and without reason.

Body lawac. The last major category of *lawac* is 'body *lawac*' (*lawac lih*). Basically this is having sexual relations with one's parent, grandparent, uncle, aunt, sibling, half-sibling, child, niece, nephew, parent-in-law, child-in-law, or sibling-in-law. Gobar punishes this by sending a thunderstorm or a crippling disease called *kelintar kayu'* which is supposed to result from a spark of lightning entering one of the offender's big toes (see Chapter 6). *Lawac lih* is a sub-class of *cemam*, improper sexual behaviour between relatives, which also includes standing or sleeping too near mature, opposite-sex relatives in the categories mentioned above. These offences are considered less serious than actually having sexual relations, and are not even considered *lawac* by some informants. The usual penalty for these lesser offences is a disease called *cemam*, the symptoms of which are fever and aching joints and muscles. This is sometimes attributed to the mixing of the shadows or odours of the relatives, without, apparently, the active intervention of Gobar.

The usual reason given for the prohibition on body *lawac* is simply that, after the first few generations of human beings had married siblings, Gobar forbade any further sexual relations between close relatives. Therefore, he punishes anyone who breaks this rule. The underlying value of the rule is that it prevents the concentration of marriage ties among close kin and therefore helps to perpetuate the widely-spreading system of social ties that makes the Batek way of life possible and practical.[23] Since the Batek do not have any

[23] I do not intend to take a position on why (or whether) all peoples have some sort of 'incest taboo'. Suffice it to say, the Batek prohibition on *lawac lih* obtains for them any universal social, psychological, or physiological advantages such a 'taboo' may be thought to have, as well as the particular advantages it has in terms of their own social system.

political or legal mechanisms capable of enforcing the rule, a supernatural sanction is useful in ensuring that it is scrupulously observed. Although body *lawac* differs from the other *lawac* acts in that it has to do with the relations among human beings rather than those between humans and the environment, the fact that the same type of prohibition and punishment applies to both shows that the social order is seen as being part of the over-all natural order established by the *hala'*.

Other lawac acts. It is *lawac* to let a mirror,[24] cooking-pot, or biscuit tin flash in the sun. It is also *lawac* to make a booming sound by beating on a split section of bamboo with a stick or thumping an inverted cooking-pot or bamboo container on the surface of a stream. Although there is no single term for these acts, they seem to form a set. The flashing is explicitly said to be like lightning and the booming like thunder. These acts are probably offensive to the thunder-god because they might seem to be mocking him or infringing his prerogatives.

Finally, any novel or unprecedented act is vaguely suspected of being *lawac*, and this suspicion is considered confirmed if it is followed by a thunderstorm. This applies when someone does something for the first time, especially something that is not part of the traditional Batek way of life. For example, it is expected that there will be at least a mild thunderstorm the first time a person leaves the forest to visit a town. This suspicion also attaches to completely unprecedented actions. For instance, we were asked not to play our radio receiver or tape recorder when thunderstorms were threatening for fear of angering Gobar. All these acts are considered offensive to the thunder-god because he is not 'used' to them. The principle seems to be that he is offended by any actions that were not established and legitimized by the *hala'*, that is to say, any activity that is not well enough established to have been worked into the mythology.

Thus, the Batek seem to believe that there is a natural order to the world which is manifested, among other ways, in the divisions of the plant and animal kingdoms. To a large extent, the Batek way of life is considered part of the natural order as well. Because this order was established by the *hala'*, it should be respected by

---

[24] One informant said this applies only to large mirrors which are like 'tigers' eyes' (*mĕt yah*).

human beings. The *lawac* prohibitions seem intended to prevent man from violating or ridiculing this order. Breaking the rules, then, leads to disorder, and the punishment for such violations is the even greater disorder of the thunderstorm and the up-welling flood. These phenomena can be seen as deliberate reversals of the creation of the earth, undermining the fundamental division between land and water. It is important to note that the connection between breaking a prohibition and the associated disaster is not a mechanical one; the punishment does not automatically follow the act. If animals or small children commit *lawac* acts, they are not punished. They must be able to understand the prohibitions before they are held responsible for observing them. The postulation of deities mediating between man and the environment, judging human actions on moral grounds, helps explain the flexibility in the connection between human acts and cosmic events.

Prohibitions to deter tigers

Tigers are not so numerous as they once were in Batek country. Very few Batek have been killed by tigers in recent years, though genealogies show a substantial number of deaths by tiger attack in previous generations. In spite of the rarity of tiger attacks today, the tiger remains the very epitome of earthly danger in the minds of the Batek. Even the bravest of hunters can lose their nerve for a few days after an encounter with a tiger. Stories about the powers of tigers are told with nervous awe. The tiger is the 'bogy' used by Batek parents to frighten children who disobey or who insist upon following them into the forest against their wishes. No doubt this practice heightens and perpetuates fear of tigers among the population, perhaps producing a degree of fear that is unwarranted by the actual amount of danger. But there is good reason to avoid tigers, and an exaggerated degree of avoidance is probably 'adaptive' for the group as long as it does not interfere with the food quest.

In addition to the practical measures taken to reduce the danger from tigers (see Chapter 1), the Batek prohibit certain acts that are thought to attract them. One such act is referring to the tiger as *pangan*, which means roughly 'man-killer'. This name is very offensive to tigers, and they will seek out and kill anyone who uses it. Fortunately there are at least five inoffensive terms for the tiger in the Batek Dè' dialect. Acts that are supposed to cause people to give off an odour like that of raw meat (*pel'èng*) are also prohibited.

These include drinking raw blood (unmixed with water) and crushing head lice after eating frogs or squirrels. I have not been able to find out exactly how crushing lice produces this dangerous odour, but it seems to have something to do with the mixing of the odour of the animal eaten and that of the person's own blood. Anyone emitting such an odour will be attacked by a tiger or, failing that, will cut himself badly with a knife or axe. The Batek Teh say the same fate befalls those who break the prohibitions on cooking certain foods together, acts which are also supposed to produce *pel'èng* odours. These prohibitions, which they call *pemali'*,[25] are essentially the same as those termed 'fire *lawac*' by the Batek Dè'. The difference is that the Batek Dè' consider these prohibitions, like all *lawac* prohibitions, to be enforced directly by Gobar and the *naga'*, while the Batek Teh, like the Mendriq, see them as enforced by the tiger as an agent of the thunder-god.

Prohibitions to prevent diseases and accidents

Irreverent rhyming. One type of humorous word-play engaged in by the Batek is called *ye'yò'*. To *ye'yò'* is to say a word followed by a nonsense word in which the syllable *bal-* is followed by the final vowel and consonant of the original word. For example, to *ye'yò'* the word for forest (*hep*), one says *hep balep*. To *ye'yò'* the term for pig-tailed macaque (*bawac*), one says *bawac balac*. To *ye'yò'* something is to mildly ridicule the thing or its name.[26] Usually this is a harmless diversion, but to *ye'yò'* certain things is supposed to cause serious diseases and is therefore prohibited.

It is prohibited to *ye'yò'* the names of foods because this will cause anyone who eats that particular food that day to contract *cika'*, severe stomach or intestinal pains (cf. Malay *cika*). The seriousness of the disease varies for different foods. *Cika'* caused by someone *ye'yò'ing* water, milk, tinned sardines, and noodles (*mee*) is always fatal. With all other foods it is less serious and may be cured by various magical medicines and spells. It is also prohibited to *ye'yò'* the *hala'* or anything closely associated with them, such as the sun, moon, stars, sky, seasonal fruit, and bees. Anyone who breaks this rule will contract *reway*, one of the most serious diseases known to the Batek. The characteristic symptom of *reway* is that the victim's head gets

[25] Dentan describes a similar set of prohibitions among the Semai which is called *pənali'* (1968: 36–7).

[26] Possibly the term *ye'yò'* is related to the term *peyò'*, 'to make a face at someone'.

very large and his body very small, which probably means his head stays the same while his body wastes away. He also has a continuous high fever. He loses his senses, as if he were in a trance, and he talks and sings incoherently. He also becomes insensitive to pain. This point is usually illustrated by saying that a victim of *reway* will take hold of burning firewood and may even put live embers in his mouth. Apparently the disease is some kind of infection of the nervous system, possibly encephalitis or cerebral meningitis, which produces high fever and delirium. Supposedly the only hope for a victim of *reway* is to find a shaman who has powerful spells and songs, one who can appeal directly to the *hala'*. Otherwise the person will certainly die.

What is dangerous and offensive about *ye'yò'*ing things, I suggest, is that by distorting the names of things, it confuses their identities and thus threatens the order of the world. To confuse categories of food must be relatively harmless, as it usually leads only to stomach pains, but to confuse the identities of the basic elements of the cosmos is highly dangerous and must be prevented. The threat of *reway* is a very powerful deterrent.

Improper social behaviour. The Batek prohibit a large number of socially disruptive and disrespectful acts, especially those that are directed toward older people. These acts are called *tolah* (cf. Malay *tulah*). They range from addressing an older person by name, rather than by a kin term or *teknonym*, to murder. Striking children is often mentioned as falling into this category. It also includes such acts as spitting on people and urinating in a stream above the camp's bathing place. Anyone who breaks the rules of proper social conduct will be punished by Tohan, the deity who originally created humans and who continues to send and take back their life-souls (*ñawa'*) (see Chapter 4). The severity of the punishment is proportional to the seriousness of the offence. One method of punishment used by Tohan is to cause the offender to fall out of a tree. This may or may not be fatal. Tohan may also send a disease, called '*tolah* disease' (*'aral tolah*), to strike down the offender. This disease is supposed to kill the body first while letting the heart and eyes live on. Apparently it is a form of paralysis. It causes lingering but certain death. If the victim's offence was a serious one, the *hala'* will refuse to take his shadow-soul after death, and it will be doomed to stay on earth in the form of a ghost (*jereng saro'*).

The concept of *tolah*, together with that of 'body *lawac'* which regulates sexual behaviour, gives a divine sanction to the norms of the social order. The fear of disease and accidents is the force behind the *tolah* prohibitions.

Conclusions

The Batek see their forest environment, both its resources and its dangers, as having special significance for them. It is not just the physical setting in which they live, but a world made for them in which they have a well-defined part to play. They see themselves as involved in an intimate relationship of interdependence with the plants, animals, and *hala'* (including the deities) that inhabit their world. Man differs from the others only in that his behaviour is less regular, and it is therefore more likely to disrupt relations among them. To minimize this possibility, man's behaviour toward the other things in the environment is regulated by a large number of prohibitions. These bring the Batek into a state of harmony with their environment. Yet it would be a mistake to think that this is due to an attitude of reverence toward the environment. They say that if they were like the superhuman beings and invulnerable to death, they would have no reason to follow the prohibitions. They do not feel responsible for the natural order the rules help maintain, but only constrained by it. Part of their envy of the *hala'* is based on the belief that the *hala'* are free of all such constraint.

4

HUMAN BEINGS

The Origin of Human Beings

The story of the creation of man sets out what are for the Batek the fundamental properties of human beings, the main determinants of the human condition, and the place of man in the cosmos. Various versions of the story differ in details, but the basic plot is the same. I present here a version given me by Penghulu Selé', an Aring man; I then discuss the significance of some of the variations in other versions.

Once two superhuman brothers, Allah (the elder) and Ta' Allah (the younger), came to earth. They each took some soil and moulded it into the shape of a human body. They called out the names of the body parts as they made them. The elder brother created a man with soil from the place where the sun comes up, and the younger brother produced a woman with soil from where the sun goes down. But the bodies were not alive; they could not stand up. So Allah went to see Tohan, who lived where the sun goes down, while Ta' Allah stayed to guard the lifeless bodies. Allah asked Tohan to give him some ñawa', the life-soul, and, after much persuasion, Tohan agreed. He gave Allah some ñawa' tòm, water life-soul. Allah took the ñawa' tòm in his hands, but on the way back he tripped and spilled it. Tohan quickly spat on the place where it fell and somehow was able to draw it back to himself, whereupon he hid it under his seat. After looking for the ñawa' for seven days, Allah went back to Tohan and asked for more, but Tohan refused. Allah borrowed some ñawa' from a banana plant; this was ñawa' 'angin, wind life-soul. He took it back to the inert bodies in a bottle (botol) and blew some of it on their fontanelles (lekèm kuy; the soft, throbbing spot on the crown of a baby's head) and some on their chests, over the heart. After the ñawa' was absorbed into the bodies, they came to life and stood up. Later these first humans married, following the instructions of Tohan as conveyed by Allah, in order to have children. The children married each other and likewise produced children until another superhuman being came down and told them it was forbidden for brothers and sisters to marry. After that people did not marry relatives closer than first cousin.

One area of variation in different versions of the story is in the number and identity of the creators. Sometimes only one is mentioned: I have heard versions in which Allah, Nabi Adam,[1] and the sandpiper bird (*kawaw kedidi'*) carried out the creation alone. Some Lebir Batek insist that Tohan created humans himself. In Penghulu Selé''s version Ta' Allah seems somewhat redundant, a mere reduplication of Allah added, perhaps, so that the creator will have a younger sibling, following the usual pattern of Batek mythical heroes. There is an Arabic-Malay expression 'Allah *ta'ala*', which means 'God most high', and the Batek seem to have construed this as referring to another person, Ta' ('grandfather') Allah.[2] In another version Nabi Adam is the older brother of Nabi Allah, but the same division of labour between older and younger brothers applies. The great variation in the identity of the creator(s) suggests that the Batek do not regard the identity of the creator as very important. Only in the case of Tohan does the being named continue to be of significance for man after human society is established. According to Penghulu Selé', Allah and Ta' Allah later withdrew to the north and south sides of the world, which in the Batek cosmology is oblivion, and they no longer play any role in human affairs. The actual process of creation varies slightly, of course, depending on whether there are one or two creators. The association of the younger brother with the female and the older brother with the male is usually found whenever there are two creators. The explicit connection of the male with east and the female with west in Penghulu Selé''s version is unusual, however; this is not a consistent association in Batek symbolism. In contrast to the variable identity of the creator, Tohan is always given as the being from whom the life-souls were obtained (though he is not always said to live in the west). This consistency probably derives from the belief that it is Tohan who gives and retrieves life-souls in the present day.

The notion that there were two life-souls, one of which was dropped, is a constant feature of all versions of the story, though the names of the two souls vary. Penghulu Selé''s water life-soul (*ñawa' tòm*) is sometimes called the 'long' life-soul (*ñawa' betét*) or simply the 'first' life-soul (*ñawa' satu'*). The complementary terms for the wind life-soul are 'short' life-soul (*ñawa' cinhạt*) and 'second' life-soul (*ñawa' dua'*). The importance of these two life-souls is that the first one,

---

[1] 'Nabi' means 'prophet' in Malay. It is optionally prefixed to the names Allah, Ta' Allah, and Adam, but never, as far as I know, to Tohan.

[2] The title Ta', oddly enough, is usually applied to the younger of a pair of heroes in Negrito stories (see e.g. Schebesta 1928: 217–18).

which was lost, would have made man immortal, whereas the one that human beings eventually received is merely borrowed (piñam) and thus provides only temporary life. The curious notion that the life-soul of man was derived from a banana plant can be understood as expressing the mortality of man. Not all versions of the story have the wind life-soul being obtained from the banana; some say that, like the water life-soul, it was obtained from Tohan, and one man provided an interesting intermediate conception, saying that it was taken from a banana plant which was inside the body of Tohan. Others go further, however, and say that not only the life-soul but also the heart and blood were borrowed from a banana plant, and this is supposed to account for the alleged resemblance, in colour and viscosity, between coagulated banana plant sap and dried human blood. (Banana sap is clear but dries to a dark brown colour.) No matter how the origin of the wind life-soul is conceived, the Batek often spontaneously compare the mortality of man to that of the banana plant, saying that, for both species, when the parent dies, the child replaces it. Skeat records that in the Semang (Kensiu) and Jakun (Mantra) stories of the creation of man there is concern over the fact that the original human beings did not die, so the earth soon became overcrowded. The deities tried various methods of reducing the population, but were finally forced to introduce death. 'By both races the same proverb is worked into the argument, viz., that it is better for the parents of each generation to die "like the Banana-tree," leaving their children behind them, than to have them in-creasing continually like the stars of the sky for multitude, as they are supposed to have done before the institution of Death' (Skeat and Blagden 1906b: 184; see also 337). Apparently the Batek Dè' merely carry the metaphor one step further: if the succession of human generations is like that of banana plants, then the life-souls of the two species must also be alike. Some of the Batek give a literal interpretation to this metaphor, saying that the human life-soul is actually borrowed from the banana,[3] though others merely express the similarity of the two souls while denying that they are the same. In any case, the Batek tradition that there were two life-souls and

[3] Occasionally one hears that the original water life-soul was taken by Tohan from a tree called kayu' bajiyuh or kayu' jerih. The term kayu' (Malay kayu, 'wood') is used only for perennial trees. The implication seems to be that perennial tree is to banana tree as water life-soul is to wind life-soul. This suggests that the life-span of a being animated by the water life-soul would be more like that of a perennial forest tree than that of the short-lived banana plant.

the immortal one was lost eliminates the problem of overpopulation before it arises.

The Batek story of the creation of man is obviously strongly influenced by Muslim-Malay traditions (see e.g. Skeat 1900: 16–23). But certain features of the story, such as the creators' being two siblings, are typically Negrito, and at least one Negrito mythical hero, the sandpiper bird (*kawaw kedidi'*), can be seen lurking behind his Muslim-named counterparts. The episode of losing the immortal life-soul is particularly distinctive, and it is fundamental to the Batek conception of man. Thus, it may be said that the Batek creation story contains both Batek and Malay elements, but the combination is unique and has a meaning of its own.

The Separation of the Races

The Batek Dè' creation story assumes that mankind was unitary in the beginning. The only account I have seen in which the different races are given separate origins is a Malay story. A Kelantan Malay claimed that the Negritos ('Pangan') arose from a ball of dirt which the first man, Nabi Adam, scraped off his body with his fingernails. This, he said, was why the Malays and Negritos should not mix (Rentse 1937: 120). One Batek gave me a slightly less derogatory story of the origin of Malays. 'There once was a Batek woman who got queasy at the prospect of eating a monkey, so she refused it. Her Batek husband became angry at her and divorced her. She went on alone until she came to a river. There she met a duck, and they got married. Their children were the first Malays.' This story neatly explains the Malay distaste for monkey and other 'unclean' foods and also the strong association of Malays with rivers, which contrasts with the Batek identification of themselves with the forest.

The separation of the Malay and Batek races and some of their cultural differences are accounted for in the following story.

A long time ago the Batek and Malays lived close together at a place near the sea in Trengganu. In those days the Batek were living on rice and other crops grown in clearings (*ladang*), and the Malays lived in the forest on wild foods (the reverse of the present situation). The Malays were jealous of the Batek who had enormous clearings and a huge surplus of food. So they set fire to the grass (*lalang*) surrounding the Batek camp. The Malays ran downstream to escape the flames and the Batek ran upstream. In some versions they both dived into the water, the Batek carrying their sacred books in their belts (or in their armpits according to the Batek Nòng) and the Malays carrying theirs on their heads. The Batek lost their books while swimming, and the heat of the fire frizzled their hair. The Malays, however, safely transported their books on their heads, and the books protected their hair from the heat. Thus, the Batek now have curly hair, and the Malays' hair is straight. In addition, the Malays stole the sacred books of the Batek as they floated by. The Batek also lost all their domesticated animals in the fire, and the Malays managed to get them. Thus, the Malays now live near the sea and have sacred books and domesticated animals, while the Batek live in the upper reaches of the rivers and subsist on wild foods.

Versions of the story of the separation of the Malay and Negrito races in a conflagration are found among nearly all Negrito groups. Sometimes other races or species are mentioned as causing the fire: the Siamese in one case (Skeat and Blagden 1906b: 219), the Chinese in one Batek Dè' account, and various species of monkeys and apes (Evans 1923: 146; Schebesta 1928: 89). Yet it is always the division between Negritos and Malays that is explained, though the distinguishing features emphasized vary somewhat. Several western Negrito versions say that the Malays managed to salvage their rice-spoons, while the Negritos could only save their digging sticks (Evans 1923: 146) or their blowpipes and quivers (Skeat and Blagden 1906b: 219), thus setting the pattern for their future economies. All versions agree, however, in attributing the curly hair of the Negritos to the fire. The Malays are the most important outside reference group for the Negritos, and often the Batek define themselves or the Orang Asli (aborigines) in general by contrast with the Malays. But the Negrito belief in a single origin for all mankind raises the problem of how such physical and cultural differences could have come about, and these stories provide a solution to that problem.

One feature of the Batek Dè' story which is not found in other accounts of the conflagration is the loss of the sacred books. However, this theme is a common one among the 'tribes of Indo-China', according to Skeat (Skeat and Blagden 1906b: 174n.), and he gives an example from the Mantra, Aboriginal Malays of Malacca (Skeat and Blagden 1906b: 346–7). Among the Batek Nòng the episode of the losing of the sacred books, which is essentially the same as the Batek Dè' tradition, occurs in the story of Nabi Noah and the flood, when the Ark is shipwrecked and all the people on board have to swim for it. Again this is a Malay story with a Negrito twist. The importance of sacred books is that they are often cited by Malays as a sign of their cultural superiority to the Negritos. The main point of the Negrito story seems to be that this cultural difference is due mainly to the deviousness of the Malays, though one informant punctuated his description of how the Batek put their books in their belts with the remark: 'Our ancestors were stupid!' It is the mere fact of having once had sacred books, as a sign of cultural refinement, that is stressed by the Batek; the actual content of the books is not known, nor is it considered important by them.

The Components of Human Beings

In the Batek view, human beings are made up of a number of components which are partially independent of each other and which have individual properties connecting them in different ways with various other things and beings in their environment. The supposed nature of these components has a powerful influence over the Batek's interpretation of human actions, experiences, and circumstances, and these ideas may be seen to lie behind some of the Batek religious practices. I first describe these components separately and then go on to show how they come together at birth, are disrupted by illness, and are separated at death.

Body

The body (*lih*) of a human being is considered by the Batek to consist principally of ordinary flesh (*séc*), bone (*tolang*), and skin (*kete'*), just like the bodies of the animals they eat. The body of a baby is supposed to develop from the blood of the mother. After death the body simply rots, like the carcass of a dead animal. Most of the solid parts of the human body are thought to be ultimately derived from the earth, the soil which was moulded into manikins by Allah and Ta' Allah. The dark brown colour of Batek skin is cited as evidence of this origin.[4] According to one story, however, the original people had no hair. Because the sun was hot on their heads, they fashioned a coarse cloth out of a type of palm-cabbage (*ta'a' bagòt*), and, when they put it on their heads, it became hair.

The internal organs are regarded as somewhat more important for life than the other parts of the body; the Batek say that all the internal organs must be present and intact for a person to be alive,

---

[4] Actually most of the soil in the forest is reddish-brown laterite. One man explained that Allah had created the first Batek from black soil and added that he also produced a pair of beings from white soil which became the Caucasians. The Batek were created first, however, and were thus the original humans.

whereas some of the other parts of the body can be lost or damaged
without resulting in death. Usually the internal organs are said to
have been obtained from Tohan or borrowed from the banana
plant, rather than moulded out of the original earth. This special
status of the internal organs is due in part to the belief that the heart
(kelangès),[5] liver (ros), kidneys (berkòl), and lungs (sop) are the main
repositories of the life-soul (ñawa').

The heart is considered the most important of the internal organs,
and it is supposed to be the first part of the body formed from the
blood of the mother. It is pictured as lying in the centre of a circle
of seven stems from which the other major organs are suspended.
The lungs surround and support the heart 'like floats on a net'. The
function of the heart is to store or hold blood (boh yǫp) and to receive
the breath. The pulse is attributed to the breath entering and leaving
the heart and thus driving the blood around the body (cf. Barnes
1974: 154–5). All animals are thought to have hearts, though they
differ in form from species to species. But only plants that have stems
and joints have a kelangès; it is the pith in the central stem or trunk.
Perhaps the pith is so designated because it seems to store the sap,
which is considered analogous to the blood of animals.

The Batek are uncertain about the functions of the lungs, liver,
kidneys, gall bladder (kemüt), and spleen (manèk), though they know
that the spleen is somehow affected by malaria. But they do understand something of the way food is processed in the digestive tract.
They see food as being gradually changed into excrement ('èc) as it
passes through the stomach ('èc puk), small intestine ('èc węc), and
large intestine ('èc ber). They do not understand the value of this
process, however, and they generally consider the necessity of eating
to be a nuisance. The Batek also say that the water they drink passes
out of the body as urine (kenom), though they do not know exactly
where or how it changes its chemical composition.

Blood (yǫp) is especially important in Batek religion. It is thrown
to stop thunderstorms, is used in some kinds of curing, and it also
appears in myths as the substance from which various foods were
created. The blood of the first humans is generally said to have been

[5] Lessons given to me by the Batek in the internal anatomy of monkeys have
shown that kelangès means the heart alone (Malay jantung) in mammals (see also
Skeat and Blagden 1906b: 463). But the term kelangès is also used to translate
Malay expressions in which states of emotion are indicated by reference to the
hati, which means heart and liver together. For example, Malay suka hati, 'to be
delighted', becomes suka' kelangès.

obtained from Tohan or the banana plant, whose sap it resembles. The blood of humans and the higher animals is thought to be stored in the heart and to be driven by the breath to all parts of the body. The blood is generally said to contain life-soul (*ñawa'*). Presumably this is acquired in the heart, which is the main seat of the life-soul. The blood of males is considered different from that of females because women abstain from eating meat and salt (and a few other minor foods) during their menstrual periods and following parturition. If a woman were to break this prohibition she would suffer from dizziness (*tewin*). One would also get dizzy from eating the blood of a female (but not a male) monkey, and therefore it is not done. Presumably female monkeys do not observe the proper food prohibitions and thus their blood becomes contaminated with dizziness-causing substances. But only the menstrual blood itself is considered dirty (*kamah*), not female blood in general.[6] Apparently it is the passing out of the vagina that is supposed to soil it, for the same blood is considered good (*bed'èt*) when it develops into a baby. The Batek do not consider menstrual blood very polluting, and women continue to carry on their usual activities and to sleep in their family lean-to during their periods. The Batek Teh and a few closely related Batek Dè', however, do not allow menstrual blood to flow into a stream, and thus prohibit bathing or washing clothes in streams during a woman's period, because they think this would anger the thunder-god. But in other respects they, like most of the Batek Dè', are not very concerned about the 'dirtiness' of menstrual blood.

The Batek Dè' generally take no special precautions in disposing of bodily excretions or those parts of the body that are removed from it. Defecation takes place in the forest outside the camp or in streams, but no attempt is made to conceal the excrement. Menstrual blood is washed out in a stream or, alternatively, in the forest by those who observe the prohibition on letting it flow into a stream. Batek children and grown men regularly shave off their hair, whenever the lice get too bad to endure, and the hair is merely thrown away, either inside or outside the camp. Older girls and women only rarely shave off their hair, however, for they think it makes them look ugly

---

[6] Some of the Batek Dè' who are closely related to the Batek Teh use a separate word, *mahọh*, for menstrual blood. Both *yạp* and *mahọh*, meaning 'blood', have cognates in other Negrito languages, but they are usually not both found in the same language (Skeat and Blagden 1906b: 536).

and old. They depend instead on frequent combing and mutual grooming to keep the lice under control. Fingernails and toenails are pared off with a knife whenever they get too long and are also casually thrown away. The Batek do not have any belief in sorcery that might work through their removable body parts, nor do they believe that any loss of power or vitality accompanies the loss of those parts that become detached in the ordinary course of events.

The Batek do make a special effort, however, to keep the body parts together during certain critical stages in the development of the child. Both the umbilical cord and the baby's first hair (which might otherwise fall out) are kept and put into a bracelet (*tabèn cas*) or a necklace (*tenwak*) which the baby wears until it is able to walk. This is supposed to prevent it from having crying fits (*sabèn*). The hair is shaved off and wrapped in a small strip of cloth which is tied to a cloth string to form the bracelet or necklace. The umbilical cord may be put in the same bundle or merely tied, without a covering, to a separate string. Either or both may be worn on the wrist or neck. Sometimes the umbilical cord is deliberately placed on the right wrist, as this is supposed to ensure that the child will become right-handed. The right hand is preferred because it is considered faster and less clumsy than the left. There are left-handed Batek, however, who are acknowledged to have developed ability or power (*bisa'*) with that hand. Similarly, a child's milk-teeth are wrapped up in a leaf of thatch and kept in a pandanus pouch until the permanent teeth have sprouted and become firm. After all the permanent teeth are in, the milk-teeth may be thrown away. Saving the milk-teeth only helps the natural process of development; there is no use in keeping a permanent tooth if it falls out in hopes that a new one will grow. These customs reveal a notion of the integrity of the body which must be maintained during early childhood to ensure healthy growth and development. Once a person is fully developed, however, there is no longer any danger in casually disposing of the detachable parts of the body.

Life-soul

Another crucial component of human beings is the life-soul, *ñawa'*, the force that animates the body. In a fully formed body, the presence of *ñawa'* is necessary and sufficient to give it life, and the departure of the *ñawa'* is equated with death. The wind life-soul, *ñawa' 'angin*, which animates man and the other mortal animals, may be characterized as the 'breath of life', which is the primary meaning of the term *nyawa* in Patani Malay (Annandale and Robinson 1903: 93–4; see also Wilkinson 1959b: 814). The Batek Dè' often describe it as 'breath', *napas*, and even literally as the 'breath of life', *napas 'o' gòs*. In the Batek Nòng version of the story of the creation of man, the term *napas* is used instead of *ñawa'* throughout, there being no water life-soul (*ñawa' tòm*) to cause confusion. In one Batek Dè' version of the creation, the prophet inserted the *ñawa'* but then had to carve the nostrils before the manikin would come to life, the first sign of life being a sneeze. Some say that all animals that breathe also have *ñawa'* which are sent by Tohan. However, the Batek Dè' do make a subtle distinction between the *ñawa' 'angin* and the physical breath (*napas*) in some contexts. Normally the location of the breath is placed in the nose and that of the life-soul in the heart. The air that is expelled in blowing, as into a blowpipe or in certain types of curing, is considered *napas* only, not *ñawa' 'angin*. Also the wind life-soul is sometimes identified with the voice, though the physical breath is not. In addition to its connection with the breath, the *ñawa' 'angin* is closely associated with the wind, *'angin*. It is said to be like wind, to be taken from the wind, and to be a small wind itself. Yet it is distinguished very sharply from ordinary wind by its power to give life. The wind life-soul of an unborn baby is borne to it by the wind, but the two are not confused. It seems best, then, to describe the *ñawa' 'angin* as an invisible force which resides in a living body and is manifested in the breath and voice.

Life-soul is homogeneous, so it can be recycled from one body to another. Tohan keeps a supply of *ñawa' 'angin*, some say in a plastic bag, and he sends it out and retrieves it as he sees fit. While the *ñawa' 'angin* is with Tohan, it has no form, but consists merely of voices and breath. When Tohan sees a baby developing in a woman's womb, he sends some life-soul to it on the wind, and it enters the body through the fontanelle. When the foetus has hands and feet, it will have life-soul (of its own) as well. But Tohan also keeps an account (*banci'*) of the ages of all human beings, and, when a person has lived sufficient years, he snatches the life-soul away, thereby causing death. Tohan may also send more life-soul to persons who are already living, thus extending their life-spans. The amount of life-soul sent out roughly balances that retrieved, so Tohan's supply of it remains relatively constant. It seems that life-soul can also be

transferred from one body to another by man. This is done by
transferring blood, the only life-soul saturated part of the body that
can be safely removed from it. This life-giving property of blood is,
I shall argue, one of the keys to its use in curing and in the blood
sacrifice.

In explaining why man is mortal, the Batek usually emphasize
that their life-soul is only a 'loan' (*piñaman*) and is merely 'lodging'
(*tompang*) temporarily in man. But this does not explain why the
wind life-soul, but not the water life-soul which was also given by
Tohan, should be periodically taken back. In some versions of the
story of the origin of man it is not even Tohan but the banana plant
which supplied the *ñawa' 'angin*, but it is never claimed that Tohan
returns it to the banana rather than to man. In fact the presumed
properties of the wind life-soul go somewhat further toward ac-
counting for the impermanence of human life. It is said to be warm
and dry, by contrast with the water life-soul which is cool and moist,
and because of this men must keep warm and eat cooked food.
Human beings are condemned to copy the sun rather than the moon,
to rise in the morning and work during the heat of the day. They
must also use fires to keep warm and to cook food. Yet heat, fire,
smoke, ashes, and cooked food are major sources of disease according
to Batek theories. Thus humans must expose their bodies to
numerous risks and debilitating influences which would have been
entirely avoided if only they had received the water life-soul.

Shadow-soul

The other fundamental component of living human beings is the
shadow-soul (*bayang*). This is a soft, transparent entity which
inhabits the entire body. Its shape is the same as that of the body,
which is merely its 'shell' or 'container'. Shadow-souls are ordinarily
invisible, though they can be seen in dreams and by shamans in
trance. But a person's shadow (also called *bayang*) is regarded as a
visible manifestation of his shadow-soul. Shadow-souls are distinctive
for each individual. When seen in dreams or trance, a person's
shadow-soul has the same appearance as the person himself. The
shadow-soul comes into existence in the womb, developing in
conjunction with the individual baby's body. After death, the
shadow-soul goes to live in the afterworld, and it retains the
distinctive features of the individual from which it came. Only
humans and superhuman beings have true shadow-souls; the only

plants or animals that have them are actually superhumans in plant or animal-form bodies.

As a manifestation of the shadow-soul, a person's shadow is considered an extension of himself beyond his body. For this reason, the shadow is subject to certain rules which overlap, to some extent, with a set of prohibitions on physical contact between certain individuals. In general, a person's shadow should not be allowed to fall upon the shadow or the body of another person. This may cause fever to afflict both parties. It is the mingling of the different shadows, or shadows and bodies, that causes the illness, not the transmission of an extant disease from one person to another through the shadows. In fact this prohibition is only casually and irregularly observed except in the case of in-laws and close consanguines who are mature and of opposite sex. In that case the mixing of shadows, like prolonged physical touching which is also prohibited, is considered improper sexual behaviour (*cemam*) and is therefore *lawac*, an offence against the thunder-god which is punished by storm or disease.[7] Even so, the Batek Dè' say they are afraid of the shadows of in-laws only at night, when their shadows are long (being produced by campfires or torches), though the Mendriq, as both dialect groups point out, fear the shadows of their in-laws at all times.

The shadow-soul can leave the body when a person sleeps. It travels on foot like a man, only it makes no noise. Any things or other shadow-souls it meets in its travels appear to the sleeper as dreams. The act of dreaming, the shadow-soul of the dreamer, and the things met are all called *tewin* in Batek Dè' (*mpa'* in Batek Teh

---

[7] In a limited context the odour of a person's body is subject to similar rules and penalties. This is in the case of marriage or sexual relations between a person and a sibling of his or her spouse or lover. It is prohibited for two brothers or two sisters to have sexual relations with the same partner without an intervening lapse of time. Thus a person cannot be married to two siblings at once and can only marry the sibling of a dead or divorced spouse after a delay of at least a month. The Batek Teh say this can never be done, though I know of one exception to the rule. The reason for these restrictions is that the smell of a person is thought to cling to a spouse or lover for a while after they separate. Thus, if two siblings have sex with the same person, the smells of the siblings will mix (*campor*). This is *cemam*, punished by the thunder-god, and it also creates an unhealthy atmosphere in which any children that might be conceived would be unhealthy and would probably die. If there are children by the first marriage, their smells also will mix in and make an even more dangerous combination. These prohibitions seem to imply that body odours, like shadows, are differentiated extensions of the individual, but this is not generally recognized or elaborated.

and Mendriq), which also means 'dizzy'. A person's shadow-soul may meet anything, but most commonly it encounters various types of food and the shadow-souls of the dreamer's friends and relatives. One's shadow-soul can also meet the shadow-souls of the dead, which return to earth from time to time. For ordinary persons, who are not shamans, dreams are the main avenue of contact with the superhuman beings (hala'). Many spells, songs, and useful bits of esoteric information are obtained in this way. In a few situations, however, dreaming can be dangerous. It is thought that tigers have such good night vision that they can see a wandering shadow-soul and follow it back to its owner's sleeping-place and kill him. Thus, when the Batek are camping in a small group and they think there are tigers around, they sometimes make a low fence of palm-fronds around their sleeping places to prevent their shadow-souls from wandering off. Ordinarily the shadow-soul returns to a sleeper naturally before he wakes up, but if it is necessary to wake someone abruptly, and he will not come around, the smoke of sweet-smelling plants ('asèp 'ayam) can be blown on the person's body to attract the shadow-soul back to it.

Dream experiences are part of ordinary reality in the view of the Batek Dè'. What one's shadow-soul sees at night, during a dream, can be found by the whole person the following morning. The dream is not an omen, however, but merely a source of knowledge which can be acted upon in various ways. If a person dreamt of a tiger one night, he would conclude that a tiger was nearby and would probably stay in camp the next day. If he dreamt of a certain edible plant or animal, he might find it the next day, but only because his shadow-soul had shown him where it was. If, however, he dreamt of a certain kind of food and then woke up with a fever, he might conclude that it does not agree with him, and he will decline to eat it in the future. This is a common source of personal food avoidances. Dreams are not normally interpreted symbolically, though occasionally a dream is said to indicate something more than just the presence nearby of the thing dreamt about. For example, I was told that if one dreamt of a cocèw flower out of season, it might mean that the floods would be early that year, for the cocèw does not bloom until after the floods, and thus the dream could not come true until the floods were over. Only in such limited instances are dreams regarded as a window on the future rather than merely a special source of information about the present.

The two souls of the Batek each make their distinctive contributions. The life-soul animates the body, and the shadow-soul helps to define the individual person. The role of the shadow-soul in dreams and after death suggests that it is the agent of consciousness and perception. Together, the two kinds of souls transform the body into a human being. Having a wind life-soul associates man with the higher animals, but separates him from the plants and the immortal superhuman beings. Having a shadow-soul sets man apart from all ordinary plants and animals and associates him with the superhumans. Thus, as defined by souls, humans are between the animals and the superhumans, and this, in Batek philosophy, is the nature—and the dilemma—of man.

Mendriq semangat: *a comparison*

A brief examination of the Mendriq soul-ideas will place the Batek notions in a new perspective, and the comparison will reveal one of the general patterns in Malaysian Negrito religious conceptions. This information was obtained from a group living as semi-settled agriculturalists on the Lah River, a tributary of the Nenggiri a few miles above Bertam (see Map 1).

The Mendriq call the soul *semangat*, the ancient Indonesian-Malay term for 'soul, spirit of life, vitality' (Wilkinson 1959b: 1053). (It may also be called *reway* following the Temiar usage.) The *semangat* is said to be shaped like its owner's body, only it is more beautiful. It cannot be seen by ordinary persons, however. Babies have *semangat* before they are born; it comes from the blood of the mother and father which mingle together to form the foetus.[8] When a person dies, his *semangat* leaves the top of his head and goes to the land of the dead, Cepèng, which is where the sun goes down. The Mendriq always say it 'returns to Cepèng' (*wék ba*-Cepèng), which seems to imply that its ultimate origin, at least, was there. When the *semangat* reaches the afterworld, it gets a new body which is young and healthy. It forgets its brothers and sisters who are still living. The *semangat* of the dead live an easy life with no work. In a living person the *semangat* is especially concentrated in the heart, chest, and veins at the elbow and wrist, where the pulse can be felt. It is also in the blood, and any loss of blood is a loss of *semangat*. All living things (including wind) have *semangat*, which is especially concentrated in

---

[8] This seems to imply that semen is seen as a form of blood, but unfortunately I neglected to pursue the matter.

the parts that can be easily killed, such as the buds of trees.[9] When a person dreams (*mpa'*), it is his *semangat* wandering abroad where it meets various *semangat*, persons, animals, and other things. It returns to the sleeper's body when the sun comes up.

The Mendriq conceive of shadows (*langòy*) as merely the natural result of sun shining on a solid body. They say a shadow cannot become detached from its body. Yet they also prohibit the mixing of the shadows of in-laws, and they say that a disease will not leave the body of a sick person if the shadows of other people are falling upon it.

The Mendriq *semangat* seems to combine most of the features of the Batek Dè' 'wind life-soul' and the 'shadow-soul'. Like the Batek wind life-soul, it is responsible for life and death, is concentrated in the heart, and is infused in the blood. Like the Batek shadow-soul, on the other hand, it goes out in dreams, and after death it lives on in the afterworld. Where the features of the two Batek souls differ, the Mendriq *semangat* is ambiguous. While the Batek life-soul is homogeneous and the shadow-soul individualized, the Mendriq *semangat* resembles its owner but is idealized, and when it reaches the afterworld it 'forgets its brothers and sisters', which in Negrito society is equivalent to saying it loses its identity. On the other hand, the Mendriq do not consider the shadow to be an aspect of the soul. Both these schemes are reasonable ways to conceive of life, consciousness, and personality, though the Batek scheme is perhaps a little sounder logically in that it provides an explanation for the continuation of life while a person is asleep and the 'dream-soul' is absent. In effect the Mendriq and Batek attribute the same 'functions' or 'duties' to souls, but the Batek divide them between two different types of souls. Also the Batek associate the soul processes more closely with external manifestations—the shadow and breath—while the Mendriq place them more inside the body and out of sight. These differences reveal a general feature of Malaysian Negrito religions: similarly conceived processes are attributed to entities which vary in number and identity. This phenomenon appears again in the conceptions of deities, where a uniform set of 'natural processes' is attributed to beings who are variable in number and attributes.

[9] The Mendriq also believe in the 'soul of rice', *semangat padi*, and 'free spirits', *hantu*, which must be propitiated when clearing and planting. These concepts were probably adopted from the nearby Malays along with the techniques of dry field agriculture.

Birth

According to the Batek Dè' theory of conception, the body of the baby develops from the blood of the mother alone. Yet they realize that conception will not take place without copulation. When the original human couple asked Allah how they could make more people, he went to Tohan to find out. Tohan sent word through Allah that they should marry and have sexual relations (*nòy* or *tòy*). Since then, people have merely followed Tohan's instructions. The Batek do not claim to know how copulation causes conception, and they have no idea of the role of semen.[10] But they do believe that the father has some kind of physical influence on the child. It is expected that male children will look like their fathers, just as female children will look like their mothers. It is also said that if a woman has sexual relations with two men in close succession, she may have twins. This is considered physically dangerous to the mother, and for this reason women are not supposed to have two husbands or lovers at once. The Batek realize that both men and women may be infertile (*manòl*), though they do not know why. They also know a number of forest medicines which are supposed to prevent or promote conception, but they have no theory as to how they work.

The Batek say they must copulate many times, usually over a period of three to four months, in order to start a baby. After a woman has gone two months without having a menstrual period, she will begin to suspect that she is pregnant (*makò'*; also means 'egg'). It is thought that the blood which would normally be expelled in menstruation has begun to collect together into a ball. After a month it is about the size of a thumb, and it continues to grow steadily. Copulation may continue, but is has no further effect. The heart is the first part of the body to develop. When the foetus has developed hands and feet, Tohan sends some wind life-soul to it. The shadow-soul comes into existence by itself about the same time. After that, the mother will be able to feel the baby moving. The baby will continue to grow and develop until it is ready to be born. There are no food prohibitions for a woman during pregnancy.

When a pregnant woman feels that she is starting labour, her husband and a few other people build her a new hut a few hundred yards from camp. It is built away from the camp to insulate it

[10] The Batek Dè' do not even have a special word for semen; it is merely included under the term *kenom*, whose primary meaning is 'urine'.

from the normal activities of the camp and also because the birth-hut is considered dirty after the baby has been born. The shelter is an ordinary thatch lean-to with a low platform floor usually made of smooth sticks, so that any waste fluids can run through to the ground. At one side of the platform a row of stakes is driven into the ground at an angle to form a backrest. The prospective mother sits on the platform, leaning back against the backrest. A midwife (*bidan*), who is usually one of the older women of the camp, sits facing her, beside her updrawn legs. Several other women sit beside and behind the woman to help support her. The woman giving birth has a cloth draped over her shoulders and across her abdomen; this keeps her warm and preserves her modesty. All men, including the husband, withdraw before the birth takes place. The midwife massages the woman's abdomen to 'gather together the baby's knees and elbows' and to draw the baby down. If there are any difficulties, the midwife may say some spells (*jampi'*) or call on someone else to recite them. If, as often happens, it is a man who knows the required spell, he recites it from a discreet distance. When the baby comes out, the midwife receives it and places it between the mother's feet. Then she gently pulls the umbilical cord until the placenta is expelled. The midwife then washes the mother and baby in cool water, which may have had medicinal leaves boiled in it earlier.[11] The mother moves aside and is covered up while the midwife cuts the umbilical cord with a sharpened splinter of bamboo (*semilu'*)[12] which has previously had a spell spoken over it to prevent infection. The end of the cord may be tied with a fine thread made from a type of rattan (*'awey riyuh*), though the Batek say this is not always necessary. The baby is then wrapped in a cloth and given to someone to hold. Then the midwife massages the new mother all over to relieve her aching muscles, and boiled medicinal leaves may be rubbed on her for the same reason.[13] The placenta is either buried beside the platform or left on it, covered with a piece of bark or bamboo. The upper Lebir Batek insist that the placenta, like a dead person, must not be buried in the ground. The new mother

[11] One type used are the leaves of a tree called *lenbet hüt* (*Ophiorrhiza discolor* R. Br.).

[12] Apparently this practice is copied from the Malays who avoid using knives for this operation for fear that the iron will harm or frighten off the soul (*semangat*) of the baby (Annandale and Robinson 1903: 97). The Batek say a metal blade would be painful to the baby.

[13] One species used is *nerper* (*Alpinia petiolata* Bak.).

and child move back into the family lean-to as soon as the woman feels able. But for three or four days after giving birth, the mother keeps a fire going above (if it is buried) or beside the placenta, returning several times a day to add fuel. This is to keep the placenta warm. It is thought that if it were allowed to grow cold, the mother would suffer from chills, and the baby would have fits of crying. Apparently the placenta is not considered to be fully separated from the bodies of the mother and child for several days after the birth. Only the mother is permitted to revisit the birth-hut. After a week or so, the placenta has disintegrated, and the hut is abandoned.

A number of precautions are taken and medicines used to prevent the mother's getting *meryèn*, the generic term for complications associated with childbirth (Malay *meroyan*). The most common form of *meryèn* is a fever with chills. Consequently the mother must rest and keep warm for three or four days after giving birth. Sometimes a stone about the size of a grapefruit is warmed in the fire and fastened to the woman's waist with a strip of cloth. Immediately before giving birth and for some days afterward, the woman is given various kinds of hot medicinal infusions, which have had spells recited over them, to warm her insides. This is also thought to promote the flow of milk. Just before or immediately after giving birth, someone paints inch-wide black stripes across the mother's forehead, upper chest, stomach, and lower back to prevent her getting fever. A similar stripe is painted across the baby's forehead for the same reason. The pigment is made by burning the leaves of certain plants[14] and making a paste of the ashes in water. These lines are renewed regularly for at least a week.

Numerous other precautions are taken to protect the health of the mother and baby. According to a few of the Batek Dè' and all of the Batek Teh a woman must not bathe in a stream for a week or so after giving birth. This, like the similar prohibition on bathing during menstruation, is intended to prevent dirty blood from entering the stream, an occurrence which would anger the thunder-god. Few Batek Dè' observe this prohibition, however. Most of the Batek women observe food prohibitions for at least a month (some say a month, others forty days, and others two months) after giving

---

[14] Most of the plants used are called merely *'obèt meryèn*, *'meryèn* medicine'. They include *Adenostoma viscosum* Forst., *Antrophyum plantagineum*, and *Tectaria singaporeana*, a fern with large simple fronds (called *hali' kengkèng* in Batek Dè').

birth to avoid getting 'dizzy eyes' (*tewin mə̀t*). The foods prohibited
are the same as those prohibited during menstruation: meat, salt,
chilies, milk, sugar, nuts, cassava, and green vegetables. As mentioned above, the navel cord and first hair of a baby may be made
into a necklace or bracelet to protect the baby from crying fits
(*sabèn*). For the same purpose a necklace may be made of a cloth
string tied to a few pieces of wild turmeric root, '*obèt dengwòng*
(Malay *kunyit hutan*). This has a spell recited over it asking the
disease to return to all those parts of the world in which it is thought
to reside. A couple may resume having sexual relations as soon after
childbirth as the mother feels well enough. They usually deliberately abstain from sex (at least on a regular basis) while the
baby is small, however, because it is feared that the mother would
not have enough milk to feed two infants.

Babies are named about a month after birth. The name is usually
given by the midwife, though some of the men insist that it is really
the father who decides. The 'original name' (*kenmòh 'asal*)[15] of a
Batek is usually the name of the side-stream near which he was
born, the name of some plant or animal seen near the spot, or the
name of a type of food eaten by the mother on the day of birth. At
adolescence the boys, and some of the girls, get 'outsider names'
(*kenmòh gob*), which are Malay words used as names (e.g. Daun,
'Leaf') in intercourse with non-aborigines. After having children of
their own, both men and women are called by teknonyms. The
baby's original name is not announced with any special ceremony,
though the midwife normally tells the parents first and they in turn
tell the rest of the camp. The midwife is usually given a few small
gifts—such as a sarong, ring, necklace, mirror, or knife—if the baby
lives.

Characteristically, childbirth is not highly ritualized by the Batek.
Their procedures are addressed mainly to the practical problems of
bringing babies safely into the world. Yet, for the mother at least,
there is the faint outline of a rite of passage. The status of a woman
does change with the birth of children. After the first child, she may
be referred to as *mabèr*, 'parent', and she will be called by a teknonym
derived from the name of her child. After the second and subsequent children, she may be called *mawòng*, 'parent of more than
one child'. The retreat to the birth-hut, giving birth, and the return

---

[15] Also called the 'childhood name' (*kenmòh 'awə̀* or *kenmòh kèn*), 'true name'
(*kenmòh betòl*), or 'flesh name' (*kenmòh séc*).

to camp may be seen as the separation, transition, and incorporation phases of a rite of passage, though only the separation phase is symbolically elaborated to any extent (by the physical distance from camp, the exclusion of men, etc.). But the husband achieves the same change of status without participating in any ritual. And the childbirth procedure is essentially the same whether it is a woman's first or tenth child, even though there is no marked change of social status after the second. Thus it must be concluded that the rite of passage is only a minor component of the Batek childbirth procedure. Of course the use of medicines and spells can be considered ritual. I examine such medical practices below.

Disease and Curing

The Batek Dè' do not have a single unified theory of disease.[16] They believe that many things can disrupt the usual smooth running of the human body, and, because the presumed causes of disease are diverse, they use a great variety of curing techniques. The general Batek Dè' term for being ill or injured is *petis*. For example, the expression used for having a headache is: '*o' petis kuy yè*', 'it is ill my head'. Most minor illnesses are described only in this way, no attempt being made to attribute them to a specific 'disease' ('*aral*; Malay *penyakit*). A few of the more serious types of illness do have specific names, however. For these, the causes, identifying symptoms, and courses of treatment are relatively widely known and agreed upon. In this section I briefly survey the main causes of disease, according to Batek ideas, and the general types of treatment used. I also describe in some detail one of the more interesting named diseases.

Causes of disease

One possible source of disease, which has already been discussed, is the breaking of the prohibitions on improper behaviour between

[16] The Batek Nòng, on the other hand, attribute most illnesses to *bès*, a large class of bodiless spirits which are explicitly compared to Malay *hantu*. They cause illness by entering one's body, and they can be driven out by a number of Malay-style exorcism rites. The *bès* have their own society which is analogous to that of humans; they even have their own headmen (*batin*). The *bès* are also supposed to have their own country which may somehow be connected with the Batek Nòng land of the dead, which is called Lembès (see also Schebesta 1928: 276) and is located where the sun goes down. The nearby Jah Hut, a Senoi people, also use the term *bès* for disease-causing spirits, and it is frequently these that are depicted in their well-known wood carvings.

relatives of opposite sex (*cemam*). Such acts may lead to Gobar's sending a crippling and sometimes fatal disease in the form of a spark of lightning which enters the foot of the offender. Less seriously, the mere mixing of the odours or shadows of certain relatives can cause them to be afflicted with a disease called *cemam*, whose main symptom is fever. Also, Tohan may send the disease called *tolah* to a person who commits a gross breach of etiquette.

Perhaps the majority of Batek diseases are attributed to things eaten. For the most part this is a straightforward and accurate assessment. It is well-known, for example, that eating too much of such foods as palm cabbage (*ta'a'*) will cause a stomach ache and bloating. A number of foods eaten by the Batek are poisonous in their natural state. These include such important foods as *gadong* (*Dioscorea hispida*), a common tuber, and *penace'* (*Pangium edule*), a large, protein-rich nut. These are processed in ways which remove or neutralize the poison, but sometimes they are inadvertently eaten before the process is complete. A number of common foods are considered harmful if eaten in large quantities, but not so poisonous that they must be processed. Some types of food are thought to disagree only with certain individuals. If a person wakes up ill after eating or dreaming about a particular food, he will most likely avoid that food in the future. Furthermore, some types of food are only considered harmful to certain people at certain times. These include the foods, such as meat, that are prohibited to women during menstruation or following childbirth. Eating any of the prohibited foods during those times is supposed to cause dizziness (*tewin*). The Batek also believe that harmful parasites or germs (*koman*; Malay *kuman*) can be eaten inadvertently along with harmless food or water. These may be present on the leaves from which food is eaten or in water if, for example, an elephant has urinated or defecated upstream from where the water was drawn. One reason the water from inside certain types of rattan is considered the best for drinking is that it supposedly does not contain any *koman*. Although the Batek may exaggerate the role of food in causing disease, sometimes blaming recently eaten foods for diseases actually contracted in other ways, the basic idea that foods sometimes contain harmful substances is well founded. Yet humans must eat or they will die, the Batek say, because they do not have immortal water life-souls.

The other major source of disease is the environment. Diseases may come from almost anything. Among the sources commonly mentioned are earth, sand, stones, wind, rain, water, and trees. The disease-causing agents supposedly enter the body through the skin or the orifices. These agents seem to be conceived of in various ways. Sometimes the cause of the illness is thought to be an inherently irritating substance. For example, if one inhales the fuzz from the surface of bamboo, this is supposed to cause a cough.[17] Also, ashes carried by smoke are thought to cause coughs and eye inflammations. Some diseases are thought to be caused by *koman* which live in the water, soil, and decaying vegetation. They seem to be pictured as like insect larvae or worms which are so tiny they cannot be seen. Ordinarily they cannot enter the body unless they are eaten, but if they come into prolonged contact with a person's skin—for example, if a person bathes in *koman*-infested water for several hours—they can gradually work their way into the body. Other disease-causing agents are vaguely conceived of as invisible, formless substances which lie inside material objects. They can only be seen by shamans, to whom they appear as clouds or mist of various colours. They are not alive, but they can pass slowly into the bodies of persons who come in contact with the things in which they reside. The transfer of such disease agents to humans is greatly accelerated if the things they inhabit are burned. Many diseases are said to come from firewood and to be released in the burning so they can enter human bodies through the smoke. Also fires are thought to draw diseases out of the ground. The heat attracts them, and they rise on the smoke. One of the reasons the Batek do not like to camp where people have lived before is that they believe some of the diseases the previous group had will have gone into the ground and will be drawn out when they make new fires. Here again it is because man has only a wind life-soul that he must expose himself to such hazards. If he had a water life-soul, there would be no need to use fires; man would not need to keep warm or to cook food.

Although food and the environment are the major sources of disease according to Batek theories, a number of other causes, such as too much sun, are cited for specific complaints. It is worth noting that both spirit invasion and soul loss, which play major roles in the disease aetiology of the Malays (see Endicott 1970) and of many other Orang Asli groups (Benjamin 1974), are of little significance

---

[17] This recalls the Batek Teh and Mendriq notion that certain kinds of chest pains are caused by tiny needles (*jarom*) that are blown into the body by the wind. Some people know how to cure this ailment by sucking the needles out.

in Batek Dè' medical theories. The closest thing to an 'evil spirit' (Malay *hantu*) in Batek beliefs is the wicked superhuman being that is supposed to cause convulsions in infants (*sabèn*; Malay *sawan*). This being is pictured as an invisible bird which can swoop down and steal a baby's shadow-soul. This is also the only disease I know of that is attributed to the loss of the shadow-soul. This set of ideas may well have been borrowed from Malays or from some other aboriginal group.

Curing techniques

The great majority of Batek curing methods involve the use of medicines (*'obèt*) made from plants. Some of the medicines are taken internally, and others are applied to the skin. The identities of the plants to be used and the way they are to be prepared and administered is learned ultimately from the superhuman beings, through dream or trance, though the information can then be transmitted from person to person. Some common medicines are known by nearly everyone and others by only a few experts. Such knowledge is readily shared, so it is not necessary for everyone to know the more unusual remedies. Hundreds of plant species are said to have medicinal properties, sometimes several different parts of a plant being used for different purposes. The Negritos are acknowledged by all Malaysian races to be the foremost experts on the medicines derived from forest plants. No doubt some of the forest medicines they use have actual pharmacological value (see Burkill 1966). This does not mean that all Batek medicines work, nor, if they do work, is it necessarily for the reasons given by the Batek. The Batek themselves admit that medicines do not always have the desired result, for a variety of reasons, so they often use more than one type of medicine, either at one time or one after the other. Nevertheless, the use of plant medicines by the Batek is not pure folly. Like much of the Batek religion, it is based at least partially on sound observation and detailed knowledge of the things in their environment.

Plant medicines taken internally can be used for most diseases; only those, such as ringworm, that are manifested exclusively on the outside of the body are excluded from this form of treatment. These medicines can be prepared in a variety of ways, depending partially on how the medicine is supposed to work. Often the medicinal parts of the plants (roots, leaves, bark, flowers, etc.) are boiled in water to make an infusion which is drunk. Such infusions are given after childbirth, as mentioned above, to warm the mother's insides. Other types of infusion are used for coughs, chest congestion, and intestinal parasites. If the patient is suffering from fever, the medicine may be given as an infusion in cold water. Usually this is done with scrapings from roots or with finely chopped leaves. Some medicines consist of fruits or small tubers. These can be eaten raw or cooked like ordinary food.[18] These medicines may be simply ingested or they may first have a spell spoken over them to improve their efficacy.

A few medicines that are not derived from plants are taken internally as well. For severe dizziness, such as sometimes results from eating inadequately processed poisonous tubers, the sufferer may be given human blood to drink. This is taken from the leg, usually of a woman, just as in the blood sacrifice. It is mixed with water and drunk uncooked. I suggest that this is meant to increase the life-soul of the sick person, though the usual Batek explanation is that the 'raw' (pel'eng) smell of the blood drives out the disease. Patent medicines obtained from the Malay rattan traders are also taken for various minor ailments. Similarly, western medicines are gladly accepted, as they are fully compatible with traditional Batek curing practices. The Batek are used to taking medicines internally, and they are willing to try new ones, for the superhuman beings often reveal new medicines to them in dreams.

Some types of plant-derived medicines are applied to the outside of the body. They are prepared and used in various ways. Commonly leaves with medicinal properties are rubbed between the palms of the hands and then smeared on the skin. This releases the sap (getah) and the odour (meni') of the plants which are often said to be the agents that cool the body or drive out the disease. Frequently the sap of a plant is extracted and used alone as a medicine. For example, the dark red sap of a very large, gnarled type of climber ('awey sikan) can be smeared on the forehead, throat, and chest to counteract headaches and coughing. As mentioned above, some medicinal plants are burned and converted into a pigment before being applied in various designs. Stripes of black pigment are occasionally pricked into the skin by means of thorns or needles, thus forming tattoos. Most commonly these take the form of a single stripe across the

---

[18] I once saw a young woman eating a tuber of a type which is alleged by the Malays, who often buy it from the Batek, to be useful for making the penis hard. When I asked her why she was eating it, she said she was just hungry.

forehead which is designed to get rid of chronic headaches. Such tattoos are also used just for beauty.

A few non-plant medicines are used in similar ways. Human blood may be rubbed on the skin to combat a disease called ke'òy (see below). One of the most commonly used external medicines is lime paste (kapur), the chalky white paste used by the Malays for chewing with betel-nut (Malay pinang). This is obtained from shops or traders or can be made by burning large quantities of snail shells and mixing the resulting white powder with water. The Batek seem to follow the Malay practices in the use of lime paste. For instance, for a headache one can put white circular spots on both temples, the middle of the forehead, and on both sides of the neck. Someone may recite a Malay spell over the lime paste ordering the 'antidote' (tawar) to enter the patient's body. Various simple patterns of spots and stripes may be applied to any part of the body that is afflicted.

The medicines of the Batek, whether obtained from the forest or from outside sources, are generally said to work by entering the body and causing the disease ('aral) or poison (bisa') to run away. Sometimes it is only the odour or juice of the medicine that is supposed to penetrate the body. Some of the medicines are also said to cool the body, producing an environment which is uncomfortable for the disease and which will therefore cause it to depart. But the Batek are pragmatic enough to use hot medicines if the patient has chills, even though Batek theory equates good health with coolness. They say that because they have wind life-souls, their bodies must be kept warm, though not so warm as they become when they have fever. The need for particular medicines for particular maladies is explained only by saying that the superhumans revealed which medicines should be used with which diseases.[19]

Another curing technique, which is closely related to the use of medicines, is the blowing of incense smoke ('asèp kemeyèn) on the patient's body. A censer is made of a split section of bamboo which contains some glowing embers and bits of fragrant resin. The curer takes handfuls of smoke, usually in his right hand, and blows it through his fist on to all the afflicted parts of the patient's body. The smoke is supposed to enter the body and cause the disease to flee.

[19] It might seem that distinctively coloured medicines—such as white lime, yellow turmeric, and grey or black ash-paste—should be used against diseases of specific colours. But the idea that diseases have colours is very vague. There is little agreement on what diseases are what colour, and no attempt is made to relate the colour of the medicine to the colour of the disease.

This is because the odour of the smoke is good (*bed'èt*) and that of the disease bad (*jebéc*), and they cannot mix. If the smoke goes in, the disease must leave. Alternatively, some say the good-smelling smoke draws the disease out of the body by attracting it, causing it to follow the smoke as it wafts upward from the patient's body.

Spells (*jampi*'; Malay *jampi-jampi*) can be used alone or with various other curing techniques. The spells used by the Batek are usually addressed to the medicine used (e.g. telling it to enter the body) or to the disease (e.g. telling it to leave the body). Batek spells are mainly in the Malay language, and they even contain a number of Arabic-Malay stock phrases such as the ending '*Laa ilaaha illal-laah*', 'There is no other God than Allah'.[20] But Batek spells are not normally addressed to superhuman beings, nor are they believed to work through the intervention of superhumans. The Batek treat spells as having power in themselves; they are thought to work directly on the disease just like the medicines with which they are often combined. Diseases are supposed to be afraid of the words of spells and to run away from them. To the outsider, most Batek spells appear to be borrowed from the Malays or at least to be modelled on Malay spells. But the Batek insist that they are sent in dreams by the superhuman beings, and that that is the ultimate source of their power.

Singing (*piñlòñ*) may also be used to treat certain serious illnesses. The songs are normally addressed to the superhuman beings. For diseases such as *cemam* that are sent by a superhuman being, the being responsible is asked to take pity on the victim and retract the punishment. For other serious diseases, the superhumans may be asked to use their own powers and medicines to aid the patient. The power of Batek curing-songs seems, then, to be based mainly on their ability to influence the superhuman beings. The super-humans are supposed to be moved by the beauty of the songs and to feel love for the people who sing them. Yet some curing-songs, like spells, seem to have power in their own right. They are supposed to cure simply by being sung over the patient. They are said to 'brush', 'bathe', or 'cool' the sick person. It seems that these songs can transmit the power of the superhuman beings from whom they are obtained in dreams.

Occasionally, for a very serious illness (*petis biyayah*), a special

---

[20] Schebesta records that all the spells of a highly regarded Lanoh shaman were in the Malay language (1928: 194), as are those of the Batek.

singing session will be organized in which a shaman will go into trance. This will be discussed in detail in the next chapter.

Ke'òy

Space limitations preclude a detailed description of all the diseases and their treatments that are known to the Batek. But one disease concept is especially interesting because it is one of the major forces responsible for the low level of conflict within Batek society. The disease called *ke'òy*[21] is an emotional depression usually accompanied by physical symptoms such as fever. It strikes persons who have had a severe fright, or who feel they have been mistreated by others, or who have been frustrated in some strong desire. Most commonly a person gets *ke'òy* if he feels someone is angry with him for no good reason. It is considered to be an affliction of the heart (*petis kelangès*) which causes it to become hot and swollen with the 'wind of *ke'òy*' (*'angin ke'òy*). It also causes the breath to become weak. This is regarded as a serious disease which can lead to death.

Ke'òy can be treated in a number of ways. Some people know spells that are supposed to relieve it. Sometimes two white arrows of lime paste, pointing upward, are painted on the chest and back of the victim. The spells and lime paste are supposed to drive the disease out of the heart. It can also be cured by removing the cause of the disease, e.g. by the alleged offender ceasing to be angry with the victim. Perhaps the most interesting treatment is the application of human blood to the body of the patient. Someone, preferably the person who caused the patient's unhappiness, cuts his leg and scrapes the blood on to five or six green leaves. He then wipes half the leaves on the patient's chest, with downward strokes, and half on his back. He can also wipe some on the patient's forehead if the disease has caused a headache. After three or four strokes with each leaf, the curer blows on it and throws it away. While wiping the blood on the patient, he may tell the heart to become cool or may just say '*ke'òy*' over and over, followed by a reference to the act that is thought to have caused the disease. When all the leaves have been discarded, the curer may place his hand on the chest of the patient, blow on it, and make motions of grasping and throwing something

[21] Possibly this name is related to the term *ko'oi* which is used for a 'familiar demon' by the Semang of Ulu Siong, Kedah (probably Kensiu) (Skeat and Blagden 1906b: 579). Being attacked by a familiar spirit, like Batek Dè' *ke'òy*, is a 'social' disease in the sense that it is caused by the action of one person toward another, rather than by impersonal forces of nature.

away. Some say the blood acts as a medicine (*obèt*), entering the heart and driving the disease or its wind out. Others say the healthy blood cools the hot, unhealthy blood. Again I would suggest, though it is not explicitly stated, that the blood given would also increase the patient's supply of life-soul (*ñawa'*), which is thought to reside mainly in the heart, and thus to make him stronger and 'more alive'. The weakness of the breath, which is one of the disease's symptoms, suggests a weakened life-soul. The blowing, grasping, and throwing away motions are supposed to get rid of the disease, its wind, or its poison (*bisa'*). If this treatment fails, it will be repeated by other members of the group until it finally succeeds.

The idea that one can cause a person to become ill and die by mistreating him helps to ensure that the Batek treat each other fairly. For in cases of *ke'òy*, the person who is deemed to have caused it is ostracized and suffers a loss of social support, while the victim is treated in a way that reaffirms the sympathy of the group for him.

Death and Burial

The Batek are fatalistic about death. They do not welcome it, but they feel there is little they can do about it. It is assumed that each person is allotted a certain number of years by Tohan, and when he has reached the proper age, which one can never know in advance, Tohan takes back his life-soul. Of course the Batek do not 'tempt fate' by reckless behaviour or by wantonly breaking prohibitions, nor do they neglect to attempt to cure diseases. But they believe that when Tohan decides they will die, there is no stopping it. The deaths, especially of old people, are taken in their stride. I could stir up no interest whatever in seeking medical help for one old woman who was dying because, as they said, her 'life span was finished' (*habis 'umor 'o'*). When a death has occurred, there is spontaneous crying, especially by close relatives and friends, but this is an individual matter; there is no ritualized mourning. In part the acceptance of death is based on the belief that the fate of the dead is a happy one, renewed life in a peaceful land where there is no work and no disease. Most Batek go to this afterworld regardless of their behaviour in this life. The only exceptions are persons who die of *tolah*, the disease sent by Tohan to punish gross breaches of proper social conduct. It is claimed that the superhuman beings

1. Batek woman performing the blood sacrifice to drive away a thunderstorm. She is doing it on behalf of her son, looking on, who is thought to have caused the storm by laughing at butterflies.

2. Batek woman applying a mixture of chopped leaves and water as a medicine to relieve her son's fever.

3. Two Batek women relaxing with their children in a typical Negrito leaf-shelter. A bamboo water container leans against the roof, and two blowpipes are suspended from the thatch on vines.

4. A singing session taking place on a bark platform. The songs, the music of the two-stringed bamboo zither on the right, and the pleasant smells of the herbs used to make the decorations are all intended to attract the superhuman beings.

5. A Batek woman digging wild yams, the staple of the Batek diet, while her daughter plays at digging above.

6. A Batek man hunting. With his bamboo blowpipe in hand, he scans the treetops for monkeys and squirrels.

refuse to take the shadow-souls of such wicked persons. The Batek do not make the distinction between 'good' (natural) and 'bad' (violent) death which is so widespread in the Malay-Indonesian world. According to such conceptions, the victims of bad death go to a separate afterworld which is usually unpleasant. The Batek do distinguish pleasant and unpleasant afterworlds, but they all go to the former, while the latter is reserved for other races.

Fate of the components of human beings

According to Batek theories, death initiates the separation of the components of the human being. The immediate cause of death is the loss of the wind life-soul which Tohan takes (*bòt*) in some way that the Batek do not fully understand. It leaves through the fontanelle of the corpse, the same place at which it entered the foetus. Tohan sends back (*pimüc*) the retrieved life-soul the next day, either to some living person or to an unborn baby.

At death the shadow-soul goes to the land of the dead which is placed either in the sky or at the western horizon. It is borne by the smoke of the incense ('*asèp kemeyèn*) which is burned by the head of the corpse. The superhuman beings from above the sky come down to help the shadow-soul of the dead person on its journey. A human shaman may sing and go into a trance so his shadow-soul can also assist the shadow-soul of the deceased. A few people say that the dead person's shadow-soul first goes to 'heaven' (*serga*'; Malay *syurga*) which is inside the earth. It is a place full of fire and boiling water and is presided over by Nabi Adam. When the shadow-soul of a Malay comes along, Nabi Adam puts it in the fire, but, when a Batek shadow-soul (and, one informant graciously added, the shadow-soul of a white man) arrives, he damps down the flames and delivers it into the hands of the superhumans. Though more usually the shadow-souls of the Batek are said to go directly to the afterworld, the souls of the Malays always go into the earth because they bury the dead in the ground.

The Batek Dè' of the upper Lebir place the afterworld in the sky. The shadow-soul of the deceased rises on the incense smoke and reaches the lowest level of the firmament in about an hour. There it is met by various friends and relatives who have died before. They transform the dead person into a superhuman being like themselves (*hala' senalin*; literally 'transformed superhuman being'). The shadow-soul is given at least two new bodies. One is human-form and looks like the deceased when he or she was a young man or woman, the most vigorous and happy time in a Batek's life. The other has the form of a tiger. These bodies can be changed like suits of clothes, and the ones not being used are stored inside the one that is. The shadow-soul may return to the grave several times over the next year or so and retrieve various bones from the corpse to incorporate in additional bodies. It returns most often during the first week after death. Some say the dead eventually acquire seven human-form bodies and an equal number of animal-form bodies (the number seven being a magical number to the Malays). The new bodies given to the dead person are animated by an immortal water life-soul (*nawa' tòm*), and they have cool dew (*mun*) in place of blood. The rejuvenated person is then taught all the songs and skills of the superhumans. After the training is completed, which may take several months, the deceased is conducted to the upper level of the firmament where the original superhuman beings (*hala' 'asal*) live. If the deceased is a child below the age of about three years (called a *kepok*), it will remain at the lower level and be raised by its dead relatives until it can understand and master the lore of the superhuman beings. Then it too will be conveyed to the level above. The Lebir people picture the afterworld proper as a vast sandy plain with no rivers and only low vegetation. It is bathed in a cool light, and the weather is always mild. The superhumans, both original and transformed, live together in many large stone houses which are like 'warehouses' (Malay *gudang*). Each has one large room inside, and the outside walls are decorated with intricate and colourful patterns. Several thousand superhumans live in each house. There are also dancing platforms made of *tekèl* bark scattered among the houses. They do not have roofs, for it never rains in the afterworld.

The Batek Dè' of the Aring River place the afterworld at the western horizon. The shadow-soul of the deceased follows the smoke upward, but then comes down again on the other side of the sea. There, in the company of the superhumans who have come to help it on its way, it follows a path until it reaches a fork. Along one branch of the path (sometimes designated as the left and sometimes the right) lies the land of the dead of other races. This is probably the same as the place of corpses from previous eras which imparts a rotten odour to the sun (see Chapter 2). That branch of the path is guarded by a being called Cel who has a body the size of a Batek but whose legs are so long that his knees reach above the firmament. The dead are afraid he will kick them into a pool of water called Tòm Cemampeng. Therefore they avoid that path and instead turn down the one leading to the land of dead Batek. The Aring Batek also picture the afterworld as a large, flat plain with few or no trees, though it is often said to be full of fruit blossoms. They also agree with the Lebir Batek in saying that the shadow-souls of the dead acquire new bodies and immortal water life-souls once they reach the afterworld. There are original superhuman beings living in the afterworld, but there is some suggestion that the dead live apart from them in a separate 'enclosure' (kota').

Both the Lebir and Aring groups of Batek Dè' agree that the dead spend most of their time singing and making decorations of flowers and leaves which they wear on their heads, wrists, waists, and other parts of the body. The Lebir people say that the dead do not eat at all, though they chew quids of betel for pleasure and also smoke cigarettes (using special fire, since there is no ordinary fire in the afterworld). Some Aring people say the dead eat seasonal fruits, though no other kinds of food, but most deny that the dead eat anything. The dead, like the original superhuman beings, are able to fly to any part of the cosmos. They occasionally come back to earth to see what their living relatives are doing. They may appear to the living in dreams or in the flesh, usually in their tiger-form bodies. During these encounters, they may teach people songs and other useful things. Shamans, who can send their shadow-souls to various parts of the universe, may meet known dead persons in the afterworld with the same potential benefits.

After the shadow-soul has left the corpse and before it has entered the afterworld, it may take the form of a type of ghost, which is called a jereng saro'.[22] This ghost may exist temporarily, just until the shadow-soul reaches the afterworld, or permanently, if for some reason it does not gain entry to the land of the dead. This may occur if the burial is not properly performed, or if, as happens very rarely, the superhuman beings refuse to take the shadow-soul of the deceased, as in the case of a person killed by Tohan for a breach of the tolah prohibitions. Thus most jereng saro' are thought to come

[22] The term jereng is quite probably related to the Malay word jerungkung. Hantu jerungkung is 'a name for the hantu bungkus (ghost in its funeral wrappings) as it rolls over the ground like a man sprawling. In Java the hantu jĕrangkong represents the last or skeleton stage of the hantu bungkus' (Wilkinson 1959a: 469).

from the dead of other ethnic groups, those that make the mistake of burying their dead in the ground, thereby trapping their shadow-souls on earth. Some say this ghost is shaped like the dead person, but is black in colour and walks like a gibbon, waving its arms overhead. When children pretend to be *jereng saro'*, they blacken their faces with charcoal and run about pulling horrible faces. Others say the ghost is like a disease, having no definite form and being invisible to ordinary men. Still others liken it to the free spirits (*hantu*) of the Malays. The *jereng saro'* attacks anyone who comes near the grave-site. It is variously described as entering the victim's body, which causes fever and death, sticking its fingernails into the victim with the same result, and flicking the victim's eyes with a fingernail, thereby causing blindness. It may also spit on a person and give him warts or other skin diseases. These ghosts are also blamed, half jokingly, for any sudden pains or cramps. It is quite common for someone to hear a sound that he interprets as a ghost calling him, even when he is in a camp far from any known grave-site. The ghost supposedly calls out *"oylah!"*, which means roughly, 'hey friend!'. When this happens, the person called makes a fist with either hand, blows into it, puts it over one ear, and says '*hay*' (which is merely an exclamation, not a word). Then he repeats the process using the same hand but putting it over the other ear. He may also shout 'don't call me!' (*yé' gan kul ba-yè'*). This procedure is supposed to prevent him from hearing the ghost and also to cause it to run away. People who hear such calls do not seem very frightened, and the ritual is tossed off almost as a reflex. Ghost-inflicted illnesses are treated with medicines, spells, etc., just like other diseases.

The corpse (*saro'*), which is left behind by the life-soul and the shadow-soul, simply rots (*sò'*) like any other meat. This fate is shared by the blood and the internal organs along with the other flesh. The bones, however, are retrieved by the dead and incorporated in their new bodies.

Burial

The Batek Dè' are apparently the last people in the Malay Peninsula regularly to practise tree-burial, though it was probably once wide-spread among the aboriginal groups. Skeat records that tree-burial was still used for shamans by the Negritos of the Sam River (a tributary of the Kelantan River below Kuala Krai) in 1900 (Skeat and Blagden 1906b: 91), and the Batek Nòng told me (in 1972) that they still employed this form of burial for shamans (batèk potew) because, if they buried a shaman in the ground, a terrible storm would occur. The Temiar say that this was once their method of burial for all persons, and some claim that it is still done occasionally in areas where they would not be subject to interference from the Malays (Geoffrey Benjamin, personal communication). Quite likely it has been the disapproval of the Malays that has caused the disappearance of tree-burial in most places. The isolation of the Batek Dè' would have permitted it to persist, or perhaps to have been revived after the Malays left their area. The rationale they give for tree-burial is that it allows the shadow-soul to escape upward and thus to arrive at the afterworld. If their bodies were buried in the ground, they reason, their shadow-souls would be trapped in the earth like those of the Malays. Tree-burial is also intended to protect the corpse from being devoured by tigers.

After a person has died, the Batek Dè' wrap the body in the prettiest and newest sarong they can find in camp. This is because the shadow of the cloth is thought to go with the shadow-soul, and the deceased will want to be well-dressed in the afterworld. Also, his tiger body will bear the pattern and colours of the cloth. Therefore it should be of distinctive colours—such as yellow, white, and blue/green—rather than red and black, which are the colours of ordinary tigers. The body should also be dressed in the leaf and flower ornaments worn in singing sessions (see Chapter 5). These act as signs (tana') which tell the superhuman beings to take the shadow-soul. If possible, a ring (cincèn) will be found and placed on a dead man's finger so that, when his wife dies and goes to the afterworld, she will be able to recognize him in his new body. If the wife dies first, a ring is put on her finger for the same reason. The corpse may be wrapped in a thin blanket. Then the most beautiful pandanus sleeping-mat of the deceased is rolled around his body, which is lying in an extended position, and tied up with rattan so even the face is enclosed.

A crude stretcher of sticks is then lashed together and placed under the corpse. The stretcher is suspended from a pole and carried by two men into the forest some distance from camp. Anyone who wants to can go along to help; the burial party would usually include most of the adults in camp. A good-sized hardwood tree (but one which is not too big around to be easily climbed) is selected, preferably at a place which is away from any heavily used paths. Some of the people set about gathering poles, bamboo, bark, thatch, and rattan with which to make a platform and lean-to in the tree. Two or three of the younger men climb up the tree to a place where the limbs branch out at a fairly flat angle. They then let down lengths of rattan and pull up the building materials as needed. A platform is made with poles for a frame and split bamboo or, preferably, *tekèl* bark for a floor. Then an ordinary lean-to shelter is constructed with the opening facing west. Sometimes a few poles are lashed into the surrounding limbs to make a kind of rail fence around the platform. Large bunches of sweet-smelling herbs (*hali' 'ayam*) are pushed into the thatch. After that, four strands of rattan are dropped down and attached to the corners of the stretcher underneath the body. The body is then pulled up and placed in the shelter, lying on its back with the head toward the west (i.e. toward the open side of the shelter). A pouch of tobacco and some *pinang* nut and betel leaf, if the group has any, are put beside the body for the pleasure of the deceased in the next world. If the deceased is a man, his blowpipe, quiver, darts, and jew's harp may be left in the shelter. The hunting equipment is for his amusement only, as there is no game in the afterworld. A dead woman will be buried with her decorated combs, flute, and cosmetics (lime and charcoal paste). A small bamboo container of water—preferably the water from inside the Malacca cane which is thought to be the same as *mun*, the magical dew of the superhumans—is deposited next to the body for the dead person to drink. No food is placed in the shelter, for the dead do not eat, and no ordinary fire is built because the dead do not like heat. But some incense-resin (*kemeyèn*) is buried on the glowing tip of a piece of firewood, and the smoke is blown on the head of the corpse and then allowed to drift upward, supposedly taking the shadow-soul with it. The Aring people sometimes throw some of the water in the container toward the west to help send the shadow-soul on its way. Finally they close in the front of the shelter with a thin fence of thatch-palm fronds. Then the men who have been working on the platform climb down and join the others on the ground. Before leaving the place, someone cuts four short sticks (called *tangkal*) and says a spell over them. These are planted in a square around the base of the tree to prevent tigers, which cannot climb trees, from shaking the body out of the tree. The people then return to their camp, and, if they are too frightened to stay in the vicinity, they pack up and move.

The Lebir Batek Dè' claim that at least some of the close relatives
of the deceased return to the grave a week after the burial and at
irregular intervals thereafter to observe the state of decomposition
of the body. As long as any bones remain, they burn incense beside
them to remind the dead person to return and get them. These visits
cease after all the bones have disappeared. (Probably they are
eventually carried off by animals.) In fact most people are too
frightened of the grave to return at all (see below).

As with most Batek religious rituals, burial is not a highly
standardized procedure. The aim of placing the body in a hut in
a tree is always the same, but the means used vary according to
practical necessities and possibilities. For example, the body may
be transported by raft or canoe if this is easier than carrying it. Also
most of the materials used may be varied or substituted depending
on what is available. The workers are volunteers who participate out
of affection for the deceased, and, as in most Batek activities, there
is no designated leader of the work-group. The blowing of incense
smoke on the head of the corpse is done by whichever of the people
on the platform wants to do it, and the recitation of spells over the
tangkal is done by whoever knows the spells. Nevertheless, certain
features of the procedure must invariably be carried out or else the
shadow-soul of the deceased will fail to gain entry to the afterworld.
The body must be deposited above the ground, it must be properly
dressed, and incense must be burned near it to guide the shadow-
soul on its journey. The burial procedure obviously constitutes, in
part, a crucial rite of passage for the dead person. According to Batek
conceptions, the deceased must be removed from this world, transmitted to the afterworld, and reconstituted there. Placing the body
in a tree, between earth and heaven, separates it from the living and
symbolizes its transitional state. The rising smoke and the gradual
disappearance of the bones can also be seen as symbols of transition.
The incorporation of the deceased into the afterworld is marked,
in the imagination of the living at least, by its acquiring new bodies
and becoming a superhuman being. The final separation between
the living and the dead is signalled by the abandonment of the grave
site and a prohibition on saying the name of the deceased. To
mention a dead person's name, especially his 'original name', is so
offensive to him that he will return to earth and pinch the heart of
the offender, thus causing him to die. Therefore, the dead are
normally referred to by their places of burial, as the 'corpse at

such and such a place' (e.g. *saro' ke-Kiap*, 'corpse at Kiap', a small stream). Though the living may have contact with the dead after a properly performed burial, it is on an entirely new basis. It is then a communication between man and a superhuman being (see Chapter 5).

Fear of the grave

The Batek Dè', like many other Orang Asli groups, usually flee the site of a death and refuse to go near a grave. But the different groups do not always agree on what they are afraid of. For example, Evans reports that the Behrang Senoi are not afraid of the ghosts of their dead friends, but of the spirits that caused the death (1923: 225). The Batek Dè' say they are afraid both of the ghost (*jereng saro'*) that may be lingering near the corpse and of the tiger that is supposed to come to eat it.

The Batek Dè' believe that if the tree-burial is properly performed, the shadow-soul will proceed to the afterworld immediately. But there is always the possibility that something has inadvertently been done wrong or that the shadow-soul has been rejected by the super-human beings. Then the shadow-soul would be thwarted in its desire to get to the afterworld, and it would take out its anger and frustration on the living. The mere possibility that a dead person's shadow-soul may become an angry ghost is enough to make many Batek Dè' afraid of graves. The degree of fear varies greatly from person to person and from one burial to another, depending, pre-sumably, on the amount of faith each person has in the efficacy of the burial procedure, in general and in particular instances. Some Batek Dè' refuse to go near any grave, though at least a few are willing to go back to the grave of a properly buried close relative. In practice, then, the Batek Dè' have some fear of ghosts at graves, even though in theory such ghosts should be rare or non-existent. The Batek Teh believe that the shadow-soul, in the form of a ghost, always lingers in the vicinity of the grave for about one week. The ghost tries to kill other people, especially the surviving spouse, so it will have company in the land of the dead. For this reason they, unlike the Batek Dè', make offerings of food and tobacco, which they place in the forest outside their camp, to induce the shadow-soul of the deceased to go on to the afterworld. Similarly, the Batek Nòng of Pahang believe that the soul stays near the grave for seven days before it can be sent on its way to the afterworld with a special singing performance. While it remains in the vicinity of the grave, offerings are made and magical barriers constructed to prevent its harming the living (Evans 1937: 267-9). Both the Batek Teh and the Batek Nòng bury the dead in the earth. Their belief that the shadow-soul lingers by the grave, and their consequent fear of the ghost, seems to be an implicit recognition that earth-burial hinders the soul in its journey to the land of the dead.

Fear of the tiger arises as soon as a person dies. It is thought that a dead body gives off a distinctive odour which can be detected by a tiger from many miles away. Fear of the tiger is especially intense when the death takes place at night, the time when tigers are usually on the prowl. Once I was in a camp when a man died at night, and all the Batek immediately moved into the centre of the camp, built up the fires, and spent the rest of the night keeping each other awake. I was considered very brave for staying in my tent which was only about fifteen feet away from the centre of camp. Occasionally, if a person dies near dusk, the other people may be too frightened even to wait until morning to bury the body. In one such case, on the lower Aring in 1971, a woman's body was just left in her shelter while the rest of the group fled, and they were too frightened to go back the next day and bury her. Usually a dead person is buried as soon as possible after death to remove the corpse, and thus the attraction for the tiger, from the group. The Batek say that after the body has been deposited in a tree, one or more tigers come and wait under the tree to lick up the putrefied ooze that drips down from the grave. Oddly enough a large tiger is said to attend a dead child and a small tiger an adult. If it can, the tiger shakes the tree until the body falls down, but the *tangkal* should prevent this. Similarly, the Batek Teh, who bury the dead in the ground, put stone pebbles as *tangkal* under the corpse and wedge a large number of sticks across the grave above the body to prevent tigers (or more likely pigs) from digging the body up. Because tigers are thought to wait under a tree-grave until the flesh has rotted completely off the bones of the dead person, the continuing fear of the grave is often explained as fear of the tiger.

Stone-ghosts

The Batek conception of man provides a clear distinction between life and death which is based on the presence or absence of a life-soul. There is an interesting exception, however, in a being that never quite achieves life yet does not become truly dead. This is the *kewą*,[23] a ghost with a body of stone.

Among the Aring Batek, when a baby is still-born or dies soon after birth (there is little agreement on exactly how soon), before it has a name, it is buried in the ground instead of in a tree.[24] This is said to be done because it would not be 'fitting' or 'appropriate' (*padan*) to put a tiny body in a large lean-to. Also some say a baby would be afraid of falling out of the tree in a wind-storm. The burial is similar to that used by the Batek Teh for all persons, but the hole is shallower, being only about two feet deep. The body is wrapped in a cloth, then a sleeping mat, and finally a roll of bark. It is placed at the bottom of the grave (there is no side-chamber as in a Malay grave) on some sticks. The mother squeezes all the milk from her breasts and places this in a tin beside the baby's head. Other sticks are wedged across the hole above the body, and a roof is made of bark and leaves. The hole is then filled in with dirt. A small shelter is built on top of the grave, and a fire is lit in front of it. Water is poured on the ground around the grave. A fence is then made around the grave by sticking stems of *boman* (*Donax canniformis*, a plant with long smooth stems often used to make sleeping platforms) into the ground in a row. Outside the fence four *tangkal* stones, which have had a spell recited over them, are placed in a square.

Sometime within the first five years after burial, the corpse of the baby becomes a *kewą*'. This is a round stone about the size of a soccer ball which has eyes, nose, and mouth but no ears, hair, hands, feet, or other human features. It moves by rolling and makes a sound like a crying baby. Some say the name *kewą*' reproduces the sound of its cry. When it finds a human being, or when someone unwittingly sits down on it, it seizes hold of the person with its mouth and sucks on him until he dies.[25] The *kewą*' sucks people

---

[23] The term *kewą*' is undoubtedly related to the Temiar term *kǝwat*, which means 'child'.

[24] This is the reverse of the present Temiar practice. Normally people are buried in the ground, but unnamed babies are hung in a cloth bag from a tree (Geoffrey Benjamin, personal communication).

[25] Skeat records that the Besisi (Mah Meri) of Selangor, a Senoi people, believe in two kinds of 'Demon of fatal Birth-sickness'. 'The one which is harmless is called Kuwak. It is believed to resemble a dwarf human being, being only three hand-spans high. It has a white body and goes naked, "barking like a deer" ("ke-e-e-eng") in the very dead of night.' They also believe in a kind of 'Grave Demon', called Kĕmuk, which 'has a globular body like the fruit of the wax-gourd ("kun-dor"). It is pallid in colour, and chases people at sight, rocking itself after them,

because it wants milk, not having had time to nurse before it died, but it will attach itself to anyone—man or woman, adult or child—and will suck any part of the body, though preferring the breasts of women and the testicles of men. It seems that its urge to suck has been so long frustrated that it has gone completely out of control.[26]

There are several means of defence against *kewą'*. The method of burial itself contains some elements which seem intended to confine the *kewą'* and cut it off from the living. Leaving all the mother's milk in the grave seems to be an attempt to satisfy the baby's longing to nurse and, at the same time, to cut it off from the mother. The fence of *boman* stems may be intended to keep the *kewą'* from leaving the grave. Once a *kewą'* is abroad, it can still be avoided, if seen in time, by running away. There are also spells that can be said to keep the *kewą'* away, which may be used if one is camping in an area where a baby has been buried. The following is the most commonly used spell for deterring *kewą'*.[27]

> *Hong anak,*
> *Mati beranak,*
> *Mati se-ekor,*
> *Tetap boman,*
> *Panjang pandok,*
> *Buat penyala,*
> *Mati mata anak.*
> *Ah.*

> Hey child,
> Dead in childbirth,
> One dead child,
> Be firm *boman* stems,

---

and making a noise which sounds like "nuh-uh-uh-uh." When it enters people they get "all abroad" and feverish, and little by little it "steals their life" ' (Skeat and Blagden 1906b: 303–4). The Batek *kewą'* seems to combine some of the features of these two beings with a few additional twists. As the Batek are on the opposite side of the Peninsula from the Mah Meri, it seems likely that these and related conceptions are widespread among the Orang Asli, though I do not happen to know of any references to such beings among any other groups.

[26] The Freudian implications of this are rich, though I am not competent to explicate them. Suffice it to say, this is a classic case of 'oral aggression' in an infant.

[27] I thank Puan Maherani Mohd. Ishak for help in translating this and other Malay-style spells.

Long and short,
Make a torch,
Die eyes of the child.
Ah.

This spell, like most Batek spells, is predominantly in Malay. The term '*se-ekor*', literally 'one tail', uses the Malay numeral classifier which, strictly speaking, is for animals, not humans. There is probably no deep significance for this usage, however, as the Batek use the same classifier ('*ay*, roughly 'body') for both animals and children. *Boman* is the plant whose stems are used for the floor of the birth hut and for the fence around the grave of a baby. The expression 'long and short' (*pandok* is Kelantan Malay for *pendek*, 'short') refers to the stems, but also is supposed to allude to the contrasting life spans of the long-lived *kewą'* and the short-lived baby. The 'torch' may refer to the fire kindled on the grave; fire is generally considered inimical to the dead and may somehow neutralize the *kewą'*. In ordering the eyes of the baby to die, the spell is in effect ordering the baby to die *completely*. This spell is probably a version of Malay spell for combating a type of demon that originates in a still-born baby (see Skeat 1900: 327, 626-7).

Even if a *kewą'* has already attached itself to a person, it can still be stopped if one knows the proper spell. A person must recite the spell, spit on his bush-knife, and then chop the *kewą'* with the knife. The spell is supposed to strengthen the bush-knife so that it will shatter the stone. The best defence against a *kewą'*, of course, is not to bury the baby in the ground at all. One woman on the Lebir said that her group put all dead babies in trees precisely because they would become *kewą'* if they were buried in the ground.

The Batek are not certain whether *kewą'* are alive or not, and there is no general agreement on what kind of soul, if any, they have. It is generally agreed that a *kewą'* does not have blood or a heart since its body is stone. The consensus seems to be that if it has a life-soul (*ñawa'*), this must be very different from ours. One woman thought it might have a breath (*napas*) but only inside the stone. Most people are unsure whether a *kewą'* has a shadow-soul (*bayang*), but one informant said it definitely does because burial in the ground would prevent the shadow-soul from leaving the body and going to the afterworld. Another said the superhumans would reject the shadow-soul of a baby because it is too small. It is tempting to interpret the demonic life of a *kewą'* as being caused by the presence of a shadow-soul in the absence of a life-soul (the reverse of the dreaming situation), but this would be giving a much too definite construction to a set of ideas about which the Batek are very uncertain. Of course uncertainty is to be expected regarding a creature that falls between the categories of life and death and human and mineral, categories which are very clearly distinguished in the Batek world-view.

5

SUPERHUMAN BEINGS

Hala' 'Asal

The *hala' 'asal* ('original superhuman beings') are the collective *alter egos* of the Batek. They are what human beings wish they were and what they would in fact have been if only they had received the water life-soul. The *hala'* have existed since before the creation of the earth, and it is assumed that they have always existed (they are given no specific origin in time or space). They do not reproduce themselves nor do they die, since they have the immortal water life-soul. They live on top of the firmament, underneath the underground sea, and at the eastern and western horizons. They once lived on both the sun and the moon, but they have not been able to stay on the sun since it became hot, soon after the creation of the earth. A few *hala'* are supposed to live on the upper parts of the stone pillars. They can go anywhere in the universe, and they often come to earth in one form or another, but it is generally agreed that there are now few if any *hala'* living continuously on earth as they did in ancient times, especially before the origin of man.

Components of hala' 'asal

The normal bodies of the *hala' 'asal* are similar in appearance to those of human beings, only more beautiful. The *hala'* look like youths (*jemaga'*) and maidens (*kedah*) and are usually dressed in the festoons of leaves and flowers that the Batek wear while singing to the *hala'*. The *hala'* can also assume any other physical embodiment they might desire, even wind and rain. When they appear on earth it is usually in the form of a person, tiger, elephant, snake, or rhinoceros. These alternative bodies are separate coverings which the shadow-soul of the *hala'* puts on and takes control of. When not in use they are simply stored somewhere, often inside the body being used. The composition of the bodies of *hala'* is unknown except in one detail. The blood of the *hala'* is clear and colourless, like water. It is said to be composed of dew (*mun*; Malay *embun*), which to the Batek has connotations of purity and coolness. Dew is found in abundance in the heavens, and it occurs on earth as the sap of the Malacca cane (*'awéy manaw*) which absorbs any drops of it that fall from above. Because the *hala'* have dew for blood and because they do not use fire, their bodies are cool. This makes them invulnerable to disease and death.[1] This coolness of the body, imparted by the *mun*-blood, is also said to make it unnecessary for *hala'* to eat. They are considered very fortunate because they can constantly travel around, visiting friends in every part of the universe, without having to worry about obtaining food. There is some disagreement as to whether the *hala' 'asal* (and the dead, *hala' senalin*) eat seasonal fruit, which, of course, differs from most foods in being eaten cold, uncooked.[2] The Lebir people usually say the *hala'* do not eat anything, though they may chew betel, and the Aring Batek say they do eat fruit but only for pleasure, not out of necessity. Interestingly, a kind of intermediate position is taken by the western Negritos. They say 'the celestial beings do not eat, but simply suck out fruits' and then throw away the rinds, which become flowers, and the seeds, which become fruits on earth (Schebesta 1957: 130–1). This implies that they do not suck fruits for nourishment, but rather to supply fruit to humans on earth. In any case, all Negritos agree that the superhuman beings do not eat cooked food, as it would be unsuitable for their cool bodies.

It is agreed by all Batek Dè' that the *hala'* have the water life-soul (*ñawa' tòm*) or long life-soul (*ñawa' betét*). It resides mainly in the heart, as does the wind life-soul (*ñawa' 'angin*) of men, but it is cool. It causes the breath to be cool and moist like clouds or mist (*kabut*) and is associated with the coolness of the *mun*-blood. This water life-soul makes the *hala' 'asal* immortal, since it is never taken away by Tohan (who is a *hala' 'asal* himself). It also makes the *hala'* much more powerful than ordinary human beings. As one man said, if we had the water life-soul, whenever we were angry, the whole river would feel the effects.

The shadow-souls (*bayang*) of the *hala'* are similar to those of humans but with a few important differences. One difference is that the shadow-soul of a *hala'* can inhabit and take control of a number

---

[1] Similarly, the Behrang Senoi (Semai) say that humans on earth are hot (*beket*) and therefore die, while those above and below the earth are cold (*senam*) and thus do not die (Evans 1923: 210).

[2] The Batek Dè' use separate terms for 'cooked' (*ncin*) and 'ripe' (*tasèk*), unlike the Malays who normally say *masak* both for 'cooked (of food)' and 'ripe (of fruit)'.

of different bodies. The shadow-souls of the *hala'* seem to retain certain anthropomorphic characteristics even when inhabiting animal bodies. Thus, *hala' 'asal* appearing in the form of tigers will have human-like facial features and will sometimes be heard singing, which distinguishes them clearly from natural tigers. There is an indirect suggestion that the personality of the individual *hala'* is also carried to the alternative bodies by the shadow-soul. This is the notion that a particular earthly shaman (*hala' té'*) can be recognized in his tiger-body by his distinctive facial features and colouration. Another difference between the shadow-souls of humans and *hala'* is that those of the former can only walk while those of the latter can fly. Even after death, the shadow-soul of a human being must be carried to heaven by incense smoke, the *hala' 'asal*, or the shadow-soul of a shaman. But a *hala'* can fly swiftly to all parts of the universe. He can send out his shadow-soul alone or the whole being can fly, body and soul together. When he wants to use a body he has stored somewhere else, the shadow-soul alone flies to where the body is waiting and enters it as if it were a *sarong* ('skirt' or 'knife-sheath'). When he wants to use the same body in another place, he 'leaps' there with fantastic speed. When a *hala'* character in a story disappears (*rayip*)[3] from earth, he leaves in this way, taking his human-form body with him.

Activities of the hala' 'asal

Hala' 'asal appear in the mythical past as creators and culture heroes. All the beings who were involved in the creation of the earth and everything in it were *hala'*. Before the advent of human beings, numerous *hala'* lived on earth in various forms. Many of the features of the present-day world, such as Batu Keñam, are attributed to the actions of these beings. After human beings appeared, certain *hala'* continued to live on earth or at least returned there from time to time, and they helped the early humans and taught them how to live. It was a *hala'* woodpecker, for example, who obtained fire for man by stealing it from the (*hala'*) sambhur deer (cf. the similar Mendriq story recorded by Schebesta 1928: 274–5). Another bird-form *hala'* taught humans which fruits they could safely eat. The rules of proper social behaviour, such as the prohibition on marrying siblings, were also sent by *hala'*. Gradually, however, the *hala' 'asal*

---

[3] The term *rayip* is derived from Arabic-Malay *ghaib* which in colloquial Malay means 'to disappear' (see Wilkinson 1959a: 365; 1959b: 934).

withdrew from the earth, though they can still communicate with man, to give him advice and instruction, through dreams.

Nowadays the *hala' 'asal*, like the dead, spend much of their time singing and decorating themselves with leaves and flowers. Their songs are not wholly frivolous, however. Some of them have the power to cure as well as to give pleasure. The *hala'* sometimes visit the earth and teach their songs and spells to human beings by appearing to them in dreams. Occasionally the *hala' 'asal* take a more direct role in curing, as when a shaman's shadow-soul carries that of a sick person to the sky so the *hala'* above can sing over it and bathe it in *mun* to make it cool. In stories, the *hala'* are credited with being able to return a dead person or animal to life by burning incense and then blowing on the head and feet of the corpse. This is said to 'bring back' (*pimüc*) the life-soul of the dead individual. Normally when human beings die, the *hala'* come down and meet the shadow-soul of the deceased at some point and help it on its way to the afterworld. The *hala'* also take a direct hand in the production of fruit by dropping the blossoms to the fruit trees on earth at the proper time each year. They also guard the very existence of the world. It is said that if the *hala'* did not constantly watch over them, the ropes of wind, rain, and lightning might snap, causing the violent destruction of the world. Similarly, the earth-snake (who is also a *hala' 'asal*) must work continuously to hold the earth together or it would dissolve in the underground sea. The rules of proper human behaviour are also enforced by some of the *hala'* to prevent the destruction that would result from man's wanton disregard of the order of nature. In short, the created order of the world has a precarious existence, according to Batek theories, and it must be actively maintained by the superhuman beings or it will revert to an earlier state of chaos.

Summary

The *hala' 'asal* are similar enough to human beings to serve as an important reference group for them. Yet they are fundamentally different from humans in several ways. In the chart overleaf I summarize some of these basic differences.

Hala'	Human
Immortal	Mortal
Cool	Warm
Do not eat	Must eat
Immune to disease	Susceptible to disease
Can fly	Cannot fly
Multiple bodies	Single body

Shamans

The relationship of humans to hala'

In normal conversation the Batek use the term *hala'* both for super-human beings and for human shamans, trusting the context to show which meaning is intended. Whenever there might be confusion, the former are termed *hala' 'asal*, 'original *hala''*, and the latter *hala' té'*, 'earth *hala''*. Yet to call any human being a *hala'*, as I have shown, is a contradiction in terms, a violation of a fundamental distinction in Batek thought. Nevertheless, the concept of the shaman as a human who is also a *hala'* is firmly established in Batek religion. Because the shaman is conceived in terms of contradictory categories, there is unusual scope for variation in this area, and the Lebir and Aring peoples attempt to resolve this contradiction in somewhat different ways.

Generally speaking, the Lebir Batek Dè' emphasize the similarities between humans and the *hala' 'asal* rather than the differences. They see human beings as becoming virtually identical to the *hala' 'asal* after death, when the shadow-souls of the dead acquire young bodies and water life-souls. The rejuvenated dead also live with the *hala'* on top of the firmament. Like the *hala'*, they spend much of their time singing and decorating themselves with flowers, and they come to earth from time to time where they are seen by the living in dreams. The Lebir people also believe that ordinary people can communicate with the *hala' 'asal* during life. Anyone can meet *hala'* in dreams and can acquire useful songs and spells from them. Also, anyone can call (*kul*) the *hala'* merely by singing and burning incense, without going into a trance. The Lebir Batek consider themselves *hala' té'* (shamans) in varying degrees, depending on how many spells and songs they have received from the *hala' 'asal*. Often an individual will be considered *hala'* only in a particular area of concern. For example, a person may know songs for bringing on the fruit season, but not know those for curing or stopping wind-storms. Thus different individuals will be called upon to use their skills at different times, depending on what speciality is needed. For the Lebir Batek, then, being a shaman is not a special status but merely a potentiality which is more or less developed by every individual.

The Aring Batek, on the other hand, seem to emphasize the differences between human beings and the *hala' 'asal*. Like the Lebir Batek, they believe that people receive new bodies and life-souls after death, but they place the dead in a special compound (*kota'*) at the western horizon, not scattered among the *hala' 'asal*. There is also a strong feeling among the Aring people that only shamans are truly capable of making contact with the *hala'*. They distinguish two types of dreams: *tewin*, which ordinary people (*kuliy*) have when they sleep, and *mpa'*, which shamans have when they sleep or trance. It is generally said that the *hala' 'asal* (and also diseases) can only be met in *mpa'*, and thus any messages from the *hala'* must come through the shamans. An ordinary person can only see such things as food, people, animals, and ghosts (both *bayang* and *jereng*) in his *tewin*. The fact that one can meet the shadow-souls of the dead but not the *hala' 'asal* in *tewin* seems to confirm that the two are seen as separate and distinct. The Aring Batek also tend to rely on shamans to send their messages to the *hala'*. They have little confidence that their own voices will reach the *hala'* without the intervention of an expert. Thus, their singing is generally a mere accompaniment to the singing or trancing of the shaman, rather than a direct communication between an ordinary human and the *hala'*.

According to the theories of the Aring Batek, a true shaman is merely a *hala' 'asal* who happens to be living on earth in human form. Such a being is very different from an ordinary human being. A true *hala' té'* could be recognized by his having the clear, colourless blood of the *hala' 'asal*. Also he would not sleep near the fire like ordinary Batek. Though he might eat cooked food while living among human beings, he would not have to. He would not live with a single group, but would continually move from one group to another, helping each in turn to solve its problems. The life of a true *hala' té'*, I was assured, is a very busy and difficult one. He must always be on the move: keeping watch over the ropes that support the world, preventing storms from getting out of hand, making certain that the fruit season is on time, and consulting with the other *hala'* (including Gobar and Tohan). He cannot even get a decent night's rest, for, as soon as he goes to sleep, his shadow-soul goes off for more consultations. Thus to the Aring Batek, being a *hala'* is a full-time job, and it would be impossible to be *hala'* in a limited way. Not surprisingly, few Aring people claim to be *hala' té'*. Even the few persons who do trance claim only to be *bomoh*, a Malay word for 'healer'. They say that their songs are authentic, obtained from the *hala' 'asal* (in dreams or trance) or learned from other shamans, but they claim only to 'copy' (*tiru'*) the actions of the ancient *hala'* when they hold a singing session. Nevertheless, at least one family and one other man are regarded as *hala'*, in some rather ambiguous sense, by the other Aring Batek. They are even thought by some to have tiger-bodies which they can enter at will, a certain sign of a *hala' té'*.

Apparently the western Negritos differentiate two categories of shamans. As Schebesta says, 'all tribes distinguish between a greater and a lesser *hala''* (1928: 228); 'the distinction seems to be that the great *Hala'* joins the *Čenoi* [celestial fairies] in the *pano'* [a shaman's hut], or becomes *Čenoi* himself, whereas the small *Hala'* (*Snahud*) is the echo of the great one and performs conjurations' (1957: 125). Such a division of shamans does not obviously exist among the Batek, though there may be a trace of it in the distinction made by the Aring Batek between the *hala'* and the *gening*,[4] the shaman's assistant. The *gening* leads the dancing and singing, especially when the shaman is in trance, and assists the shaman in various ways. He is credited with being able to call the *hala' 'asal* with his songs and cure minor ailments by singing and blowing incense smoke on the patients' bodies. Yet he is definitely not the equal of the *hala'*: he does not trance, has only *tewin* dreams, and has no tiger-body. He studies with the shamans only, not with the *hala' 'asal*. The distinction between the shaman and the shaman's assistant breaks down among the Lebir Batek. They use the term *gening* or *hala' gening* for

---

[4] The term *gening* is probably related to Malay *gending*, which means 'support; second; medium. Esp. of a shaman "helping out" a spirit at a seance' (Wilkinson 1959a: 350).

all persons who trance during singing sessions, and this may include the majority of the participants. Yet even they recognize differences in the powers of individual *hala' té'*. Only the most accomplished shamans are believed to have tiger-bodies; perhaps they can be equated with the 'great *hala*" of the western Negritos.

Characteristics of shamans

Among the Batek of the upper Lebir, most of the adult men and many of the women are considered shamans to some degree. The role of shaman is just one of many social roles played by the average mature Batek; it does not set one off as a special type of person. Even among the Aring Batek, who sharply distinguish shamans from ordinary people, the shamans do not stand out from the crowd. It has often been reported that Negrito shamans do not reveal themselves to outsiders, and the identities of the shamans can only be found out indirectly or after long acquaintance with a group (see e.g. Skeat and Blagden 1906b: 227; Schebesta 1928: 242; Evans 1937: 191). The two most important shamans of the Aring Batek display no outward signs of their special status nor any obvious personal peculiarities. One is a man about thirty years old who is the most active member of a family of shamans. He has been married several times and has children by two of his wives. He has a rather retiring personality and does not seem above average in intelligence. He is somewhat conservative in outlook, showing little enthusiasm for farming or any other change from the traditional hunting and gathering way of life. He specializes in trancing to get fruit blossoms from the *hala'*. He has no special influence over the group aside from that derived directly from his role as fruit shaman. The other is a man about fifty-five years old who is a headman (*penghulu*) as well as a shaman. He is a natural leader, a highly intelligent person with an outgoing personality. He has had the same wife for many years, and they have four grown children. He is quite progressive in his outlook and has been co-operating with the J.O.A. in their agricultural schemes in recent years. He is well-known as a curer as well as for being able to trance and communicate with the *hala'*. He is a very influential man as Batek go, though his influence is due as much to his general wisdom and leadership ability as to his shamanistic powers. Although these two men are quite different from each other, they are both 'typical' Batek and are not socially or psychologically aberrant in any way.

To be a shaman, one must know some songs of the type that can be used to communicate with the superhuman beings. Among the Lebir people, the number of such songs a person knows is considered to be a rough indication of the degree to which he is a shaman. To the Aring Batek, a knowledge of songs is necessary but not sufficient to make one a *hala' té'*. They say a shaman must also be able to trance and send his shadow-soul to visit the *hala' 'asal*. The Lebir people consider trancing a highly desirable skill in a shaman, but not absolutely necessary for effective communication with the superhumans.

Both groups of Batek Dè' agree that shamans have clear blood (*mun*), like that of the superhuman beings, as well as the ordinary red blood of humans. Some Aring people say the 'white' blood of the shaman is only in his heart, and the rest of his body contains red blood. The Lebir people claim that shamans have both kinds of blood all over their bodies. Perhaps they identify lymph with the clear blood of the *hala'*. They say the amount of clear blood a person has varies with the amount of shamanistic knowledge and power he has.

Both groups also agree that some shamans at least have tiger-bodies that they can use in the forest. The Lebir people attribute this characteristic only to the most accomplished shamans, not to everyone who knows a few songs. The tiger-body of the shaman is similar to that of a natural tiger except that it resembles the human shaman in its facial features and colouration. At night, when the human body of the shaman is asleep, his shadow-soul goes to the tiger-body and it wakes up. In the morning the shadow-soul returns to the human body, and the tiger goes to sleep somewhere deep in the forest. When the shaman trances, his shadow-soul may also enter the tiger-body, and the shaman-tiger, along with its *hala'*-tiger friends from Batu Balok, is sometimes seen or heard prowling around the camp during a singing session. The shaman uses his tiger-body for roaming about in the forest or for travelling to Batu Balok to visit the *hala'* there. He may also use it to travel to other Batek camps where he will listen to their singing or eavesdrop on their conversations. The shaman-tiger acts as a guardian for the shaman's group. The Aring Batek say that if there were no shaman-tigers (or *hala'*-tigers from Batu Balok) to protect them, they would be molested by ordinary tigers whenever they went out of camp. The shaman-tiger is like an ordinary tiger in that it is vulnerable to death, though it will not die of disease because it knows all the necessary cures. It tries to keep out of sight of men, fearing that it may not be recognized and will be killed. It is afraid of people's spears, but is still more afraid of snares. It can pull out the spears and heal the wounds with forest medicines, but, if it is caught in a snare, it will surely die. When the tiger body is killed, the human body dies as well. My informants remember two cases in which this was thought to be the cause of a shaman's death. Of course the death of the human body also results in the death of the tiger.

One important feature of shamans among the western Negritos is absent among the Batek. This is the possession of a magical stone, either a quartz crystal (*cebuh*) or a neolithic blade (*batu karei*) (Schebesta 1957: 124, 127, 134–6), the so-called 'thunderbolt' of the Malays (Skeat 1900: 276). 'The *Cebuh* is a miracle stone, a *batu Cenoi*, a *Cenoi* stone because it comes from the *Cenoi* [celestial fairies]. The *Cenoi* live in it. Anyone who has a *Cebuh* is automatically a *Hala*" (Schebesta 1957: 124). *Cebuh* stones may be found in the rolled-up leaves of the *palas* palm (*Licuala kunstleri*) where they are formed from dew or rain-water. Alternatively, Ta Ped'n (a deity of the western Negritos) can breathe such a stone into the body of a *hala'*. The *hala'* keeps it in his chest, but can remove it at will. The *cebuh* stone is used for curing. The shaman holds the stone on the head of the patient and then blows through his fist. This supposedly blows the *cenoi* out of the stone and into the patient's body, thus driving out the disease (Schebesta 1957: 135). The Batek know nothing of magical stones of any kind, but there seems to be a trace of the *cebuh* stone in some of their beliefs about *mun* (heavenly dew).[5] Supposedly a shaman can bring back a small lump of *mun* (about the size of a thumb) from the land of the *hala' 'asal*. It is like ice (Malay *air batu*), and, while he can show it to other people, they cannot take hold of it or it will melt and disappear. The *hala'* stores it in his chest and takes it out whenever he needs it to cool the body of a person who has fever.

Activities of shamans

To summarize briefly, the most important activity of Batek shamans is communicating with the *hala' 'asal*. They act as the leaders in

[5] Cuisinier reports that a Malay shaman in Kelantan, who apparently was of partially Negrito ancestry, had among his equipment some translucent stones which were called *guliga embun*, 'bezoars of dew' (1936: 38, 47).

singing sessions, and they may trance and send their shadow-souls to meet the superhuman beings face to face. Most shamans also perform cures, as curing is merely the application of knowledge—of songs, spells, and medicines—that is obtained, at least ultimately, from the *hala' 'asal*. The Lebir people consider all curing to be the acts of shamans (*hala' té'*) and thus all persons who know any cures to be shamans to some extent. Among the Aring Batek, on the other hand, there are many more people who practise curing than there are acknowledged shamans, though the shamans monopolize the most powerful curing technique, namely trancing and enlisting the direct aid of the superhumans (see below). In both their human and tiger forms, shamans try to protect the well-being of their groups. The activities of shamans are all modelled on what the Batek imagine to be the behaviour of the *hala' 'asal*. During their shamanistic performances, the performers identify closely with the superhumans, but for living human beings this unity with the *hala'* can only be a temporary condition.

Becoming a shaman

According to the Lebir Batek, any person who has sufficient ability and interest can become a shaman. To do so, he must learn shamanistic songs and spells and must acquire the clear blood of the *hala'*. The Aring Batek, on the other hand, believe that only persons who are descended from shamans have the potential to become shamans themselves. They claim that the clear blood cannot be acquired; it can only be inherited from a shaman parent. The inheritance of the *hala'*-blood is bilateral. Supposedly both men and women can be *hala'*, and they pass on that potentiality to all their children of both sexes. In fact, most acknowledged *hala'* are men, and it is usually one of the *hala'*'s sons who replaces him when he dies. Yet there is one Aring family in which the father, who is still alive, and three of his sons and one daughter are all considered *hala'*. The emphasis on heredity among the Aring Batek is quite consistent with their conception of the shaman as qualitatively different from ordinary human beings.

The Batek believe that the songs and spells of the *hala'* have power in their own right, and it makes no difference how one obtains knowledge of them. The Lebir Batek believe that *hala' 'asal* may appear in a person's dreams and teach him various songs, spells, and also the identities of plants that have medicinal properties. No doubt a person who is interested in such things and thinks about them a lot will have such dreams more often than other people, but all Lebir Batek can and do meet *hala'* in their dreams from time to time. Knowledge received through dreams can be supplemented by deliberate study with persons who have the required knowledge. Occasionally a person will even travel to another group, such as the Batek 'Iga' at Kuala Tahan, to study with a particularly knowledgeable person. There is no formal teacher–pupil relationship established, however, and no payment by the pupil is expected. Such knowledge is not secret and jealously guarded as it is among Malay magicians (see e.g. Cuisinier 1936: 3, 6, 12, 14, 15, 28). Knowledge acquired from a human teacher is considered just as valuable as that obtained in a dream, though its power rests ultimately on the assumption that it was originally received from the *hala'* *'asal*. The Lebir Batek believe that a person can become a minor shaman merely by obtaining shamanistic knowledge in these ways. But the Aring people regard such learning as only the means by which persons who have the innate potential to become shamans can develop that potential.

Both the Lebir and Aring Batek consider the most effective knowledge and power to be that obtained from *hala'*-tigers, which may be either dead humans or *hala'* *'asal* in their tiger-form bodies. The most usual way of making contact with a *hala'*-tiger is to wait at the grave of a dead person, on the seventh day after death, and to sing until the deceased appears in his tiger-form body.[6] The Aring Batek claim that this only happens if the deceased was a shaman and a parent of the person waiting. The Lebir Batek, on the other hand, say that this should work with any dead person, for they believe that all Batek become *hala'* and acquire tiger-form bodies after they die. In practice, however, most Lebir people would be afraid to wait at the grave of anyone other than a parent or grandparent, in spite of the expressed view that *hala'*-tigers in general are harmless to humans. The person waiting at the grave must be alone, and he must show no sign of fear when the *hala'*-tiger approaches. The novice orders the tiger to come near, and then he burns some incense and blows the smoke on it. This causes the *hala'* to assume his human form. Then the *hala'* teaches the novice all sorts of useful

---

[6] This method of obtaining magical knowledge is common among the Orang Asli groups of the Peninsula (see e.g. Wilkinson 1932: 127; Schebesta 1957: 124n., 153).

songs and spells and shows him how to send his shadow-soul to any part of the universe. He also admonishes the novice to take care of his fellow Batek and not to beat his wife or children. He then gives the novice a tiger-form body of his own and teaches him how to enter and use it. The tiger-body has any pattern of markings its owner wants. The Lebir Batek say that the *hala'* also gives the novice some clear blood. The *hala'* takes a lump of *mun* about the size of a soccer ball out of his own chest and places it in the heart, eyes, and ears of the novice. The *mun* in the heart takes away the need to eat while the instruction is going on. The *mun* in the eyes and ears enables the person to see and hear the *hala'* even from hundreds of miles away. This initial training may take as long as a week, during which time the novice remains by the grave. When the instruction is finished, the novice again blows incense smoke on the *hala'*, and he returns to the form of a tiger. These meetings may be repeated any number of times, and the siblings of the novice may also get instruction from the deceased parent. Arrangements for future meetings may be made at the grave or later through dreams. By repeated meetings, the novice will acquire more and more songs, skills, and *mun*-blood and thus will become increasingly effective as a shaman. I do not know if people actually seek shamanistic power in this way, though all my informants insist that they do.

The Lebir Batek also believe that people can get shamanistic knowledge from *hala'*-tigers that are *hala' 'asal* in their tiger-form bodies. Such *hala'*-tigers may be met accidentally or deliberately summoned. If a person working in the forest happens to come across such a tiger, which can be recognized by its intricate markings, he can blow incense smoke on it and cause it to change to its human form. Many Batek carry a small amount of incense in their pouch of personal effects just so they can take advantage of such chance encounters. The *hala'* may then teach the person some useful song or spell, or he may just ask how that person's group is faring. After a little while, the *hala'* will revert to his tiger form and go on his way. A person can deliberately summon a tiger-form *hala' 'asal* from Batu Balok by the following method. He must go into the forest alone, during the daytime, with only a bit of incense and a piece of cloth to sit on. He then sings until a *hala'*-tiger comes. He changes the *hala'* to human form by blowing incense smoke on it, and the *hala'* then teaches him some *hala'* lore. The *hala'* also gives him some *mun* so that he will not have to eat during his training. At nightfall, the *hala'* goes back to Batu Balok, and the novice returns to his camp. But he does not sleep. Instead, he sits on a bark platform and sings all night. In the morning he returns to the forest and meets the *hala'* again. This process is repeated for a week, until the person's training is complete and he has become a competent shaman. The day after his training is finished, he begins to eat again.

Death of shamans

To the Lebir Batek, the death of a shaman is like that of any person except that a shaman may decide for himself when he is ready to die, and he voluntarily gives up his life-soul (which is ordinary wind life-soul) for the benefit of the group. The shaman is given an ordinary tree-burial. When his shadow-soul reaches the afterworld, it receives several new bodies, as does the shadow-soul of every Batek. The tiger-body is just one of several animal-form bodies—including elephant-, snake-, and rhinoceros-shaped ones—that it may use while in the forest.

To the Aring Batek, on the other hand, the death of a shaman is very different from an ordinary human death. In theory a true *hala' té'* cannot die, for he has a water life-soul. But shamans do at least appear to die, though the condition is strictly temporary. My informants were not certain about what kind of life-soul an ordinary shaman has while living among men. In any case, after his apparent death, the shaman's life-soul goes to Raja Yạh, the king of the tigers, rather than to Tohan. The survivors leave the body of a dead shaman in his own shelter, as they were told to do by the *hala' 'asal* long ago. They place the corpse on several sleeping mats (seven is the ideal number) and cover it with a sarong and a cotton blanket. It is not bundled up like the body of an ordinary person. The people place many kinds of good-smelling leaves in the hut, most of them inserted into the thatch. They also make two small censers (usually a split piece of bamboo containing hot embers and some fragrant resin) and place one on each side of the body. No ordinary fire is kindled because *hala'* cannot take the heat. Also it is not necessary to place water in the grave because the body of a *hala'* is already cool. The dead shaman's hut is not closed up in any way. As soon as the body is properly arranged and the incense burning, the surviving members of the group abandon the camp. This is because they are afraid of the *hala'*-tigers which are expected to arrive soon after the death of a shaman, even though *hala'*-tigers should not, in theory, be dangerous to humans.

If a son of the dead shaman wishes to take his place, he may stay behind at the grave.[7] Soon a number of *hala'*-tigers, who are relatives (*kabèn*) of the dead shaman, arrive from Batu Balok. They recite spells over the body, and Raja Yah sends a water life-soul to it, thus causing the shaman to come back to life. Some informants say that his body then changes into that of a tiger. The first sign of the change is that he begins to walk about on four feet like his friends. Gradually his body becomes furry and takes on the shape of a tiger. His head is the last part to change, and some of his facial features continue to show through after the transformation is complete. This metamorphosis takes about a day. According to other informants, the shaman's shadow-soul merely enters his tiger-body for good when he is brought back to life, leaving behind the dead human body. From then on the shaman will be a *hala'*-tiger.

The *hala'*-tigers derived from dead shamans are essentially the same as the tiger-bodies of living shamans except that they do not have to share a shadow-soul. Thus they are entirely independent of human beings and can be active at any time of night or day. They normally live at Batu Balok where, some say, they take the form of human beings. When they are roaming about in the forest, however, they are in their tiger-form bodies. In either form they speak like Batek. If the former *gening* ('assistant') of a dead shaman meets the shaman in the forest after he has become a tiger, the *gening* can recite a spell and blow incense smoke on the tiger and thus return him temporarily to human form. The *hala'*-tigers, like the tigers of living shamans, act as guardians for the Batek, only they are not associated with any particular Batek group. They sometimes approach Batek

---

[7] This type of burial and the beliefs surrounding it are very similar to those of the 'Sakai tribes of the Perak-Pahang border', i.e. the Semai (Wilkinson 1932: 127). It is very common among the Orang Asli for shamans to be given a different kind of burial from ordinary persons (see e.g. Skeat and Blagden 1906b: 91, 207–8; Evans 1927: 26; Schebesta 1928: 228). Sometimes this is because the shaman is supposed to go to a different afterworld or take a different route to the same afterworld. In other cases the special form of burial is meant to facilitate the shaman's transformation into a tiger. Interestingly, the Kintaq have two kinds of shaman, both of which receive a special form of burial. One type is buried in the ground in a squatting position with the head protruding from the grave but covered, and the other type is placed on some sort of platform. The former goes to the land of the *cenoi*, and the latter becomes a tiger (Schebesta 1957: 152–3).

camps at night and watch and listen to the people, especially when they are having a serious singing session. The shaman can make use of them in curing. When he is in a trance, his shadow-soul can carry the shadow-soul of the patient out to the *hala'*-tigers and have them recite their potent spells and sing their songs over it. The *hala'*-tigers are afraid to come right into camp because they, like shaman-tigers, are capable of being killed. If people mistakenly kill a *hala'*-tiger, however, its shadow-soul merely returns to Raja Yạh where it is given a new body. Then Raja Yạh may send out some other *hala'*-tigers to take revenge on the human killers. Thus, human beings must be very careful to kill only ordinary tigers, not that killing tigers is something the Batek frequently do.

Shamans and tigers

As the foregoing description shows, both groups of Batek Dè' posit a close connection between shamans and tigers both before and after death. The connection is especially emphasized and elaborated by the Aring Batek, perhaps because of their closer ties with the Mendriq, who explicitly state that shamans are descended from the original tiger (Schebesta 1957: 121). Many of the other indigenous peoples of the Malay Peninsula assume some sort of association between shamans and tigers, though the nature of the connection varies. Both the rural Malays and the western Negritos believe that certain shamans can be possessed by a tiger-form spirit in a spirit-raising seance (see e.g. Skeat 1900: 436–44; Cuisinier 1936: 68; Evans 1937: 196, 201; Schebesta 1957: 121, 139–40). In the Malay case the possessor is a free spirit (*hantu belian*) (Skeat 1900: 447) and in the Negrito case a *ćenoi* (Schebesta 1957: 139). These tiger-spirits take control of the shaman and cause him to growl and act like a tiger though his body remains that of a man. In some respects this is the reverse of the Batek notion of a living shaman having an alternative tiger-form body. With the Batek it is the 'spirit' of the shaman, his shadow-soul, which goes out and takes control of the tiger. Both schemes seem intended to harness the power of the tiger for the benefit of man, but the spirit-possession system gives more control to the tiger than to the shaman. The notion that shamans become tigers of some sort after death is widespread among the Orang Asli groups of the Malay Peninsula (see e.g. Skeat and Blagden 1906b: 227; Schebesta 1928: 274; 1957: 152–4; Wilkinson 1932: 127). The exact nature of these tigers is not clear from the literature, though it is quite likely that they, like the *hala'*-tigers which come from dead Batek shamans, are tiger-form bodies inhabited by the shadow-souls of shamans (see Skeat and Blagden 1906b: 227).

The Batek notion of the shaman-tiger, in which the shadow-soul of a living shaman enters and controls a tiger-form body, is quite distinct from the Malay concept of the were-tiger, in which certain persons (especially Korinchi Malays) are thought to change into tigers and roam about killing and eating people and domestic animals (see e.g. Skeat 1900: 160–3). According to this belief, the body of the person actually changes into that of a tiger and back again (Clifford 1897: 66–8). Basically the Malay and Batek ideas differ in two ways: first, the were-tiger is a man's body transformed while the Batek shaman has two bodies at once; and, second, the were-tiger is evil while the shaman-tiger is usually good. But there are some convergences between the two sets of ideas which may explain why the Malays often attribute the power to become a tiger to Negrito shamans (see e.g. Clifford 1897: 202). I was told that it would be possible for a wicked shaman to use his tiger-body to perform evil deeds, such as killing his parents-in-law. My informants remembered one such shaman who had lived on the upper Tahan River. His tiger-body killed several persons before it was killed by people in Perak, where it was not recognized as a shaman-tiger, and this, of course, caused the death of the shaman back on the Tahan. This story reveals some of the suspicion that is often attached to a person who has magical powers, even though shamans are generally considered beneficent by the Batek. Another convergence is that the body of the shaman is said by some to actually change into that of a tiger *after death*, when he becomes a *hala'*-tiger and goes to Batu Balok. The confusion of the shaman-tiger with the were-tiger may well be perpetuated by the Negritos themselves, who do not necessarily discourage such an interpretation by the Malays. Skeat met a Negrito on the Aring (undoubtedly a Batek Dè') who gave him a detailed description of how a shaman could change himself into a tiger, go about raiding the local cattle pens, and then return to human shape. This man was later revealed by the local Malays to be such a shaman himself (Skeat and Blagden 1906b: 227–9). This story, as Schebesta points out (1957: 147), is clearly a description of the common Malay belief in the were-tiger. The reason it should have been told by a Batek, even though it is a misrepresentation of the Batek belief, is no doubt quite simple. It is to the advantage of the Batek to be feared by the Malays as it ensures them a certain amount of respect and consideration which they otherwise would not get. For a similar reason, they are not at great pains to debunk their equally undeserved reputation as the possessors of powerful black magic.

Why should there be such an intimate connection between the shaman and the tiger in the beliefs of the Batek Dè' and many other Orang Asli groups? I think it is due to the convergence of several cognitive and emotional features of the relationship between humans and tigers. The Batek are highly ambivalent toward tigers. On the one hand, they greatly admire them for their awesome strength and speed. These qualities make the tiger a very appropriate symbol for the notion of superhuman power on earth, which is personified in man by the shaman. But the Batek greatly fear tigers as well. The identification of the shaman with the tiger seems to be a way of converting the danger of tigers to power for man. The belief that some humans control tiger-bodies and use them to protect the human community, even against other tigers, certainly helps to reduce the people's fear of tigers. This idea, by a neat twist, turns the power of the tiger against itself. But it is an exercise of imagination and hope, and it is not entirely successful. Even though in theory *hala'*-tigers are beneficent to the Batek, in fact most Batek are afraid of them except when they believe they have some close personal tie with a particular *hala'*-tiger.

Communication with the Superhuman Beings

Methods of communication with superhumans

Usually ordinary speech does not reach the *hala' 'asal*. The only exceptions I know of are the extemporaneous speeches that are made to stop thunderstorms if there has been no breach of a *lawac* prohibition. These are spoken loudly, to carry over the noise of the wind, but are otherwise like ordinary speech. These orations are addressed to the *hala'* in general or sometimes to Angin, the wind personified, or Gobar, the thunder-god. Usually they are rambling and slightly indignant discourses to the effect that the Batek love the *hala'* and do not deserve to be annihilated by falling trees. One clever ploy that is sometimes used is to remind Gobar that he once lived on earth, eating tubers like a man, and he had to be pulled up Batu Keñam by the *hala'* sisters. This shames him so much that he stops the storm. Normally the speeches also contain denials that anyone has broken a prohibition. Only certain people are credited with the ability to reach the *hala'* in this way. They are not chosen or trained in any way; it just becomes known that their words generally get results, that is, they cause the storm to stop.

There are only a few instances in which standardized spoken formulas are addressed to the *hala' 'asal*. The invocations that accompany the blood sacrifice would fit this description (see below). The only Malay-style spell I know of that is addressed to the *hala'* is also meant to stop thunderstorms. It runs as follows:

> *Ahoh! Suara jin,*
> *Kerana Siti Bueh,*
> *Kerana Siti Batu,*
> *Benang lepas, benang sunyi,*
> *Itu asal engkau,*
> *Kalau engkau menang pekataan aku,*
> *Aku kena sumpah engkau,*
> *Sidi guru,*
> *Sidi aku,*
> *Kerana guru,*
> *Sidi berkat,*
> *Katalah gantong kuasa Allah.*

> Oh! Voice of genies [refers to wind],
> Because of Lady Foam [name of rain],
> Because of Lady Stone [name of thunder],
> Thread finished, thread quiet [refers to the rope of wind],
> It was originally you,
> If you disobey my words,
> I shall have to curse you,
> Effective for teacher,
> Effective for me,
> Because of teacher,
> Effective blessing,
> Say due to the power of Allah.

Immediately after reciting the spell, one is supposed to hiss sharply several times to send the spell to the heavens. My informant, a young man of about twenty years old, said he had received this spell from the *hala'* in a dream. But it has a very Malay cast to it, quite apart from its being mainly in the Malay language, as are most Batek spells. The references to genies, 'ladies' of foam and stone, and cursing are quite alien to Batek conceptions of thunderstorms. The fact that all spoken communications with the *hala' 'asal* occur during storms may be significant. Possibly the *hala'* pay special attention to the people they threaten with storms, and thus they would receive a type of message under those circumstances which ordinarily would not reach them. The Batek do not use any kinds of spoken 'prayers' to the superhuman beings, unless these attempts to stop storms are so considered.

Odours, both good and bad, are often used to communicate with the *hala' 'asal*. Incense and good-smelling leaves and flowers are used extensively for this purpose, either alone, as at burials, or along with other forms of communication, as at singing sessions (see below). The Batek Dè' also burn various substances during thunderstorms on the theory that the smoke will reach the *hala'* and influence them to stop the storm. Most of the substances burned are considered good-smelling. They include the leaves and roots of some of the plants used for bodily decoration (*hali' 'ayam*; mostly species of wild ginger), fragrant woods (*geharo'*; Malay *gaharu*), and incense resin (*kemeyèn*). The Batek usually make do with whatever good-smelling substance comes to hand, but the more sedentary Mendriq keep a supply of dried roots of one fragrant plant (*kasay*) to be available for burning in case of a thunderstorm. The substances to be burned are merely thrown into the cooking-fire. Someone may recite a brief invocation such as: *kayu', kayu', kayu', pangku' ketò' yè'*, 'wood, wood, wood [referring to *gaharu* wood], hold up my sky'. The rationale for this practice is that the deities will be pleased by the sweet-smelling smoke and will take pity on the people who sent it to them. The opposite reasoning seems to lie behind a related practice of the Aring Batek. If a very severe thunderstorm lingers over a camp even though no offence has been committed by members of that camp, a few people may burn some of their hair. They take a stick with glowing embers out of the fire, for it is prohibited to burn hair over a cooking fire, and place a small number of hairs, which can be given by anyone, on the embers. Someone gathers the smoke in his fist (either hand) and blows it first downward, to the earth-snake, and then upward, to the thunder-god. No spell or other words are recited. This smoke is thought to smell bad (*jebéc*). The superhumans are supposed to stop the storm because they want the Batek to stop producing that horrible stench.[8]

The most commonly used method of communicating with the *hala' 'asal* is singing (*piñlòñ*). Such singing can occur in a very informal setting or in a well-organized singing session. Just one or two persons singing while wearing a few good-smelling leaves is considered by the Lebir people to be a legitimate attempt to 'call' (*kul*) the *hala'*. In special singing sessions (see below), the singing is done by a group of people following a leader. The session may be devoted entirely to singing, or the singing may be used to send a shaman into trance. The songs (*haka'*) of the Batek are improvised by the singer around a certain theme. There are a limited number of tunes, so many songs have the same or similar tunes. The words are partially Malay and partially Batek, some of the latter being special or obscure words heard only in songs. Interspersed among the words are a large number of meaningless melodic syllables used for balance and to fill out a line. A particular song will be character-ized by a number of set phrases or lines, but their order is entirely optional. Also, a clever singer will add new lines on the same pattern as he goes along. Perhaps the most common pattern is to have variable lines of verse alternating with a fixed line of refrain. When more than one person sings, the leader usually starts the verse, and the 'chorus' joins in a few beats behind him, either repeating what he has sung or producing some variant of it which takes off from his first few words. The effect is something like a round in which the various parts are subtly different. The congruence is of course closer on the refrain than on the verse. Batek songs are generally pleasing to the western ear, though somewhat monotonous as a group. The main reason songs reach the *hala' 'asal* while spoken words do not is that the songs are 'beautiful' (*bed'èt*). They attract the attention of the *hala'* and may induce them to come down to earth to listen. At special singing sessions, sweet-smelling herbs and incense smoke are used as added attractions. Also, several types of musical instruments may be played (see below). Theoretically the songs appeal to the *hala'* because they are their own songs, which men have learned from them in dreams. Because the songs give them pleasure, they are favourably disposed toward the people who sing them and will

---

[8] Some of the Semai burn hair to prevent lightning from striking their houses, and others burn 'evil-smelling rubbish to scare away the storm' (Evans 1923: 201).

try to help them. The songs themselves reveal, though sometimes only indirectly, what the singers desire.

Both the Lebir and Aring Betek regard trancing[9] as the most effective means of communicating with the *hala' 'asal*. According to Batek theories, trancing is a sort of controlled dreaming, in that the shadow-soul can be deliberately sent to any part of the universe. It is guided by the songs that accompany the trance, different songs being used for different destinations. The shadow-soul is variously described as flying or being carried by the incense smoke, the wind,[10] or the *hala' 'asal*. It may also use its tiger-body to make journeys on earth. The shadow-soul of the shaman is able to meet any of the *hala' 'asal*. In this way the shaman can negotiate directly with them, and, because he is a friend of the *hala' 'asal*, he can get whatever help and information he needs. The great advantage of trancing over ordinary dreaming, of course, is that in the former the shaman can decide what *hala'* to visit and can determine the topic of discussion, whereas in the latter the dreamer plays a passive role, without any influence over which, if any, *hala'* will visit him or what information it will impart.

Trancing is always accompanied by singing. The songs simultaneously guide the shadow-soul and describe its journey. Normally trancing takes place in special singing sessions, with a group of singers following the lead of the shaman or his assistant (*gening*). In an emergency, however, such as someone suffering a serious accident, some shamans can sing themselves into trance on the spur of the moment. The songs that accompany trancing are very difficult to translate. They contain many words that have no equivalent in the vernacular language. Some of these words, I suspect, are distortions of words from the language of the Semaq Beri, a non-Negrito aboriginal people who live immediately to the south of the Batek. The Semaq Beri have a highly developed form of 'soul-leaving' shamanism, and some aspiring Batek shamans have been known to go to them to study their songs. Other words are standard Batek or Malay but have entirely different meanings in songs than in normal speech. In addition, many words are distorted for harmonious effect,

[9] Trancing is called *lupa'* (literally 'to forget'; cf. Malay *lupa*) by both groups and is also called *mpa'* (also means 'to dream' for shamans) by the Aring Batek Dè'.

[10] Some Aring people say it is 'threads of wind' (*benang 'angin*) that carry the shaman's shadow. This recalls the notion of the western Negritos that the shaman climbs or is pulled to heaven on fine threads which are like cobwebs (Schebesta 1957: 139). The Batek Nòng compared these threads to plastic rope.

either consistently or only in certain contexts. The full meaning of a song is, of course, much greater than the sum of the superficial meanings of its individual words, for each word suggests a whole range of meanings to a listener fully versed in the culture. Each song has a distinctive set of lines and allusions, though they may be sung in different orders and repeated any number of times. Woven around these fixed elements are various improvisations on the theme which are introduced by the song-leader in a particular performance. The length of the song coincides with the length of the soul's journey, which is usually between a quarter of an hour and an hour. The following is a highly condensed version of a Lebir Batek Dè' trancing song. It is a song for making a general tour of the universe just to get other useful songs. The translation offered is very tentative, as I could not get satisfactory glosses for a number of the individual words.[11]

1. 'Òy 'amòy, 'òy 'amòy, 'òy 'amòy, 'òy 'amòy,
   'Òy, serway bayang, serway lakòh, lèh teman,
   Celah lòrong nang kèy watuh, nang kotikeh, lèh teman.
   'Òy 'amòy, 'uhehh . . .
5. 'Òy, ka-semilang puco', ka-semilang lentam,
   Ka-semilang lapis, ka-semilang liku', lèh teman.
   'Òy 'amòy, 'uhehh . . .
   'Òy, serway bayang, serway lakòh, lèh teman,
   'Entah keyeh, kasim benar ranòn teman, hehh . . .
10. 'Òy 'amòy, 'òy 'amòy . . .
   Celah lapis liku', lèh teman,
   Celah kabur Tingring, kabur Redam,
   Ropeh bagay ranòn teman, 'ehehh . . .
   'Òy, 'òy, lamòng kabur ganti', kabur tingkah,
15. Ranòn kabar tingkah so'al lèh teman,
   'Òy, bagay celah lòrong, òy.
   'Òy 'amòy, 'ehehh . . .
   Lamòng kabur ganti', 'òy 'amòy, 'eheh . . .
   'Òy 'amòy, 'ehehh . . .
20. 'Òy 'amòy 'entah keyeh kasim benar pantòn, 'òy,
   'Entang keyeh, kasim benar so'al kapungabis,

---

[11] I thank Encik Abdullah bin Sepien for his help in deciphering the Kelantan Malay expressions in the song. This song contains a slightly higher proportion of Malay words than most Batek trancing songs.

Bagay pantòn teman,
'Òy, 'entang kolayin, lakòh kolayin, lakòh bayang.
'Òy 'amòy, 'ehehh . . .
25. *'Òy, serway bayang 'òy, 'òy serway lakòh 'òy,*
'Òy 'amòy, 'ehehh . . .
'Òy, celah kabur Tingring,
Celah kabur lapis, ranòn teman.
'Òy 'amòy, 'ehehh . . .
30. *Ka-semilang lentam, ka-semilang puco', 'òy,*
'Òy, celah lapis liku', leh teman.
'Entah keyeh, kasim benar ranòn,
'Entah keyeh, kasim benar pantòn, 'òy.
Serway bayang, 'òy 'amòy, 'ehehh . . .

1. Oh come, oh come, oh come, oh come,
   Oh, carry my shadow-soul, carry it on a journey, take me,[12]
   To the passage at this time, at this moment, take me.
   Oh come, . . .
5. Oh, all around the land,[13] all around the sea at the horizon,
   All around the firmament,[14] all around the underground sea,[15]
      take me.
   Oh come, . . .
   Oh, carry my shadow-soul, carry it on a journey, take me.
   Very genuine, send true songs to me, . . .
10. Oh come, oh come, . . .
   The passage to the underworld,[16] take me,
   The passage through Tingring,[17] the land of Redam,[18]
   As described in my song . . .
   Oh, oh, send me up to the land of *hala'*, sound the log drum,

[12] The shaman uses the term *teman* (Malay for 'follower, companion') as the first person singular pronoun to indicate his close but subordinate relationship to the *hala'*.

[13] Literally 'to nine mountaintops'. *Puco'* also means 'shoot of a plant' and refers symbolically to the log drum.

[14] Literally 'to nine layers'. *Lapis* here means layers of the firmament (it can also mean layers of the earth), and it also refers symbolically to the mats on which the singers sit.

[15] Literally 'to nine corners'. *Liku'* also refers symbolically to the bark platform.

[16] This suggests the tortuous journey through many 'layers' (*lapis*) and 'corners' (*liku'*) of the earth.

[17] This is supposedly a pool of water on top of Mount Tahan which forms an entrance to the underworld.

[18] This is a tall mountain which nearly reaches the firmament.

15. The song and the sound of the drum are my concern,
     Oh, and so is the passage, oh.
     Oh come, . . .
     Send me up to the land of *hala'*, oh come, . . .
     Oh come, . . .
20. Oh come, very genuine, give me true verses, oh,
     Very genuine, give me true subject matter as just mentioned,
     The same as my verses,
     Oh, to somewhere else, journey somewhere else, journey shadow-
       soul.
     Oh come, . . .
25. Oh, carry my shadow-soul oh, oh carry it on its journey oh,
     Oh come, . . .
     Oh, the passage to the land of Tingring,
     The passage to the firmament, my song.
     Oh come, . . .
30. All around the sea, all around the land, oh,
     Oh, the passage to the underworld, take me.
     Very genuine, send me true songs,
     Very genuine, send me true verses, oh.
     Carry my shadow-soul, oh come, . . .

Some typical features of Batek songs can be seen in the original version of this song. A certain poetic harmony is produced by grouping similar phrases together and by sometimes using rhyming words in similar positions (e.g. *ranòn*, 'song', and *pantòn*, 'verse'). Some words may even be distorted to make them rhyme. For example, it is common in Batek songs for the endings of many words to be changed to *-ng* (e.g. *semilang* is substituted in this song for Malay *sembilan*, 'nine') which has this effect. Conversely, the same word may be given different endings in different places, apparently just for effect or variety (e.g. *'entah*, 'very', is sometimes pronounced *'entang*).

The superficial meaning of this song is reasonably clear from the translation. The shaman wants to be sent to all parts of the universe and to be given new songs by the *hala'* in each place. A second level of meaning appears in the early part where the terms used for different areas of the world refer also to the log drum, mats, and bark platform used in the ceremony. There is a suggestion here that the ceremonial setting is a microcosm, but this notion is not developed anywhere. The explicit explanation given is that the shaman wants the *hala'* to carry the shadows of the ceremonial equipment as well as his own shadow-soul to the different places mentioned. This song also incorporates instruction to the other participants in the ceremony when the shaman sings 'sound the log drum'. No doubt there are other levels of meaning to this song that I do not know about. The meanings of Batek trancing songs are complex in part because the songs are addressed simultaneously to the shaman's shadow-soul, the superhuman beings, and the other performers.

Batek trance is not usually deep; the loss of consciousness is not complete. However, this varies somewhat from person to person and time to time. Usually a shaman in trance just goes on singing, with eyes shut, describing in song the journey of his shadow-soul. Sometimes the shaman stops singing when he goes into trance, but continues to sit with eyes closed, swaying in time to the music. It is said, though I have not seen it, that shamans sometimes dance and then fall down in a stupor. I suspect that this last technique is influenced by the Mendriq who seem generally to use deeper trance than the Batek (see Schebesta 1957: 148–9). No alcohol or drugs are used by the Batek to induce trance, though good-smelling leaves are worn and incense burned, and their odours may have some small effect on the shaman's state of consciousness. Batek shamans do not normally answer questions when they are in trance. This is consistent with the theory that the shadow-soul is absent from the body at that time. The shaman is not aware of his surroundings while in trance, but he may be able to recount the adventures of his shadow-soul after he revives.

It is worth noting that the shamanism of the Batek Dè' is basically of the 'soul-leaving' type. In this respect it is similar to the shamanism of the Orang Asli peoples to the south of them, such as the Semaq Beri (Knud-Erik Jensen, personal communication), Temoq (Peter Laird, personal communication), and the Orang Hulu, a Jakun people of northern Johore (Andrew Hill, personal communication). Yet, in the Lebir notion that any person may be visited by *hala'* in dreams, there may be a trace of the generalized spirit-mediumship of the Malays and the Orang Asli to the north and west of the Batek, including the western Negritos (see e.g. Evans 1923: 150–1, 160–7; Schebesta 1928: 26–7, 273; 1957: 121, 132, 237–40). It seems that the Batek lie on the border between the peoples practising 'soul-leaving' shamanism and spirit-mediumship, and they are influenced, though unequally, by both.

Singing sessions

Several times a year the Batek organize formal singing sessions which, if shamans are involved, may culminate in trancing. One or more singing sessions are held each year near the end of the floods, in January and February, to bring on the fruit season. Songs are sung for all the important species of fruit. Typically the songs describe and praise the fruit and ask the *hala'* to send it in abundance (see pp. 57–8 for an example of a fruit song). If there is a shaman present, he may send his shadow-soul to the *hala' 'asal* to plead with them personally to send a large number of fruit blossoms. He may also go to Gobar, the thunder-god, to get flowers from the stone pillar (either Batu Keñam or Batu Balok) on which he lives. He must use deception to do this, for Gobar does not willingly give up his fruit blossoms. During the fruit harvest, in July or August, at least one more singing session is held. This is essentially a celebration and a way of giving thanks to the *hala'* for the fruit which is so greatly loved by everyone. The songs sung are intended merely to give pleasure to the *hala'* and to attract them to the singing session to renew the bond between them and mankind. People may trance and send their shadow-souls to the land of *hala'* just for the pleasure of it, to see their *hala'* friends and relatives (many shamans even have husbands or wives among the *hala' 'asal*) and to reacquaint themselves with the fabulous places where the *hala'* live. The shamans may ask the superhuman beings to guard the Batek from general misfortune. These somewhat unfocused singing sessions, which occur at least once a year, are the closest thing to 'worship' of the *hala'* that exists among the Batek.

Special singing sessions may be organized at any time of the year if someone is desperately ill or if large numbers of people are ill. The songs used are intended to attract the *hala' 'asal*, both human-form and tiger-form, to the singing session. It is hoped that the *hala'* will join in the singing and thus drive off the disease. A shaman may trance in order to go to the *hala'* and get a diagnosis and the spells and songs needed to cure the disease. After coming out of trance, he will try whatever medicines and curing techniques the *hala'* showed him. The shaman may bring back a lump of heavenly dew (*mun*) from the superhumans (probably a bit of sleight of hand) which he can massage into the patient's body to cool it. In cases of extreme illness, the shaman may carry the shadow-soul of the patient to the *hala' 'asal* for their personal attention. They will sing over it and cool it with *mun*. The shaman may also send his shadow-soul to find and retrieve the shadow-soul of a victim of *sabèn*, the disease in which the shadow-soul is stolen by a supernatural bird.

Very occasionally a special session will be performed during the floods if the flooding is too severe or goes on too long. The singers plead for the *hala' 'asal* to stop the rain.

A formal singing session is usually planned a few weeks in advance. The organizers, who include any interested persons, try to get as many people as possible to camp together for the ceremony, so that there will be many hands to share the work and many voices to carry the songs to the *hala'*. A singing session can be performed anywhere, but the site chosen must be located where outsiders will not find it and interfere with the ceremony. The actual preparations for a singing session may take several days. The men usually build the bark platform on which the singing takes place, and both men and women work on the large shelter that covers it. Older people spend much of their time making decorations and equipment. Food-getting activities go on as usual. There is no attempt made to build up a surplus of food, for the ceremony usually only lasts one night, and there is no feasting associated with it. Perhaps this is because the *hala'* do not eat, and singing sessions are above all a time when the Batek identify with the superhuman beings.

The Batek Dè' believe that a singing session can only be successful if it is performed on a bark platform. The platform (*lantéy*; cf. Malay *lantai*, 'floor') is composed of a number of logs about eight inches in diameter, lying parallel to each other about three feet apart, a series of smaller poles lying across the logs at right angles, and sheets of bark from the *tekèl* tree (*Shorea sericea*), lying on the poles. The bark is reddish-brown, about a half inch thick, and is rather soft and fibrous. The sheets are five to six feet wide, being stripped whole from the trunks of good-sized trees, and as long as the platform. The platform may be any size, depending on the number of singers expected, but twenty by thirty feet is about average. This type of platform is used because it is good to dance on: it keeps the feet from getting tired or cut, and it produces a pleasant thumping sound as the people dance. The raised position of the platform seems to symbolize the separation of the performers and their equipment from the ordinary world. Supposedly the shadows of the platform and all the ritual paraphernalia on it arrive at the land of the *hala'* *'asal* along with the shadow-souls of the singers who trance. Unless the weather is very dry, the Batek build a large lean-to shelter (*hayą' tebew*) over the platform to keep rain off the performers and equipment. It is shaped like an ordinary sleeping shelter, only it is much bigger, about twenty feet high at the upper edge and big enough at the base to cover the whole platform. It is made of ordinary thatch, usually *cemcòm* (*Calamus castaneus*), but the support poles are much longer and have many more rows of thatch than those of a normal shelter. The roof is usually four or more sections of thatch wide (each section is about seven feet wide, the length of a palm frond). The thatch of the *hayą' tebew* is stuffed with bunches of good-smelling leaves, and sometimes a special T-shaped rack of wooden poles is placed toward the front of the platform and covered with similar bunches of leaves. Usually the Batek construct a 'log-drum' (*balèn*) at the back of the shelter. This is a straight green log about five inches in diameter which is stripped of its bark and suspended by rattan cords from two sticks which are driven into the ground at a 45° angle. The log hangs about eighteen inches above the platform, and two or three people sit cross-legged in front of it and beat out a rhythm on it with short sticks and sections of bamboo. Such a drum produces a ringing sound similar to the beating of a metal jerry-can, which is occasionally used by the Batek Teh as a substitute for the log drum. The bark platform and large shelter are thought to be the same as those used by the *hala'* *'asal* for their singing sessions. That is why two of the first plants dropped to earth by the *hala'* *'asal* were the *tekél* tree, for its bark, and the *cemcòm* palm, for its thatch.

The participants in a singing session wear a number of special trappings (*halat*; Malay *alat*, 'equipment') made of leaves, flowers, and bark. A sort of wreath (*pemolang*) is worn on the head. This is usually made of *palès* palm leaves (*Licuala* spp.) twined together with various good-smelling leaves (*hali'* *'ayam*)[19] and flowers.

---

[19] Any good-smelling leaf is called *'ayam* by the Batek Dè' (not to be confused with Malay *ayam*, 'chicken', which is termed *hayam* in Batek Dè'). If more discrimination is desired, the 'species' name is added, e.g. *'ayam renam*. Most *'ayam* species are herbs, many being wild gingers (*Zingiber* spp.). Some of the most commonly used types (which, unfortunately, I have not identified) are *baròk*, *sayang, renam, pengasih, cingcong, sari'*, and *manyèng*. These terms often occur as the true Batek names of both men and women.

Occasionally it consists of a woven band of pandanus with *'ayam* leaves inserted in it. Two 'bandoliers' (*tenéwek*), thick loops of crushed and twisted plant stems hung with large bunches of *sayang* leaves (*Zingiber* sp.),[20] are draped over each shoulder and under the opposite arm so that they cross on the chest and back (see Collings 1949: 96–7 for Khmer parallels). Bracelets (*tabèn cas*) and bicep bands (*cinǫs* or *kenlah*), plaited from *palès* palm leaves, are worn to hold bunches of *'ayam* leaves. Such leaves may also be inserted into the waist-strings of the men's loincloths. Often a sort of whisk of *'ayam* leaves is held in each hand.[21] Some of the participants may lack one or another of these decorations, though most wear them all. The same sorts of things are worn by men and women. These special trappings are intended to make the dancers look pretty and, more importantly, to produce a powerful mixture of good smells that will attract the *hala' 'asal* to the performance. The leaf whisks are waved back and forth by the performers to keep themselves cool as they dance. These elaborate decorations, which may make the dancers look like moving bushes, are supposed to be the same as those worn by the *hala' 'asal* when they sing and dance.

Batek singing sessions always take place at night when it is cool. Some even say there is *mun*, i.e. drops of dew, in the air at night. Incense is burned somewhere on the platform and a few small wick-lamps or resin torches may be used, but ordinary fires are not allowed near the platform because any heat would drive the *hala' 'asal* away. Singing sessions usually begin between 7.00 and 8.00 p.m. and go on for anywhere from a few hours to the whole night. There is no formal beginning to a session. A few people merely assemble at the platform and start singing, and this acts as a signal to others to put on their regalia and join them. The singers sit on some pandanus sleeping-mats that have been placed in the centre of the platform. If available, the mats used are ones with colourful plaid patterns made with dyes. These are considered more attractive to the super-human beings than plain mats. A few volunteers, usually women,

[20] The Batek Teh dance on a bed of *sayang* leaves instead of a bark platform. This protects their feet and also gives off a strong, sweet smell as it is crushed by their feet.

[21] Very similar trappings to these are worn by nearly all the Negrito groups on 'festal occasions' (see e.g. Skeat and Blagden 1906b: 124–6). Also some Semai shamans wear essentially the same garb as the Batek dancers (Evans 1923: 212). In the Semai case, the shaman attempts to attract a 'familiar spirit' (Evans 1923: 213); perhaps the decorations are meant to aid in this.

start beating out a rhythm on the log drum using sticks and joints of bamboo. Someone may join in with a bamboo zither (*'amang*); this consists of an open length of bamboo about two inches in diameter and two feet long with two strings usually made of nylon fishing line. It is strummed, purely as a rhythm instrument. Palm-wood jew's harps (*gingòng*) and bamboo mouth-flutes (*pensòl*) may also be played, though they are used more in small-scale singing sessions where they are not so nearly drowned by the singing and dancing.

The songs used at the beginning are intended to attract the *hala' 'asal*, both human-form ones from above and below the earth and tiger-form ones from Batu Balok. Some songs explicitly ask the *hala'* to come, but others attract them by their beauty alone. The fragrant odours of the decorations and incense also drift out and entice the *hala'* to come to the ceremony. Once the singing gets going, a few people stand up and begin to dance in a circle round the seated singers. The dancing is a sort of shuffle which usually consists of two sliding steps in succession with one foot and then the other; the dancers' bodies sway forward and backward in time to the music. As the number of dancers increases, the bark platform resonates with the thumping of their feet. Both the dancers and the people sitting sing. Gradually the excitement of the performers builds up. After an hour or two of dancing and singing, the *hala' 'asal* are supposed to have arrived and to be lurking unseen in the shadows, adding their exquisite voices to the singing.

As one song is finished, another begins. Different people take the lead in singing the songs they each have received from the super-human beings. Eventually a shaman starts a song to send his shadow-soul to the land of the *hala'*. He chooses an appropriate song to suit his destination. Normally he just sits and sings, with his eyes shut, and gradually loses his senses. The Aring Batek say his shadow-soul flies out of his body under its own power, while the Lebir people say that the *hala' 'asal* who have come to hear the singing carry it on its journey. Usually the shaman continues to lead the singing while he is in trance. Among the Aring Batek, however, the shaman some-times falls silent, and his assistant takes over. The shaman, or his assistant, sings of the exploits of the shaman's shadow-soul, and the rest of the people sing along, following his lead. They vicariously participate in the experiences described in the song, and some people claim that the shadow-souls of everyone on the platform accompany that of the shaman on its journey. In this way the imaginary experience of visiting the *hala' 'asal* is shared by the whole group.

Some songs describe how the shaman's shadow-soul goes to the sky and is led by the *hala' 'asal* on a path through the firmament to the world above. Others describe a journey down through the bottoms of deep river pools to the land beneath the 'skin' of the earth. In such places, the shaman's shadow-soul visits the *hala' 'asal* and the dead. It discusses the people's problems with them and seeks any help that is needed. It also just travels about, marvelling at the wonderful sights. When the shadow-soul becomes tired, it begins the journey back to earth. Some of the people singing burn incense to attract the shaman's shadow-soul back to his body. Among the Aring people, the shaman's assistant may throw parched rice (*bertih*) on him to help wake him up.[22] If there is an ill person to be treated, the shaman will then perform any curing rites the *hala'* have taught him, and the rest of the people will help by singing whatever songs the shaman leads them in.

The process of trancing may then be repeated by the same or a different shaman. Often shamans will have visited most of the regions of the universe by the time the singing session is finished. The session ends whenever the people get too tired to continue or when they feel they have accomplished their purpose. There is no special closing ceremony.

Blood sacrifice

When a thunderstorm passes directly over a Batek camp, the inhabitants usually take some kind of action to try to stop it. If no one in camp has broken a *lawac* prohibition, it is assumed that the storm was intended as punishment for some other group. In that case, the members of the unfairly threatened group will try to influence the *hala'* to stop the storm by means of impromptu speeches, spells, burning incense or hair, or some combination of these measures (see above). Oddly enough, the Kelantan Batek do not sing to the beings who control the storm. However, the Batek Nòng of Pahang do. Although they are reported by earlier sources (Evans 1927: 18; Schebesta 1928: 276) to have used the blood sacrifice and they still remember it perfectly well, they say they now only sing to Jawac (the thunder-maker) and the earth-snake (who causes the up-welling flood) for ordinary offences (*talañ*;

---

[22] This is probably an adaptation of a Malay custom (see Skeat 1900: 441).

equivalent to Batek Dè' *lawac*). For *ceman* offences (improper sexual conduct), which are considered more serious, a shaman must make an offering of two small pandanus mats which have coloured designs on them. The shaman goes into a trance, and his shadow-soul (*'oway*) carries the shadows of the mats to Jawac and the earth-snake. This is considered 'payment' (*'opah*; Malay *upah*) in compensation for the offence. It makes the deities happy, so they stop the storm.

Among the Batek Dè', if a *lawac* offence has been committed by a member of the camp, someone must make the blood sacrifice or else the storm will not stop until a tree has fallen and killed the offender and anyone else in the way. Persons who break *lawac* prohibitions are not generally subject to serious reproach, so such violations are not concealed. In principle, the offender should perform the sacrifice and offer his or her own blood. Often, however, the actual or alleged offender is a small child who is barely old enough to understand the *lawac* rules. In that case, one of the parents cuts his or her own leg and then wipes the blood on the leg of the child before throwing it to the thunder-god. In this way, the blood takes on the odour of the child, and the deity is deceived into thinking that the actual offender has paid for the offence. Children are not cut because the parents fear that they might become ill from it. The children are frightened by this procedure, however, and it impresses upon them the seriousness of breaking *lawac* prohibitions. Usually the mother performs the blood sacrifice for a child, though the father will do it if the mother is absent or if her attempt does not succeed in halting the storm. Women claim that the men are not brave enough to do it first. Adults of both sexes do not often break *lawac* prohibitions themselves, at least not when they are camped near potentially dangerous trees, for they know the rules and believe that they will be punished for breaking them.

The blood sacrifice is known as 'throwing blood' (*'alòy yạp* or *songkac yạp*) to the Batek Dè'. The performer first takes a small knife and taps the point or cutting edge lightly against her shin. Either leg can be cut, but usually it is the left leg of a right-handed person and the right leg of a left-handed person.[23] When a few small cuts have been produced, the blood is scraped on to the blade of the knife. The leg must be freshly cut; it is *lawac* to use already flowing

---

[23] Supposedly only the legs are cut because cutting them is less likely to cause illness than cutting other parts of the body.

blood from a recent leech bite. A small container, usually a plate or tin but sometimes a split section of bamboo, is partially filled with water from the rain running off the thatch of the shelter or from a bamboo water container. The blood is then washed off the knife blade into the water. For fire *lawac* (the improper mixing of foods during cooking) and blood *lawac* (letting certain types of blood go into a stream), some of the blood and water mixture is then poured on the ground near, but not on, the cooking hearth. This blood is intended for the earth-snake and is supposed to ensure that the earth will remain firm. While pouring the blood mixture, the person may say something like: *tòn tòm jin, ya' yè' nan-kiyom té', pangku' té' yè'*, 'there is your water, grandmother beneath the ground, hold up my earth'. This may be shortened to just: *ya'*, 'grandmother'. The invocation may be omitted entirely, as the blood offering is thought to be effective by itself.

For fire *lawac* and blood *lawac*, the rest of the blood and water must then be thrown upward, and, for laughing *lawac*, throwing it upward is all that is required. That blood is intended for the thunder-god and is meant to make him stop the thunderstorm. Some Aring Batek throw it separately to east and west, for the two beings who make up Gobar (see Chapter 6), though there is no agreement as to the order in which it should be done. The Batek normally throw it only once in each direction, though the Mendriq say they pour it on the ground four times and throw it upward three times, apparently to make up the Malay mystical number seven. As they throw the blood mixture upward, the Batek usually shout *pak*, which is a word, now obsolete in normal speech, meaning 'catch' (see Skeat and Blagden 1906b: 554). This is often followed by a phrase such as: *mòh pangku' ketò' yè'*, 'you hold up my sky', or *mòh mereda' ketò' yè'*, 'you decrease my sky'. The latter phrase refers to the storm that has taken over the sky. The person performing the rite may also add something like *yè' bayèr kenring pesaka' mòh*, 'I pay the blood inheritance from you'. *Kenring* is a special word for blood, used only in this context. Probably it is the adjective *kering* (Malay *kering*), 'dry', with an infixed -n- making it 'the drying agent', that which is meant to dry up the rain. Perhaps the most commonly used invocation, both while pouring and throwing the blood mixture, is *nèng dosa' kerana' yè'*, 'there is no offence (or sin) because of me'. This seems to mean that the blood offering cancels out the offence. It is not to deny that the offence was committed, because, if the person considered herself (or her child) innocent, she would not have performed the rite at all. The invocations used while throwing the blood upward may also be omitted without reducing the effectiveness of the rite. The invocations merely make explicit some of the ideas connected with the blood sacrifice which are thought to be perfectly understood by the deities anyway.

After pouring and throwing all the blood and water mixture, the person performing the ritual may wipe the remaining blood off her leg with a good-smelling leaf, usually from some kind of wild ginger plant. She then puts this on a firebrand and burns it. As the smoke rises, she says: *jing, jing, jing, rabòn yè' hali' sayang, banrang ketò' yè' 'on, 'om pangku' ketò' yè' 'on*, 'listen, listen, listen, my fumigant is the *sayang* leaf [or whatever kind of leaf was used], brighten my sky there, hold up my sky there'. The smoke is supposed to be very good-smelling and therefore to be pleasing to Gobar. The leaf itself has a good odour, and the burning would remove the 'raw odour' (*pel'èng*) from the blood. Apparently the distinctive odour of the blood identifies the smoke with the person sending it.

There are several theories about how the blood reaches the deities in the blood sacrifice. Some say only the 'shadow' (*bayang*) of the blood, its red radiance, actually gets there. The lightning fetches it, like a camera taking a photograph, and carries it up to Gobar. Others say it is just the odour of the blood that arrives. The odour spreads upward like smoke, and also descends into the earth. Still other informants say the blood as a whole reaches the deities. Though the water in the mixture merely falls on the ground, the 'core' (*buku'*) of the blood is propelled into the sky by the throwing and into the earth by the pouring. Some say the blood thrown upward is received and carried to Gobar by the lightning.

There are also several different views of how the blood sacrifice accomplishes its purpose. One informant claimed that the blood does not go to the earth-snake and the thunder-god at all. He said that when a person breaks a *lawac* prohibition, *lawac* blood arises in his body. The blood sacrifice merely gets rid of some of that bad blood. Most Batek believe that some part of the blood reaches the deities, but many say they do not know what the deities want the blood for. It merely makes them happy to see that people have thrown it and to see that they are afraid. Some Batek say that Gobar is happy to get the blood because he uses it to cause the wild seasonal fruits to ripen. This notion is usually associated by the Batek with the view that it is only the *bayang*, the red colour of the blood, that reaches the deities. Gobar mixes the colour into the fruit blossoms or copies it on the skins of the fruits. This reddening causes them to ripen. Informants who say that only the odour of the blood reaches the deities claim, on the other hand, that the deities stop the storm because they do not like the smell; they are afraid of it. They say the odour is *pel'èng*, the odour of raw meat. It is not considered as bad-smelling as menstrual blood, but it is unpleasant none the less. Many Batek say that Gobar drinks the blood, and this makes him happy. Therefore he takes pity on the people who sent it to him. The earth-snake is also said to drink it or to send it to the thunder-god for him to drink. The deities drink the blood raw. This view is quite consistently associated by the Batek with the idea that the blood as a whole reaches the deities. These different views of how the blood sacrifice works are fully formed alternative conceptions, not just confused renderings of a single 'correct' interpretation.

The meaning and significance of the Negrito blood sacrifice has attracted some general interest among anthropologists. The deeper significance of the rite has been explored by Needham (1967) and Freeman (1968). Needham suggests that one of the reasons blood is used as the offering in this case is that it is a 'natural symbol', something that exerts a 'primordial impress on the unconscious mind of man as a natural species' (1967: 284). Freeman has proposed that the act of cutting oneself is a psychologically appropriate response to the terrifying danger of a thunderstorm (1968: 377). The more specifically cultural meaning of the rite for the Batek must, of course, be sought in the context of their own cultural conceptions. To the Batek, blood is a substance with somewhat contradictory properties. It is highly valued because it is essential for human life. It is infused with life-soul (*ñawa'*), and it is generally regarded as having come directly from the *hala'* (it is even termed an 'inheritance' from them in blood sacrifice invocations) rather than from the earth like most parts of the body. The *bayang* of the blood, its bright red radiance, seems to symbolize its life-giving properties. This is the aspect of the blood that contributes to the fruit supply. At the same time, blood carries the odour of raw meat. This is not only unpleasant in itself, but it has strong associations with danger, as it is the odour that attracts tigers. Thus, the Batek seem to be attracted to blood and repulsed by it at the same time. This ambivalence is quite similar to the ambivalence they feel towards Gobar. They consider him good because he produces fruit and bad because he punishes them for violations of the *lawac* prohibitions. This ambivalence is expressed in the curious belief that Gobar produces fruit, but human beings can only get it by stealing it. In a sense Gobar symbolizes the natural order which he maintains, for they both have their beneficent and dangerous sides. Blood, then, is an especially appropriate offering to make to Gobar because it expresses at once the positive and negative attitudes of the Batek toward him. The different interpretations of the blood sacrifice given by the Batek merely express these attitudes separately and in combination. Throwing blood to Gobar and his subsequent drinking of it re-establish a bond between man and deity that the *lawac* violation has broken. Ordinarily the Batek are at pains to associate themselves with the *hala'*, but Gobar is an exception. Because of their mixed feelings toward him, they resist entering into an intimate association with him unless they are threatened with the prospect of sudden death. The blood sacrifice binds the Batek not only into the highly appreciated fruit cycle, which Gobar in part maintains, but also into the restrictive system of *lawac* prohibitions, which he enforces.

6

DEITIES: DESCRIPTION

It seems that all the Negrito groups believe in a class of immortal superhuman beings, though the designation and divisions of that category vary somewhat from group to group. Most groups use some selection or combination of the terms *hala'*, *cenoi*, and *puteu* (or their cognates) to cover the class of beings called *hala'* alone by the Batek Dè'. The specific fields of reference for each term vary for different groups, however, often in intricate overlapping patterns. For example, the Batek Nòng use the term *potew* for all the superhuman beings, but they single out the 'fruit fairies' with the term *cemròy*. The term *hala'* is used specifically to indicate those *potew* who have lived on earth in human form and have now become guardian tigers. Schebesta found that the western Negritos used the term *hala'* primarily for shamans (1957: 120–56 *passim*), and they called the other superhuman beings by the Malay expression *orang hidop* ('living persons', i.e. 'immortals') (1957: 10). Perhaps this is a sort of *lingua franca* designation used by the western Negritos to overcome the differences in the connotations of the terms used in their individual languages. In any case, Schebesta says 'the *orang hidop* are also generally regarded as *Hala'*, which means that they were *Hala'* at the time they still lived on earth. The deity [Ta' Pedn], too, is a *Hala'* and, to be sure, the greatest of all' (1957: 122). He adds further that 'all beings embued with supernatural powers, who, however, are always personified, are *Hala'* and hence also *Cenoi*' (1957: 122). It seems that these terms refer to a single class of beings, and whether they are called *hala'*, *cenoi*, or *orang hidop* depends on which of their characteristics is to be emphasized: their magical powers, their connection with fruit, or their immortality. The overlapping of these terms suggests that the western Negritos, like the Batek Dè', consider there to be a fundamental unity of superhuman beings ranging from the 'deities' to the shamans.

It is arbitrary and artificial to separate out a class of 'deities' from the superhuman beings of the Negritos. Nevertheless, Evans refers to some of them in this way (1937: 138–58 *passim*), and Schebesta, while expressing reservations about Evans's use of the term 'deities' (Schebesta 1957: 10), has no such reservation about terming one of the superhuman beings (Ta' Pedn) 'the deity' (*die Gottheit*) (e.g. 1957: 122, 133) and 'God' (*Gott*) (e.g. 1957: 132). In fact there are perfectly good reasons for treating the more powerful and individualized superhuman beings separately in some contexts, even though such a grouping does not correspond to an explicit 'native category'. Certain of the superhumans stand out clearly from the faceless, nameless mass of *hala'* (or *orang hidop*). These are the beings who are seen as having a continuing influence over the lives of the Negritos and as being the dominating personalities in superhuman society. They are individualized to the extent that they are given personal names or titles, and they have distinctive personalities and other characteristics. Although they are superhuman beings, with all that that implies, they are also much more. Therefore I shall further examine those superhumans who are individualized and of continuing importance to man in an attempt to explain their full significance in Negrito religious conceptions. Whether they are called 'deities' or not is unimportant; I retain the term as a useful working label without implying that they fit all the connotations of the English term. Perhaps it should be noted in advance that they are least like deities in our sense of the word in that they are not venerated or worshipped. In fact some of them are less respected than the great mass of anonymous superhuman beings.

In this and the following chapter I broaden the inquiry to include all the Negritos of the Malay Peninsula. One reason for this is that the conceptions of the Batek Dè' cannot be fully understood except in relation to certain general patterns in Negrito deity concepts which are not evident in the beliefs of any particular group. Also, there has been a great deal written about the deity concepts of the Malaysian Negritos (see e.g. Evans 1937: 138–58; Schebesta 1957: 10–34; Freeman 1968), and yet I do not think they have been completely and correctly explained. I therefore add my own data from the Batek (of all dialect groups) and the Mendriq to that already published by other researchers, which is mainly on the western Negritos, and attempt a complete reinterpretation of the subject.

Deities of the Batek Dè'

Thunder-god

The thunder-god of the Batek Dè' is called Gobar, which is also the term for thunder itself. The name 'Gobar' is probably derived from Malay *gobar*, 'gloomy, overcast (of sky)'. The deity is associated with dark, threatening clouds as well as with the actual thunderstorm. He is said to be the same as Karei, the name given the thunder-god by the Batek Teh and most western Negritos. When thunder occurs, the Batek Dè' say 'Gobar is making noise' (Gobar *'o' kenglüng*) and 'Gobar is angry' (Gobar *'o' marah*). In everyday discourse, thunder and thunderstorms are attributed to Gobar, and he is referred to with the third person singular pronoun *'o'*. Yet it is often said in story-telling contexts and in discussions of the cosmos that Gobar is actually two *hala'* beings. (Like the Batek, I shall refer to Gobar in the singular except when his duality is especially pertinent.) The Aring Batek generally say that Gobar is two brothers who are named Mạwạs (the elder) and Nạwạs (the younger). The Lebir people usually describe Gobar as two brothers, who are both known only as Gobar, but they occasionally refer to them as a brother and sister or a married couple.

Both the Lebir and Aring Batek Dè' agree that Gobar once lived on earth in human form. He even ate tubers which were dug for him by his aunt (*be'*). The following is a brief summary of his exploits on earth before he became the thunder-god.

In the early days when some of the *hala'* then living on earth were being changed into tubers and seasonal fruits, Gobar (or Mạwạs and Nạwạs in Aring versions) decided he wanted to become a honey-bee. The existing *hala'* bees warned him that they would burn him if he did, because he had smoked them out of their nests before to get their honey. But he ignored them. He climbed a tree and hung beneath a limb as if he were a bees' nest. The bees then flew up to the branch carrying torches and began to burn him. He could not take the heat and fell screaming to the ground. That is why he now has bumpy skin and is one reason his voice is now so loud. Gobar was very depressed by this incident. He wandered on, going here and there, until he came to a tortoise (*hawang; Testudo* sp.). The tortoise startled him with its loud roaring voice. Gobar was jealous of the tortoise and proposed that they exchange voices. The tortoise refused, but Gobar took his voice anyway, and that is why the tortoise is now mute. Gobar went on until he met a *hala' kalèp* fruit. This is a type of fruit that bursts open with a loud 'pop' when it is mature. Gobar wanted his sound as well. The fruit *hala'* also refused to give it, but Gobar took it anyway. He even took the popping sound made by the *kalèp hala*''s blowpipe. Gobar went on until he came to the stone pillar that is now called Batu Keñam. The two *hala*' sisters who had originally built it as a shelter wanted to leave because the spider-hunter bird had turned it into stone. They ordered Gobar to live on the stone pillar and look after it. Then Gobar either climbed or jumped up Batu Keñam or was pulled up, on a string of wind (*tali*' *'angin*), by the *hala*' sisters or by his younger brother. In another version of the story, he shot a series of earth balls into the sky with his blowpipe. These formed a chain which he then climbed up.

According to the Lebir people, the two brothers who make up Gobar still live in a cave half-way up Batu Keñam, and the elder brother makes thunder toward the west while the younger brother makes it toward the east. The Aring Batek say the brothers later moved to Batu Balok, on the upper Relai River. Some say they then separated, the elder brother going to live on the ground at the eastern horizon and the younger brother at the western horizon.[1] When Gobar first went to live on Batu Keñam, his aunt went into the ground and became the earth deity, who is partially identified with the *naga*' that supports the earth. She is now called Ya' ('grandmother, old woman') by human beings.

The Aring people say that Mạwạs and Nạwạs make thunder by spinning stone tops (Malay *gasing*) which, according to some stories, they made from the earth-balls they shot into the sky. They are said to compete with each other to see who can make the loudest noise, and Nạwạs, the younger, usually wins. (He is also considered the cleverer of the two brothers.) I have never seen Batek using stone tops, but they occasionally make tops out of wood. When these tops are spun on a sheet of bark, they give out a roaring sound which could easily be likened to thunder. The Lebir people generally say that Gobar makes thunder with his mouth (it is the same whether he is spoken of as one or two persons). They often mention the remarkable contrast between the big voice of Gobar and his small body, which is no bigger than that of an ordinary Batek. Some informants claim, on the other hand, that Gobar's voice is no louder than a normal person's, but it is amplified by the 'rope of lightning' (*tali*' *kilat*) along which it travels. Lightning (*kilat*) is described by the Aring people as either the flashing of the cloth strips (*penjo*', 'breechcloth') used as a top cord or the light

---

[1] Neither the Lebir nor the Aring Batek consistently associate one brother with one direction and the other with the other direction; they are merely associated with opposite directions on the east-west axis.

reflected from the deities' bush-knives or daggers, worn in their waistbands, as they spin the tops. The Lebir people say that lightning is the reflection (*bayang*) of Gobar's red loincloth or of his red shirt which he borrowed from the *hala' kelkül* fruit (a fruit that is red when ripe) who formerly lived on Batu Keñam.

The image of the thunder-god (or gods) is rather complex. The Aring Batek describe Mạwạs and Nạwạs as looking like Batek 'youths' (*jemaga'*) when they were on earth. But the name Mạwạs recalls the word *mawas*, the Malay name for the orang-utan, which is known in the Malay Peninsula only as a fabulous giant ape which has, as an integral part of one forearm, an iron blade with which it cuts down trees (Skeat and Blagden 1906b: 283, 283n.). It also resembles the term *mawa*, one Malay name for the gibbon. After leaving the earth, both Mạwạs and Nạwạs are described as being black-skinned and young like a child below the waist, but old above the waist, with a long beard. However, one Aring man said that the two *hala'* who make up Gobar (whom he described as a married couple) look like water monitor lizards (*pacẹ̀w*) and live at the edge of the sea at the eastern and western horizons. According to the Lebir Batek, Gobar had human form when he lived on earth, and he retained this basic form after he went to live in a cave on Batu Keñam. But he now has bumpy skin, the legacy of his encounter with the bees. Also, he is now extremely old. Some say he is toothless, and that his skin is white and like iron.[2] Both the Aring and Lebir people agree that Gobar wears a red shirt. It is the reflection of this shirt that causes the red glow on the clouds at sunset. The many variations and inconsistencies in the images of the thunder-god do not disturb the Batek, probably because his primary manifestation is auditory, in the thunder, and visual images are only of secondary importance.

One important activity of the thunder-god, in conjunction with the earth deity, is the punishment of any Batek who breaks *lawac* prohibitions. All *lawac* acts are supposed to be punished by a thunderstorm, from Gobar, and a flood from the underworld, caused by the earth deity. According to the Aring Batek, when Gobar went up the stone pillar and his aunt went to the underworld, they made a specific agreement to punish *lawac* acts. Gobar told Ya' ('grandmother' as she is now called) that whenever humans laughed

---

[2] Some very old Batek lose pigment in parts of their skin, especially around the hands, leaving them with spots of 'white' skin.

at certain animals (e.g. leeches) she should dig upward underneath the camp of the offender and cause water to spurt up, dissolving the earth around him. At the same time, he would loose the wind and rain and create a thunderstorm in which the offender would be crushed under an uprooted tree. If humans did not commit these offences, however, she should 'hold back' (*tahan*) the underground waters, and he would hold back the forces of the heavens. He also instructed Ya' and all the other *hala'* to be on the look-out for breaches of the rules and to inform him if any were seen. The prohibition on incest seems to have been added later. The following story tells how this came about.

The earliest human beings had married their brothers and sisters because they did not yet know that it was prohibited. Once a *hala'* came to earth from the moon, where he then lived, and settled among the people. He dreamt that Gobar did not want people to marry their brothers and sisters (i.e. his 'shadow-soul' went to Gobar and was informed of this) and that henceforth they should seek their spouses outside their immediate families.[3] To break this rule was *lawac*, punishable by flood and storm. In addition, Gobar might afflict the offender with certain diseases which would cause pain and sometimes death. After the *hala'* informed the people of this and they understood, he went back to live on the moon.

There are apparently two types of disease used by Gobar as punishment for improper sexual behaviour (*cemam*). For less serious violations, such as merely standing or lying too near a prohibited relative, he sends the disease called *cemam* (like the English 'cold', *cemam* is the name of the disease and the alleged cause of it). Its symptoms are fever, stiffening of all joints and muscles, and sometimes death. There seems to be a feeling that the act of *cemam* itself, which is seen as the mixing of the odours and shadows of the offenders, is enough to cause the *cemam* disease without the direct intervention of Gobar. The other type of disease seems to be reserved for persons who have actually committed incest. It is caused by tiny sparks of lightning which lie in the forest under the leaves. A person who has committed incest will step on one of these and it then enters his big toe (of either foot), causing an illness which prevents him from standing up or walking. The Aring Batek call this disease *kelintar kayu'* after its supposed cause. The word *lintar* is Malay for 'lightning' (short for *halilintar*), and *kayu'* means 'tree' and 'wood'. According to this interpretation, the sparks of

---

[3] The Batek, unlike most Negritos, allow marriage of first cousins.

lightning that enter the victim's foot are splinters of wood which Gobar fashioned from some of the earth he shot into the sky. They are propelled to earth with a breechcloth, probably used as a sling. There is an obvious similarity between the spinning of the top to cause thunder and the hurling of the *kelintar kayu*' in that both implements come from the original earth and both are propelled by a breechcloth. The connection is confirmed by the belief that the flashing of the breechcloth in both cases causes lightning.

Another important activity of Gobar is looking after the fruit flowers on Batu Keñam or Batu Balok[4] and controlling the earthly fruit seasons (see p. 56 above). At the proper time of year, Gobar signals to the *hala*' to start taking the fruit blossoms to earth. He does this by making thunder during the day, but without causing a storm; this is the distant rumbling one actually hears in Kelantan in March and April. Soon after this thunder is heard, the flowers begin to appear on the fruit trees. This goes on for several months as the different species come into bloom. If the people are worried that the fruit crop will be inadequate, they hold a singing session and send the shadow-soul of their shaman to steal some more blossoms.

Considering that Gobar is the pre-eminent figure in the Batek pantheon, their attitude toward him is surprisingly irreverent. They take great delight in telling how he was burned by the bees, and they consider it amusing that he is covered with ugly bumps as a result. Gobar is considered less *hala*' than the 'genuine' or 'true' *hala*' (*hala*' *biyayah*) who live on top of the firmament. That is why, according to some accounts, the two *hala*' sisters who created Batu Keñam had to pull Gobar up to the cave. Perhaps the placement of Gobar only half-way up the stone pillar is meant to symbolize his inferiority to the *hala*' above the firmament. Yet even though Gobar is not respected, the rules he enforces are. The Batek generally follow the various prohibitions because they are afraid of the thunderstorm. They do not fear Gobar personally, however, unless they have broken a rule. Gobar is not regarded as cruel or arbitrary in his punishments, though he can, it seems, make mistakes. If a thunderstorm passes over a camp when no one has broken a prohibition, the Batek are indignant and do not hesitate

---

[4] The Aring people who say that Mawas and Nawas have now moved to the eastern and western horizons still seem to associate them with the fruit blossoms on Batu Balok.

to call out to Gobar that they have done nothing wrong. This is usually sufficient to get him to diminish the storm. The fruit blossoms Gobar sends to earth are sent more out of duty, one might say, than out of compassion for mankind. He is not swayed by personal appeals for extra flowers because he wants to keep them for himself. That is why the shaman must steal them. Thus, Gobar is not loved for the benefits he gives to man any more than he is hated for the punishment he metes out. He seems to be regarded merely as the agent by means of which the prescribed punishments are carried out and the seasonal fruit cycle maintained. He has little leeway for acting for or against man of his own volition, either inside or outside the context of these processes.

Earth deity

The earth deity of the Batek Dè' is a single being with a double image: an old woman and a giant snake (naga'). The Aring Batek emphasize the old woman image, though they verbally identify her with the naga'. She is the aunt of Gobar who went into the earth when Gobar went up Batu Keñam. She now lives in the under-ground sea, directly under the centre of the earth. She is normally called only Ya' ('grandmother, old woman') by the Batek, though one informant thought that her proper name was 'Arac, which is similar to the name given her by the Batek Nòng—Raròc.[5] To the Lebir Batek, the earth deity is simply the naga' (the 'turtle-snake') that supports the earth. They do not have the story of Gobar's aunt going into the earth. It is called Ya' merely as a courtesy, because it would be offended if it were called a naga' or snake. They generally picture the naga' as a huge snake which is sometimes said to have large horns (like those of the dragons that are often pictured on Chinese medicines and other goods). This is the naga' through which the sun passes on its journey under the earth. It is not known whether this being is male or female. Though the naga' looks like a snake, it speaks like a Batek. There are many lesser naga', both male and female, who live in the underground sea, in rivers, and in pools on mountains. Ordinary snakes are said to be special friends of the naga', and that is one reason adduced for the prohibition on eating them.

---

[5] These names are probably related to the name 'Arud' which is given by the 'Sakai-Jakun' of the Tekam River in north central Pahang (probably the people now called Semaq Beri) to an old woman who lives in the underworld with her pet dragons in a house made of the bones of the dead (Evans 1923: 209–10).

The earth deity supports the earth and keeps it from being dissolved in the underground sea. The old woman is said to 'hold back' the underground sea, and the *naga'* is pictured as holding the earth on its back. But the earth deity can deliberately let the waters burst through the earth to punish any Batek who breaks prohibitions. The old woman does this by digging upward with her digging-stick underneath the offender. The *naga'* accomplishes the same thing simply by shifting slightly, thus letting part of the earth open up. The earth deity collaborates with Gobar in punishing the wrong-doing of man. In the story of the Aring people, Gobar and the aunt made an explicit agreement to his effect. They both watch out for transgression and inform the other when any are seen. Then together they punish the offender using thunderstorms and upwelling floods. For most offences, both Gobar and the earth deity receive a portion of the blood sacrifice which is made to stop the storm and flood.

The Batek are ambivalent toward the earth deity, just as they are toward Gobar. They realize that both are necessary for the well-being of man, but they dislike being punished by them for their misdeeds.

Tohan

The name 'Tohan' is obviously derived from Malay 'Tuhan' which means 'God'. The Batek Dè' generally picture Tohan as looking like a Batek because, they say, the first human beings were modelled after him. He is like an old man with black curly hair and brown skin. His distinctive feature is that he has grass growing on his back and a small green spot on the back of his neck where tiny trees are growing. This is the 'sign' (*tana'*) that he is Tohan and one of the original superhuman beings (*hala' 'asal*). He is generally spoken of as one being, though he may have several bodies in different places. Some say he lives with a wife who looks like him and is also called Tohan. There is little agreement about his location. Some Batek say he lives where the sun goes down and others say where the sun comes up. Still others claim that he moves back and forth between those two places or that his shadow-soul cycles between separate bodies which remain at the places of sunrise and sunset. The Aring Batek generally maintain that the life-soul, which Tohan sends and retrieves, goes west at death like the shadow-soul. But those Aring people who place Tohan in the east reconcile these two ideas by saying that the life-soul goes under the earth, like the sun, to reach the place of Tohan. The differences of opinion on the location of

Tohan do not vary systematically between the Aring and Lebir groups. Tohan is considered to be unrelated to Gobar and the earth deity and independent of them, neither subordinate nor super-ordinate. Unlike them, he seems not to have spent any time on earth in any form.

The main concern of Tohan is the maintenance and continuation of human life. It was he who gave the life-soul to the first couple and sent them instructions telling them how to reproduce. He is now the custodian of human life-souls (*ñawa' 'angin*). He is said to sit with a plastic bag full of *ñawa'* (some say the bag even has a zipper) and to take out a bit whenever a baby begins to develop and send it on the wind into the mother's womb. He can also send more life-soul to a living person to increase his years of life. He constantly replenishes the supply of life-soul in his bag, however, by taking back the life-souls of persons who have lived their allotted number of years, thereby causing their death. Tohan also punishes people for gross breeches of proper social conduct (*tolah*) (see pp. 81–2 above).

The Batek are ambivalent toward Tohan as well. Although he gives life, he also takes it away, sometimes at rather inopportune times. And if he had not withheld the water life-soul after Allah dropped it, man would not die at all. The Batek seem to think of Tohan as rather distant and unapproachable. I have never heard of shamans trying to influence Tohan as a method of curing. The attitude seems to be that when a person's time is up, Tohan takes his life-soul, and there is nothing that can be done about it.

Other beings

There are a few other beings in the Batek Dè' pantheon who might arguably be classed as deities. One is Tahun, a superhuman being who is responsible for the production of seasonal fruit (*kebü' tahun*). He is supposed to look like an ordinary Batek, but his skin is a bit reddish in colour, perhaps because that is the colour of many seasonal fruits when ripe. Those Aring Batek who mention Tahun say he lives on Batu Balok. He watches over the fruit blossoms there and drops them to earth, or sends other *hala'* down with them, when Gobar rumbles. The few Lebir Batek who describe Tahun as a single being say he lives on top of the firmament. When Gobar rumbles, Tahun's chest bursts open, sending fragments of his shadow-soul to all the fruit trees (of all species) on earth. After the fruit has begun to develop, the pieces of Tahun's shadow-soul return to his human-form body. Most Batek, however, leave Tahun out of their descriptions of the process of fruit production. Usually it is said that the fruit blossoms are sent by the *hala'* in general or by numerous *hala' tahun*, 'seasonal fruit superhumans', following orders from Gobar (see p. 56 above). Tahun seems to be mentioned mainly by those Aring people who place Gobar at the eastern and western horizon. He takes over the position of Gobar as the sender of fruit flowers from Batu Balok, but he does this only when Gobar signals to him with the distant rumbling thunder.

The attitude of the Batek toward Tahun and the *hala'* who bring fruit is very positive. The great love of the Batek for fruit seems to spill over on to the beings who supply it (unless, as in the case of Gobar, the supplier of fruit is also a punisher). These beings are considered generally sympathetic and helpful to man. It is they who initiate most of the useful dreams that come to the Batek. These beings, while not individualized enough to be called deities (except in the case of Tahun), are very important in the lives of the Batek. To a large extent the Batek's optimistic outlook on life is due to their belief that the cosmos is thickly populated with helpful and sympathetic beings, a radical difference from the Malay belief that the world is full of 'evil spirits' (*hantu*).

Two other beings who could be considered deities are Angin, 'Wind', and Ujan, 'Rain'. They occasionally appear in stories as living on earth in human form, and some informants say that they now live on Batu Keñam or Batu Balok, still in the form of men. They are the beings who send out the wind and rain in the thunderstorm, following orders from Gobar. Yet more commonly these tasks are said to be performed by Gobar himself. He sends out the wind and rain by opening the doors of the caves in which he keeps them or, according to other stories, by propelling them down the ropes of wind and rain.

The question of whether Tahun, Angin, and Ujan are deities or not does not hinge on whether they fit my definition of a deity but on whether they exist at all. When they are mentioned, they are both individualized and of continuing importance to man, but more often than not they are left out of descriptions of the processes in which they are supposedly involved. Then Gobar is said to produce the storm, including the wind and rain, and the fruit, though with help from the anonymous *hala'* above the firmament. The personified beings—Angin, Ujan, and Tahun—appear to be mere epiphenomena of the forces which they are supposed to control. In each case Gobar is the ultimate cause, and the existence of Angin, Ujan, and Tahun depends on whether a proximate cause is hypothesized as well. When they do exist as separate beings, they act only under orders from Gobar.

I do not regard such mythological figures as Allah, Ta' Allah, Nabi Adam, and the sandpiper bird as deities because they are of no significance to the Batek today. They appear only in stories of ancient times, and have now withdrawn from contact with man. Although they are individualized, they are essentially similar in the parts they play to the myriad unnamed *hala'* who are supposed to have spent some time on earth.

Structure of the Batek Dè' pantheon

The location of the deities in the Batek Dè' pantheon conform to the two main axes of the Batek cosmos: up-down and east-west. Generally pairs of related beings are placed on one of these axes, in opposite directions from the centre. When viewed as a unitary being, Gobar is complementary to the earth deity with whom he shares the duty of enforcing the *lawac* prohibitions. He is above the earth on the central axis (either Batu Keñam or Batu Balok) and she is below it in the same position. But there is a partial division of Gobar which associates him with east and west as well. The division of Gobar into two beings is only weakly developed by the Lebir Batek. They do not give the two beings separate names, and they place them together in a cave on Batu Keñam. They are associated with east and west only to the extent that their voices—the thunder—go out in those two directions. The Aring Batek make a sharper distinction, giving the two beings separate names (though their unity is implicit in the fact that the names rhyme), and some go so far as to place one in the west and one in the east at ground level. This scheme places Gobar on the east-west axis while leaving the unitary earth deity at the bottom of the up-down axis. Tohan is also placed on the east-west axis, though he is sometimes said to be at one end of it and sometimes at the other (or to move back and forth). This disagreement regarding his location may well be due to the fact that he is a unitary being who is not paired with any other superhuman being. There is no other deity to occupy the opposite end of the east-west axis from him and thus to form a stable relationship of complementary opposition.

Celestial Deities of Other Groups

Batek Nòng

The Batek Nòng, like the Batek Dè', have a pair of principal celestial deities who are subsumed under a unitary entity in some contexts. Normally they attribute thunder and other meteorological phenomena to *ketò'*, the 'sky' (Malay *langit*). They say, for example, 'the sky thunders' (*ketò' 'o' gerger* or *ketò' 'o' kof*) (cf. Schebesta 1957: 25) and 'the sky is going to rain' (*ketò' 'o' mah hạc*). Although *ketò'* was not personified by my informants, Schebesta was led to believe that *ketò'* was a deity and in fact was the 'supreme being' of the Batek Nòng (1928: 276). But the Batek Nòng also say that a being named Jawac makes the thunder by throwing down a string with a stone on the end (*tali' sawoh*; probably Malay *tali sauh*, 'anchor cord'). The stone makes the noise, and the string is the lightning. Jawac is said to look like a pigtailed macaque (*bawac*; Malay *berok*; *Macacus nemestrinus*), the 'coconut monkey', and to be covered with hair, including a long beard. But he speaks like a Batek. He is supposed to live in the lowest layer of clouds and actually to carry (*yey*) them from the sea where they are produced by the action of the wind upon the waves. Jawac is said to 'open up rain, to break open the clouds' (Jawac '*o' boka' lesem, 'o' pecah kabut*) and to 'make the wind' ('*o' di' 'angin*). Jawac has a younger brother named Jawéc who lives on the 'fruit island' above the clouds and sun. Unfortunately I did not find out what he looks like. Jawéc watches over the fruit island and the *cemròy* ('fairies') that live upon it. When the *cemròy* hear thunder (presumably in the spring), they drop the flowers to earth, and the flowers become fruit. Jawéc is sometimes called Ta' ('grandfather, old man') Jawéc, although he is the younger brother, just as the Batek Dè' consider Ta' Allah to be the younger brother of Allah. Although Jawac and Jawéc are clearly distinguished, their essential unity is indicated by the similarity of their names. Like the names Mạwạs and Nạwạs, the mention of one immediately calls to mind the other.

The Batek Nòng also believe in a *naga'* who lives underground and is called Ya'. She is said by some informants to be the wife of Jawéc and by others to be the wife of Jawac. (This ambiguity, like the rhyming names, further demonstrates the unity of the two brothers.) Jawac co-operates with Ya' to punish humans who break the *talañ* prohibitions, which are similar to those called *lawac* by the Batek Dè'.

He causes a punitive thunderstorm, and she dissolves the earth beneath the offender with an upsurge of water. Jawéc does not participate in the punishment, but merely informs the others when he sees humans breaking the prohibitions. I was not told any stories in which these beings appear on earth, and one informant explicitly denied that they could be identified with any of the heroes in the stories I did collect. But there is some evidence that two of these mythical heroes, Teng and Bonsu (Malay *bongsu*, 'last-born'), are somehow equivalent to Jawéc, the guardian of the fruit island. Evans writes that Teng and Bonsu are two brothers who 'live above the seven layers of the sky. Bonsu looks after fruits and flowers. His fruits fall from above, and his flowers also, and become fruits and flowers on earth . . . Teng also looks after fruits and flowers' (1927: 17). That Jawéc should be represented here by two brothers can be understood as merely another instance of the bifurcation of deities, a common pattern in the religious conceptions of the Malaysian Negritos.

Although the celestial deities of the Batek Nòng are generally similar to those of the Batek Dè', there are some interesting differences in detail. One important difference is that the Batek Nòng brothers are distinguished on the vertical axis, rather than in terms of east and west, the younger brother being above the older. This ties in with a difference in the division of labour between the brothers. Among the Batek Dè', both Mạwạs and Nạwạs make thunder, in opposite directions, and both are involved in the making of fruit. But among the Batek Nòng, only Jawac makes thunder and only Jawéc makes fruit. Finally, the Batek Nòng regard the earth deity as the wife (*ji'*) of one or the other of the celestial brothers, while the Batek Dè' consider her their 'aunt' (*be'*), as she was called on earth.

Batek Teh and Mendriq

The pantheon of the Batek Teh and the closely related Mendriq is structurally simpler than the foregoing: there is only one major celestial deity, the being called Karei. The Batek Teh always equate Karei with Gobar, rather than with Mạwạs or Nạwạs, whenever they are comparing their ideas with those of the Batek Dè'. The Batek Teh say that Karei is as large as a mountain, wears golden clothes, and carries an enormous sword made of gold and iron with which he cuts down trees and kills spirits (Malay *hantu*).

Thunder is thought to be his voice and lightning his shadow or reflection (*bayang*), just as the rainbow is the 'reflection' of the *naga*' under the earth. Karei is supposed to sit above on the clouds except during the time of floods when he retires to the top of Batu Hala' on the upper Relai River (equivalent to Batu Balok of the Batek Dè'). When Karei withdraws, the *naga*', seen as a huge snake, comes out of the ground and causes the rivers to overflow. The time when Karei is out on the clouds includes the fruit season, and it is said that when he rumbles in the distance, he is causing flowers to come to earth and become fruit. When the first fruits of certain species and the first honey are brought in each year, some incense must be burned and a spell recited or Karei will send a tiger to kill the person who gathered them or will cause him to fall out of a tree. Karei and the *naga*' co-operate to enforce *lawac* prohibitions, by causing storms and upwelling water, but they are not regarded as related. Karei is supposed to have once lived on earth in human form. In some stories he is accompanied by his younger brother 'Wind' (Angin). Eventually they ascended to heaven by climbing a tall tree and shooting balls of earth into the sky until they formed a rope which the brothers climbed up.

I did not find out the Mendriq image of Karei, but Schebesta records that he is 'black, tall, and has long limbs', which suggests that he still has the form of a *siamang* (a type of gibbon; *Hylobates syndactylus*), the form he had when he ascended to heaven (1957: 24). I was told that he makes thunder (which is also called *karei*) by gathering together wind from all directions at one spot and forming an enormous cloud which becomes hot and black like the large cauldron used for cooking the food of Chinese coolies (Malay *kawah Cina*). Thunder is the rumbling of the fire and lightning the sparks thrown out. Karei sits at the *hayạ' lawac* ('*lawac* shelter') which is in the sky and is made of clouds. He watches to see if people are breaking *lawac* prohibitions, and, if they are, he causes a storm. He is aided by a bisexual *naga*' underground which causes water to spurt up and dissolve the earth underneath the offender. Sometimes he calls the tiger to perform the punishment; he does this by rumbling at night. But when Karei rumbles during the day, first in the east and a few weeks later in the west, he is giving seasonal fruit flowers to the world. During the floods, when he is not heard and the fruit season is over, the fruit trees bathe and become cool and healthy. According to Schebesta, the Mendriq think that Karei once lived on earth, where he was called Rinjén or Putéu, with his wife Takel and their son Hanei (1957: 24). He gives the following story.

> *Rinjén* formerly lived on earth. Once, in the shape of a siamang, he met his wife *Takel* and his son *Hanei*. He kindled a fire at which all three warmed themselves. *Rinjén* kept turning around in front of the fire until he was thoroughly warm and then rose up to heaven where he still lives. After that he was called *Karei*. *Takel* made her dwelling in the interior of the earth. *Hanei*[6] went into the forest and became the tiger (1957: 24).

Probably the *naga'* is somehow associated with Takel, though the latter was never mentioned to me. Neither Schebesta nor I was told of any other major beings in the Mendriq pantheon, though there are several *hala'* birds mentioned in stories who act as 'culture heroes'.

Thus the celestial deity of the Mendriq and Batek Teh, Karei, is essentially a unitary being who both sends fruit and enforces *lawac* prohibitions by means of thunderstorms. The basic arrangement of beings is on the vertical axis with only traces of horizontal differentiation, for example, in the Mendriq notion that thunder must come from east and west before fruit flowers appear. The connection between the thunder-god and the tiger is closer in these two groups than in others. All groups believe in the existence of some *hala'*, tigers, but the Mendriq and Batek Teh seem to regard all tigers as instruments of the deity.

Western Negritos

The pantheons of the western Negritos, whom I have not visited personally, seem to be generally more complex than those already described. Yet I think the elaboration takes place along lines already revealed in the ideas of the eastern Negritos. Much of the complexity seems to arise from attempts to fit beings from the pantheons of adjacent groups, and even in a few cases from Malay folk-tales, into one's own cosmology without displacing the beings already there. Some of the complications probably resulted from the desire of the investigator to get a synthesis of pantheons which would not normally have been brought into conjunction, as in the meeting

---

[6] This should probably be *haney 'ap*, 'Friend Tiger' or 'Mister Tiger'. *Haney* is the standard appellation for the characters in Mendriq and Batek Teh stories. It is probably derived from Malay *handai*, 'comrade'. Penghulu Selé' (Batek Dè') claimed that any stories in which the term *haney* was used were Malay stories, but the Mendriq seem to use it in all their stories, including those of a very typically Negrito cast.

arranged by Schebesta between his Jahai and Lanoh informants (1928: 187–8; cf. Evans 1937: 143). This complexity occurs even when the different beings are, in some sense, the same beings but with different names. For example, the Mendriq, who are on the eastern edge of the block of western Negrito groups (see Map 2) have a simple pantheon in which the thunder-god is called Karei and the earth-god Takel. The Kensiu, on the western edge of that block of dialect groups, have a similar, almost as simple, pantheon, but the thunder-god is called Ta' Pedn and the major earth deity Manoij (Schebesta 1928: 250–5; 1957: 21–3). The Negrito groups in between—the Kintaq, Lanoh, and Jahai—incorporate all four of these beings into their pantheons in various arrangements. I shall briefly outline these schemes as set down by Evans and Schebesta and reserve for the next chapter the discussion of their significance. One note of caution: much of the disagreement among informants is over the 'kinship' connections among the beings rather than their locations, images, or actions. This emphasis seems to have come from the investigators and to go against the grain of the Negrito conceptions. Certainly ordinary notions of descent and marriage do not apply, for the superhuman beings of the Negritos have always existed and do not reproduce in the ordinary human way. Perhaps more important, 'kinship terms' are used in a broadly classificatory manner by the Negritos, e.g. the term for 'elder brother' normally applies to all cousins who are older than ego (or in some cases, whose parents are older than ego's parents) and, indeed, to all male Negritos of ego's generation who are older than he is. The terms for 'mother' and 'father' and especially those for 'grandmother' and 'grandfather' (*ya*' and *ta*' in Batek Dè') are used very broadly as honorific titles for revered older persons (see also Schebesta 1957: 22). The use of such titles for superhuman personages does not necessarily imply that they are seen as being involved in a kinship system, and I strongly suspect that the great variation in information recorded on the relationships among the *hala*' beings is due to each informant having to improvise an answer to an unnatural question, one for which his culture does not provide a ready reply. What, then, can we conclude from statements of the type 'Karei is the father of Ta' Pedn' or 'Karei is the elder brother of Ta' Pedn'? I think one can say only that terms denoting relative seniority indicate some degree of dominance of the elder over the younger. The less senior being is sometimes seen as more sympathetic to man and may act

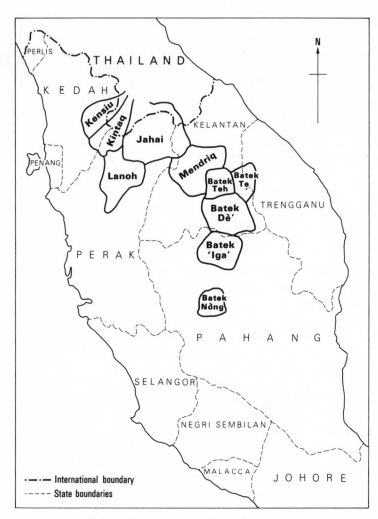

Map. 2. Locations of Negrito Dialect Groups

as an intermediary between man and the dominant older figure. Thus, calling one being the 'son', 'younger brother', and even the 'servant' of another (e.g. Schebesta 1928: 218) are very similar statements to a Negrito, indicating merely that one being has some kind of authority over the other.

Kensiu. The Kensiu of Kedah (mentioned above) regard Ta' Pedn as the main celestial deity and Ya' Manoij as the earth deity,[7] though several minor 'grandmothers' are also occasionally mentioned (Schebesta 1928: 251; 1957: 22–3). Ta' Pedn is supposed to look like a Malay raja but to be as white as cotton (Skeat and Blagden 1906b: 210). Ta' Pedn lives above, and it is he or one of his subordinates (Ćapong or Kělbö) who makes thunder (which is called *kaei*). It is made by swinging a rope or vine against one of the heavenly planks, the noise being the hitting of the plank and the lightning the flashing rope. Ta' Pedn uses thunderstorms to punish human beings for committing offences; the first peals of thunder are a summons to perform the blood sacrifice (Schebesta 1928: 252; 1957: 23). Ta' Pedn is supposed to boil the sacrificial blood and give it 'to the fruit trees so that it becomes various fruits for the use of man' (1928: 254). As with the Mendriq, the same being is the enforcer of prohibitions and the fruit-giver. Ta' Pedn and Ya' Manoij are said to have lived in the firmament together (in his early report Schebesta says they were married (1928: 251)), but to have descended to the earth after it was created by the dung-beetle. Later Ta' Pedn returned to heaven and Ya' Manoij went into the centre of the earth (Schebesta 1928: 251–2; 1957: 22–3). In one report, Ta' Pedn was said to have a younger brother, Kalchegn, who lives above him and 'holds the liana to which the sun is tied and swings it around' (Schebesta 1928: 250).

Kintaq. The Kintaq of southern Kedah and northern Perak believe in three major celestial deities—Kaei, Ta' Pedn, and Begjeg (also spelled Bagjeg, Begreg, Bajiaig, etc.)—two wives shared among them—Jalan and Jamoi—and two major earth deities—Ya' Takel and Ya' Manoij. The two celestial wives are explicitly said to be Malays, i.e. to come out of a Malay folk-tale (Schebesta 1928: 220; 1957: 19). The male celestial deities always appear in stories in sets of two, but the members of the pair are not always the same. In one story Kaei is the older brother and Ta'

---

[7] Skeat records the name 'Takell' for this being (Skeat and Blagden 1906b: 210), but Schebesta, working twenty-five years later, was given only 'Manoij'.

Pedn the younger (Schebesta 1928: 217). In another story Kaei and Begjeg appear together, and, though it is not explicitly stated that Kaei is older, it is he who gives the orders (Schebesta 1928: 219–20; 1957: 19). Similarly, descriptions of the pantheon usually only include two of these beings at a time, often making them the husbands of Jalan and Jamoi (Evans 1937: 143; Schebesta 1928: 219; 1957: 18–9). The pairings always establish Kaei as superior to Ta' Pedn and Ta' Pedn as superior to Begjeg. The problem for the Kintaq seems to be to fit three male beings to two positions in the stories and to two wives. One elaborate solution given to Schebesta (and diagrammed by him (1928: 218)) manages to incorporate all three celestial males, the two celestial wives, and the two 'grandmothers'. Although this scheme is probably somewhat atypical, a work of individual ingenuity, I quote Schebesta's account of it in detail because it clearly shows the principles used by the Negritos to order their pantheons.

Over the *rankel* [the fruit blossom wheel on top of Batu Ribm] dwells Begjag, a younger brother of Kaei; he is the ruler of Ligoi, the place of the winds. Below the *rankel* a beam or bridge, called *galogn*, stretches through the firmament from east to west, and upon this the sun pursues its course. This is also the dwelling-place of Kaei and Ta Pedn. Kaei sits at the eastern end on a mat, with his wife Jalam [*sic*] beside him. Ta Pedn lives on the western end, also sitting on a mat, his wife Jamoi beside him (1928: 217–8).

A second place lies under the ground to the east, where Manoid lives, the grandmother of the three male heavenly dwellers, Kaei, Ta Pedn, and Begjag (1928: 219).

In the third place, in the west, below Ta Pedn, sits Takel, the grandmother of the three heavenly women, Jalan, Jamoi and Chemioi (Chemioi is the wife of Begjag) (1928: 219).

This elegant scheme merely extends to a greater number of beings than previously seen the principle of opposing the members of pairs of beings on the east-west and up-down axes. Appropriately, the only unpaired figure—Begjag—is placed in the centre, over Batu Ribm. A much simpler, and probably more typical solution to the problem of fitting three beings to two positions (and wives) is that given to Schebesta on his later (1939) visit to the Kintaq. His informant then said that Kaei and Ta' Pedn were just different names for the same being and that Begjeg (Begjag) should be placed on the *galog'n* opposite Ta' Pedn (1957: 23). The lord of *ligoi*, the place of winds, was said to be a *hala'* named Ćimioi, who was earlier given as the wife of Begjag, rather than Begjag himself (1957: 18).

There is good reason to believe that this is a more typical conception of these matters for the Kintaq than the more elaborate scheme described above. In fact, the only story recorded in which Kaei and Ta' Pedn appear together apparently came from the same informant as that scheme (1928: 217). In all other stories *either* Kaei *or* Ta' Pedn is paired with Begjeg, the perennial younger brother. Moreover, the characteristics and behaviours attributed to Kaei and Ta' Pedn extensively overlap. According to Evans, Ta' Pedn is white (1937: 142), and Kaei is said to be 'fair in colour and covered with white hair' (Schebesta 1928: 220). Both Kaei and Ta' Pedn are supposed to cause thunderstorms as punishment for transgression of certain rules (Schebesta 1928: 221; Evans 1937: 142). Also Ta' Pedn controls the heavenly fruit in one account (Evans 1937: 148), and Kaei is supposed to have created the *rankel* from which all fruit comes (Schebesta 1928: 217, 220). The *cenoi* are said to love Ta' Pedn (Schebesta 1928: 218) and to be his subjects (Evans 1937: 142), but also to serve Kaei (Schebesta 1928: 225). It may well be that the introduction of the name Kaei for this being (rather than for thunder alone) was due to Schebesta's own use of the term which he had picked up among the Jahai and Lanoh (Schebesta 1928: 250). Evans uses the name Ta' Pedn alone (he spells it Tapern and Tak Pern) (Evans 1937: 141–9 *passim*). This makes it all the more remarkable that one of Schebesta's informants should have been able to integrate Kaei into the pantheon so neatly. Although Kaei-Ta' Pedn is supposed to 'command' thunder (which is termed *kaii* or *kaei*) and to cause it to occur when men misbehave, the actual work of making the noise is sometimes said to be done by his subordinates. Schebesta was told that a dragon called Tanyogn lies near Kaei, and it makes thunder by roaring and lightning by spouting water into the air (1928: 222). Evans records that Ta' Pedn makes thunder by commanding a stone to roll across some boards in heaven (1937: 142). But later informants (in 1935) said that 'Chemam, who lives below Tak Pern, makes thunder with his top-spinning' and that 'a person called Ang-lah also makes thunder (*kaii*) on a plank with a stone and thread' (1937: 143). Chemam, of course, is the term for 'incest' and the disease used to punish it among the Batek. Evans adds some interesting details concerning Chemam: 'Chemam, who looks like a gibbon (*mawah*), makes thunder with his mouth, . . . but when he gives sickness he looks like a Malay' (1937: 184).

Lanoh. The Lanoh live to the south and slightly to the east of the Kintaq, in Ulu Perak. It is somewhat difficult to separate the ideas of the Lanoh from those of the Jahai in Schebesta's work because much of his material was obtained in a mixed camp, and the informants obviously made some effort to accommodate their beliefs to those of the other group (see Schebesta 1928: 187–8). I therefore give slightly more weight to the material of Evans on the Lanoh and to the reports of Schebesta's Lanoh informants who were not part of that mixed camp. The Lanoh seem to regard Karei as the older brother of Ta' Pedn; they are similar in many ways, but are not merged (Evans 1937: 144; Schebesta 1928: 188–9; 1957: 14). By one account they are said to be married to Jamoi and Jalan, who live on the *galogn* in the sky (Schebesta 1928: 186–7; Evans 1937: 144), but others have Karei married to Manoij (Schebesta 1928: 188, 189; 1957: 14) and Ta' Pedn to Takel (Schebesta 1957: 14), both of whom live in the earth. Either way, the symmetry of the more elaborate Kintaq pantheon described above seems to exist here. In addition, the Lanoh recognize a being named Kapig'n (Schebesta 1957: 14), which means 'above, firmament' (Schebesta 1957: 11). He is said to be another younger brother of Karei (Schebesta 1928: 189). Karei is supposed to look like a *siamang* (gibbon) (Evans 1937: 144; Schebesta 1928: 188; 1957: 14), and both he and Ta' Pedn are covered with long, white, shiny hair (Evans 1937: 144). Other informants said Karei looks like a Malay (Schebesta 1957: 14), and even a Malay 'chief or prince' (Schebesta 1928: 185). When human beings commit offences, Karei is supposed to cause thunder (Schebesta 1928: 185, 189, 1957: 14; Evans 1937: 144) (how he does it is not stated), and Ta' Pedn 'throws down a huge quartz crystal which goes into the earth, and the waters well up from the hole it makes and drown the offenders' (Evans 1937: 145). The Lanoh say that

Karei inflicts four types of punishment: in the first he strikes the evildoer with lightning or fells tree-trunks to the ground; the second method is to send the tiger against the sinner to tear him to pieces (the tiger is Karei's policeman); thirdly, he sends certain diseases to follow the sin; and fourthly, for certain sins he insists on the blood sacrifice (Schebesta 1928: 189).

Blood is also sacrificed to Manoij (Schebesta 1957: 14). The sources do not say who is thought by the Lanoh to produce the seasonal fruit. According to Lanoh stories, Karei and his younger brother Ta' Pedn once lived on earth. One day they went on a fishing expedition up the Perak River. When they stopped for a smoke and a meal, they stuck their fishing rods in the ground, and when they looked up, the fishing rods had become mountains, the present Gunung Kenderong and Gunung Kerunai. The next night they made a circular hut in which they performed a magical ceremony, and then they ascended to the sky. Before they went to the sky, there was no thunder (Evans 1937: 144).

Jahai. The Jahai, who live east of the Kintaq and Lanoh in northern Perak and north-eastern Kelantan, consider Karei to be the father of Ta' Pedn[8] and also of Begreg and Karpeg'n (Schebesta 1928: 185, 186; 1957: 11, 13). One Jahai informant argued, however, that Karpeg'n was merely the 'firmament', the natural phenomenon, and he is left out of some schemes (Schebesta 1957: 11, 12). Manoij, who is Karei's wife, and their daughter Takel live in the earth (Schebesta 1928: 186; 1957: 11). Karei and Ta' Pedn seem to be separate and clearly distinct beings among the Jahai. Both are said to be shiny and bright like the sun (Schebesta 1928: 188; 1957: 13, 14), but Karei is also described as looking like a *siamang* (Schebesta 1928: 188; 1957: 14). Normally both are said to live in the sky (Schebesta 1928: 185, 186; 1957: 13), but one informant said that, while Ta' Pedn sits on a beam in the sky, Karei lives below in a cave (Schebesta 1928: 187; 1957: 14), perhaps meaning that he lives on Batu Ribm. Karei is the thunder-maker; he produces it by beating a rope (or vine) upon the ground while playing with his children (Schebesta 1928: 185; 1957: 15). The kind of play they engage in is not described. Karei communicates with Manoij by means of lightning, which also is not explained (Schebesta 1928: 188; 1957: 13). He and Manoij demand the blood sacrifice when men break his commandments (Schebesta 1928: 185-7; 1957: 12, 13, 15), and because of this Karei is considered 'evil', though it is admitted that he only punishes men when they misbehave (Schebesta 1928: 186; 1957: 12). Ta' Pedn is considered good; he intercedes on behalf of mankind, begging Karei to recognize their

---

[8] Schebesta was told by one informant in 1939 that in *čenoi* songs the name Karei is replaced by other names, such as Ta' Pedn and Jalan. Schebesta concludes that '*Karei* and *Ta Ped'n* are one and the same person' although 'in everyday life, people clung to the opinion that *Ta Ped'n* was the son of *Karei* and that *Karei* was the greatest of the *orang hidop* [immortals]' (1957: 15). There is no other evidence that the Jahai identify Karei with Ta' Ped'n, and there are many statements to the effect that they are distinct beings. I would argue that these *čenoi* songs came in from more westerly groups such as the Kensiu, among whom the thunder-god is named Ta' Pedn.

repentance and to stop the storm (Schebesta 1928: 186; 1957: 12).
Ta' Pedn is supposed to produce fruit and vegetables, while Takel
makes the tubers that grow in the ground (Schebesta 1957: 15), and
he is thought to be the creator of water, fire, and trees, though not of
the earth (Schebesta 1928: 187; 1957: 12, 13, 15). Yet Karei is
unequivocally stated to be superior to Ta' Pedn, who acts as Karei's
'servant' in his acts of creation (Schebesta 1928: 187; 1957: 12, 13).
It appears that the Jahai have a division of labour between Karei
and Ta' Pedn which is similar to the Batek Nòng division between
Jawac and Jawéc, the first member of each pair being the thunder-
maker and the second the fruit-producer. And in both cases the
subordinate being appears relatively benevolent, probably because
he is detached from the punitive role, and he becomes an intermediary between man and the thunder-maker.

It seems that the western Negritos merely distribute the various
activities and images of the celestial deity to a greater number of
beings than do the eastern Negritos. They give a separate identity,
for example to a specialized sky being (Kalchegn, Kapig'n, or
Karpeg'n) who is concerned primarily with maintaining the order
of the cosmos (e.g. holding up the sun), a duty which the Batek
assign to all the *hala' 'asal*. Also, the Kensiu and Kintaq have
specialized beings that actually make the thunder, though they act
under orders from Ta' Pedn. Regardless of how numerous the beings
are, however, their distribution, like that of the eastern Negrito
deities, tends to follow the simple pattern of vertical and/or
horizontal (east-west) differentiation of pairs of beings, with unitary
beings placed on a central axis.

Earth Deities of Other Groups

The Negrito earth deity combines features of a human female (the
relative of the thunder-god who went into the earth) and a *naga*, an
enormous dragon or snake which is found in the cosmologies of most
of the peoples of Indianized South-East Asia and Indonesia. The
relative importance of the two images differs for different Negrito
groups. The image of the earth deity as a human female seems most
prominent among the western Negritos. She is normally called 'Ya''
('grandmother') alone by the eastern Negritos, but the western
Negritos add a proper name, most commonly Manoij or Takel. The

image held of her by all groups seems simply to be that of a Negrito woman, the form in which she appeared on earth when the thunder-god also lived there in human form. The main difference from group to group is not in the image of the 'grandmother', but in the number of them. The Mendriq and all of the Batek dialect groups have only one. The Kensiu have one major earth deity, Ya' Manoid, but various minor grandmothers are occasionally mentioned. The Kintaq, Lanoh, and Jahai are generally reported to have two. Yet Evans records one version of the Kintaq pantheon in which there are three grandmothers who live in the earth: Yak Takel, Yak Manoid, and Yak Lepeh. The use of proper names for the grand-mothers is most frequent among the groups that have more than one, where the use of 'Ya'' alone would be ambiguous. The arrangement of the Ya' under the earth follows the same principles as the arrangement of the celestial deities above it. When there is only one, she is placed in the centre (e.g. the Aring Batek Dè'), and, when there are two, they are either placed one below the other (see e.g. Schebesta 1957: 15) or in the east and west (see e.g. Schebesta 1928: 219). There is some tendency for the number and arrangement of the earth deities to parallel those of the celestial deities, but the two sets of beings are at least partially independent. The example of the Aring Batek who place the two thunder-gods at the eastern and western horizons and the single Ya' in the centre of the world shows this independence clearly.

One of the main activities of the Ya' in all groups is causing localized floods which are used to punish persons who violate the *lawac* prohibitions by dissolving the earth underneath the offender's camp. These are called *henwéh* (or some cognate) by many of the Negrito groups (Evans 1937: 173, 174, 181), though the Batek Dè', like the Kintaq and the Kensiu (Schebesta 1957: 95), call them *talañ*, the term used by some groups (including the Batek Nòng) for the prohibited acts (i.e. as equivalent to *lawac*). All groups clearly distinguish these from ordinary floods (*banjil*). I do not know of any detailed descriptions in the literature of how the Ya' produces such floods, but the Batek Dè' picture of her digging upward under the offender's camp with her digging-stick is probably fairly typical. The notion of an earth-woman who punishes wrongdoers by flood may show ancient Buddhist influence. In the Buddhism of northern Thailand there is a story of an 'earth mother' named Dharaṇi who came up and destroyed Māra, the Buddhist embodiment of evil, by pulling her hair and thus causing a flood (Davis 1974: 172; Porée-Maspero 1961: 913). One version even states that she was awakened, before performing this act, by a thunderbolt from Buddha (Davis 1974: 286–7), just as Karei is sometimes said to communicate with Manoij through lightning (Schebesta 1957: 13).

Schebesta argues that one or another of the Ya' is responsible for the tuber crop just as one of the celestial deities is responsible for the fruit crop (1957: 15), and he thinks that the portion of the blood sacrifice which is given to the earth deity goes into the tubers as, in some schemes, the blood thrown upward goes into the fruit (1957: 92). This connection is not explicitly made by the eastern Negritos, as far as I know, but it is plausible in view of the general symmetry between the celestial and earth deities. The Aring Batek clearly associate the Ya' with tubers for they say that she was digging them for her nephew Gobar before she went into the ground.

The Hindu concept of the *naga* is extremely rich (see e.g. Bosch 1960), and it has been further elaborated in South-East Asia. Not all the Negrito groups associate all the attributes of the *naga* with the earth deity. Some of the typical features of the *naga* may not be known at all by a particular group, and some of them may be split off and attached to beings other than the earth deity. As I have mentioned, the Aring Batek have adopted little more than the term itself, but other Negrito groups have taken over more of the typical *naga* associations. The eastern Negritos seem to emphasize the *naga* image more than do the western Negritos, though it may be that the importance of the *naga* has everywhere increased since the time of Evans's and Schebesta's reports, which are my main source of information about the western Negritos. The Mendriq spoke to me only of the *naga'* (they, like all Negritos, pronounce it with a final glottal stop), whereas they had described their earth deity to Schebesta as a woman named Takel (Schebesta 1957: 24). A description of the Batek Teh ideas about the *naga'*, which I know well, will show some of the range of these associations and will show how some of these ideas could easily have become attached to the flood-making female earth deity. The Batek Teh picture the *naga'* as an enormous snake, about the size of a train. They do not know what sex it is. The *naga'* is coloured red on its back, yellow on its belly, and green in between. Its clothing is made of gold, with which it is always associated. The rainbow is the shadow or reflection of the *naga'* which is cast into the sky above. This idea is held by all the

Batek dialect groups and most of the other Negrito groups as well
(see Schebesta 1957: 66–70). The Batek Teh say that any rain falling
through the rainbow is 'hot rain' (Malay *hujan panas*) and can cause
fever, but this is basically a Malay belief, and the Batek actually
show little, if any, fear of hot rain. The *naga'* is assigned several quite
different living places, which suggests that there are more than one
naga'. The Batek Teh sometimes acknowledge this, in fact, but they
usually speak as if there were only one. The *naga'* is sometimes said
to live in the underground sea. It is also said to live at the bottom
of a deep pool, called *manko'* (Malay *mangkuk*, 'bowl'), which is on
Gunung Tahan, the highest mountain in the Peninsula.[9] This pool
is the bathing place of the *hala'* and is said to be full of gold. *Naga'*
(probably more than one) also live in the headwaters of the major
rivers. Sometimes these *naga'* rush down the rivers, causing floods
and landslides. This association of the *naga'* with mountains, floods,
landslides, and rainbows is found also among the Malays (Skeat
1900: 14–15) and certain other Malaysian aborigines (e.g. Evans
1923: 208). The widespread distribution of this association of ideas
may be indicated by the following report from the Kédang people
of Lambata, an island near Timor in eastern Indonesia. The *ular
naga* ('*naga* snake') of Kédang 'lives near the top of the mountain.
No one seems to have seen it, but it was described as being very big
round, and was said to come out of its hole at the top of the mountain
during the rainy season. A very large destructive flash-flood is said
to be caused by the emergence of the *ular naga'* (Barnes 1974: 39).
The Kédangese also believe in guardian spirits in the form of snakes
which live in springs. They are not called *naga*, but the resemblance
to the Malay and Batek Teh ideas is obvious: 'A rainbow (*nado-tado*)
seen near the spring is this snake. Rainbows are particularly associated with gold and are one of the forms which may be taken by the
snake-like guardian spirit within gold' (Barnes 1974: 62).

The Batek Teh seem to view the punitive acts of the *naga'* as being
like causing a landslide underneath the offender. The dissolution of
the earth in both cases is described in the same terms: *tè' 'o' rentoh*,
'earth collapses' (Malay *tanah runtuh*). In fact the spots that have
been pointed out to me as having been destroyed by the *naga'* are
always the places where a riverbank has collapsed. Unlike the usual
conceptions of the Ya', the Batek Teh *naga'* is associated not only

[9] This is probably the same as the pool called Tingring in the Batek Dè' trancing
song given above (p. 147).

with localized punitive up-wellings of water, but with floods in general. In fact, there are indications that the Batek Teh, like many of the peoples of Cambodia and Thailand, associate the *naga'* with the whole of the rainy season. They describe the alternation between the rainy season, when there are floods but little thunder, and the less rainy seasons, when thunderstorms are prominent, in terms of the movements of Karei and the *naga'*. They say when Karei retires to Batu Hala', at the beginning of the flood season, the *naga'* comes out into the rivers, and, when the *naga'* goes back into the headwaters, Karei goes out to live on the clouds.

Another Batek Teh conception which has to do with the *naga'* is the notion that there is another world underneath the rivers in which *naga'*-people go about in human form, only taking the shape of snakes at night. That world is in all particulars a duplicate of the one on the surface of the earth, but the rivers we know form the sky of the *naga'*-world. The *naga'*-people are like us except that they eat all their food raw and do not use fires. If a human shaman dives down there, he must be brave or the *naga'*-people will kill and eat him. But, if he is brave, he will be given food and wives. This conception is almost identical to one recorded for the Land Dayaks of Sarawak, even down to the ordeal which a human visitor must go through (Geddes 1961: 100–3). I am told by Gérard Diffloth (personal communication) that some groups of Semai (Senoi aborigines) in the Peninsula have a similar belief, and no doubt other peoples in Indonesia have it as well. It appears in one Batek Dè' story also, but in a very abbreviated form. It is not mentioned for any other Negrito group in the literature, and it may be a conception that has come in from non-Negrito sources in the recent past.

For the Batek Teh, like the Lebir Batek Dè' and possibly the Mendriq, the *naga'* attributes of the earth deity overwhelm the human ones. The Aring Batek Dè' and the Batek Nòng seem to maintain a fairly even balance between the two images, and the western Negritos emphasize the image of the old woman. One can easily see the overlap between the notions of a being that lives in the headwaters of rivers and causes floods and landslides and an underworld deity who punishes human misbehaviour by dissolving the earth under the offender with an upsurge of water from the underground sea. The images of the *naga'* and the 'grandmother' may seem rather incompatible, but the common association with underground water and floods seems powerful enough to override those differences in what must be regarded as more superficial imagery.

Tohan

The name Tohan did not come up in my investigations of any group other than the Batek Dè', but this may have been simply because I did not go deeply enough into the matters with which he might be associated, such as sending souls to babies, with the groups I did not visit for extended periods. I am quite certain, however, that he has no place in the Batek Teh pantheon. Tuhan appears in the reports of Vaughn-Stevens, a controversial collector for the Berlin Ethnographical Museum who worked with the Kintaq in the early 1890s (see Skeat and Blagden 1906a: xxvi–xxvii; Schebesta 1957: 6), as a deity who, along with 'Ple', is subordinate to Kaei (Schebesta 1957: 21; see also Skeat and Blagden 1906b: 209, 209n.). But Vaughn-Stevens seems often to have mixed reports from different ethnic groups ('Ple' is probably a Temiar deity), so it is difficult to know what to make of this reference. Tuhan is not mentioned by later investigators of the Kintaq. The main function of the Batek Dè' Tohan seems to have been performed by the thunder-god among the people investigated by Vaughn-Stevens. He writes that 'before they leave the presence of Kari the souls sit in the branches of a big tree behind his seat and there wait until he sends them away' (quoted in Skeat and Blagden 1906b: 5).

Other Beings

Not all the Negrito dialect groups have a specialized fruit deity like Tahun of the Aring Batek. Sometimes the production of fruit is attributed to the thunder-god, as in the cases of the Mendriq and Batek Teh Karei and the Kensiu Ta' Pedn. But Jawéc of the Batek Nòng and, I will argue, Ta' Pedn of the Kintaq, Lanoh, and Jahai can be classed as basically fruit deities. All groups seem to have 'fruit fairies' (called *ćenoi* by the western Negritos, *cemròy* by the Batek Nòng, and *hala' tahun* by the Batek Dè' and Batek Teh) who bring the fruit blossoms to earth (see e.g. Evans 1937: 142–305 *passim*; Schebesta 1957: 130–2). Among the western Negritos they have the added importance that they are the 'spirits' that possess the shamans in a type of spirit-raising seance (the *pano'* ceremony)

(Schebesta 1957: 129). Wind (*'angin*) and rain (*'ujan*) are not generally deified among groups other than the Batek, though occasionally there is a deity such as the Kintaq Begreg who is described as the ruler of *ligoi*, the 'place of the winds' (Schebesta 1957: 17–8). All groups know a number of minor superhuman beings who appear in stories in human or animal form. I do not treat these as deities, however, except when, as in the case of the thunder-god, they later become associated with a continuing process which affects the lives of the Negritos today.

7

DEITIES: INTERPRETATION

Previous Researchers

Evans

Evans says 'I have in writing of the Negrito gods previously spoken of them as ancestor deities and, on the whole, I do not think I shall withdraw this description' (1937: 140). He says the Menik Kaien and Kintaq Bong deity Tapern (Ta' Pedn) 'appears to be a kind of deified tribal ancestor' (1937: 141). He cites as evidence two stories in which the heroes, including Ta' Pedn and Begjeg, have various adventures on earth and then ascend to the sky where they now live as deities (1937: 140, 141, 232–3). He adds that in 1935 he asked the Kintaq about the term 'Tata', recorded by Schebesta as a title for Ta' Pedn, and he 'found that "ancestor" is the correct translation' (1937: 151).

Evans does not explain exactly what he means by 'ancestor deity', but the evidence he adduces suggests that he means merely that the people think the deities were once men. Certainly he does not argue that there is anything like an 'ancestor cult' in which deceased members of the group are remembered and their ghosts thought to become deities. The Negritos I have met seldom know anything about their deceased relatives beyond the second ascending generation, and there is no attempt made by individuals or groups to claim descent from particular or generalized ancestors, deified or otherwise. Nor does Evans give any evidence to the effect that the deities are thought to have been the parents of any human beings. As Schebesta points out, 'nothing is said about the procreation of human beings by the *orang hidop* [Batek Dè *hala*']. Human beings owe their existence to some act of creation, or their presence is accepted without much thought about their origin' (1957: 48). But even the relatively weak contention that the deities are thought to have once been men is not supported by the evidence. It is never said in the stories he cites that the heroes are ordinary human beings, but only that they lived at one time on earth among the ancestors of the Negritos (see Evans 1937: 141, 232–3). In fact the miraculous actions of the heroes in the stories make it plain that they are superhuman beings, and one of the characters in the second story is explicitly called a *halak* (*hala'*) (Evans 1937: 233). Many *hala'* beings are thought to have come to earth at times in the past, but they are clearly distinguished from ordinary persons by their possession, according to the Batek Dè', of immortal life-souls (*ñawa' tòm*) (see also Schebesta 1957: 52, 59). The deities and other *hala'* beings are normally said to have existed since before the creation of the world (e.g. Schebesta 1957: 35), whereas human beings are generally said to have been created, at a later time, by the deities (Schebesta 1957: 48–52). Thus it would be impossible, in terms of this set of beliefs, for the deities to have arisen from dead humans since the deities were in existence before any humans. The only sense in which Evans's interpretation of the deities as deified ancestors could be true is if it were said that the idea of a deity is a glorified memory of a person who once actually lived but whose former humanity is now denied by making him a member of a class of beings who are immortal and have existed since before man came into being. Such a convoluted interpretation is not proposed by Evans, and there is no evidence for it.

The evidence of the title given Ta' Pedn is at best ambiguous. The term *tata* may well mean 'ancestor', as Evans says (1937: 151), as well as 'little grandfather' (Schebesta 1957: 18), just as one Malay term for ancestor—*nenek*—also means 'grandmother' and 'great-grandmother'. But the term *tata*, like the common Negrito term *ta'* ('grandfather, old man'), can be used as an honorific title for any respected older man (see Schebesta 1957: 11n., 22, 34, 52) and could very appropriately be applied to a deity.[1] The Batek refer to the earth deity as 'Ya'' ('grandmother, old woman, great-grandparent, ancestor') without any implication that they are related to her in any biological or quasi-biological way. Similarly, the Negrito custom of calling themselves the 'grandchildren' (Batek Dè' *kañcò'*) of a deity does not imply that they consider themselves to be descended from the deity in the ordinary sense.

---

[1] It might be argued that the honorific title *ta'* is already contained in the name Ta' Pedn, so an additional 'Ta'' or 'Tata' would have additional meaning, perhaps signifying 'ancestor'. I think this is merely a reduplication of the honorific title, however, resulting from the incorporation of the term 'Ta'' into the proper name, but I cannot be certain since I have not visited any groups which use the name Ta' Pedn.

Schebesta records a Kintaq story in which Kaei and Manoid create the first humans from clay, and he comments: 'Although in this legend it is definitely stated that Kaei and Manoid were not the parents of the first man and woman, but created them, the Kenta nevertheless call themselves the grandchildren of Kaei' (1928: 221). It seems that the use of such titles as *tata* for deities, if they carry the meaning 'ancestor' at all in that context, must be taken in a metaphorical rather than a literal sense.

Schebesta

Schebesta was a member of the *Kulturkreislehre* school of ethnology which centred round Fr. Wilhelm Schmidt of the University of Vienna (Benjamin 1973: v; Evans-Pritchard 1965: 104), and he interprets the Negrito deities in terms of Schmidt's theory of primitive religion. According to Schmidt, the 'primitive cultures' of the world, the 'food-gatherers', represent an earlier stage of human development than the more complex societies (1931: 238), and they therefore retain more traces of the religion of ancient man than do others (1931: 257). The most prominent feature of early religion, he suggests, is the idea of a 'high god', a 'Supreme Being' (who is obviously similar to the Christian God), in a system of monotheism. He writes:

Comparing the primitive cultures with the later ones we may lay down the general principle that in none of the latter is the Supreme Being to be found in so clear, so definite, vivid and direct a form as among the peoples belonging to the former . . . This Supreme Being is to be found among all the peoples of the primitive culture, not indeed everywhere in the same form or the same vigour, but still everywhere prominent enough to make his dominant position indubitable (1931: 257).

This Supreme Being is supposed to live in the sky, though not to be identified with it, and he is said by most peoples to have formerly lived on earth with men (1931: 264–6). His form is said to be either imperceptible to human senses or like that of a human, but remarkable in some way (1931: 266–7). The names given to him express such ideas as fatherhood, creative power, and his connection with the sky (1931: 267–9). His major attributes are: immortality, omniscience, beneficence, righteousness, omnipotence, and creative power (1931: 269–73). He is the giver and enforcer of moral law (1931: 274–7), and he is worshipped in some way, such as by prayer, sacrifice, or formal ceremonies (1931: 277–82).

Schebesta examines the deities of the Malaysian Negritos and comes to the conclusion that Ta' Pedn is the 'supreme and peerless lord of heaven' and that Karei is an 'interloper in the circle of the celestial *orang hidop*' (1957: 32). He admits that Karei is considered more important and superior to Ta' Pedn by most groups (e.g. 1957: 12, 14, 18, 21), but contends that

> there has been a change in the conception of god among the Semang. *Karei*, the personified natural phenomenon [thunder], supplanted an earlier celestial deity to such an extent that he now occupies first place, but the former *orang hidop* remains at his side. Ta Ped'n remained within the scheme, but he did not influence the minds and imaginations of the natives to the extent that the feared thunder god *Karei* did. This has gone so far that *Karei* is often conceived as dualistic: sometimes he is the threatening, malevolent one, the thunderer, but again the benevolent, helpful Ta Ped'n whom he superseded may be vaguely discerned in him (1957: 32; see also Schebesta 1961: 118).

Schebesta bases this conclusion on a number of pieces of evidence. One consideration is that Karei is regarded by some as being wicked and evil, and he is hated and feared (Schebesta 1957: 12, 14, 31), while Ta' Pedn is supposed to be kind and benevolent (Schebesta 1957: 31, 32) and to intercede for human beings 'when *Karei* rumbles too violently with thunder' (Schebesta 1957: 12). Also *Karei* is sometimes pictured as a 'wild beast' such as a *siamang* or gibbon, and Ta' Pedn is not, at least not explicitly (1957: 31). Another 'decisive factor is that *Karei* is often assigned a different dwelling in heaven from that of *Ped'n*. He dwells below in a cave, whereas *Ta Ped'n* lives on the *galog'n* in heaven' (Schebesta 1957: 32). 'Still more important is the circumstance that the celestial *Cenoi* are associated only with *Ta Ped'n*, never with *Karei*. *Karei* is unknown in the *Cenoi* language' (Schebesta 1957: 32). 'Finally, creation, in so far as it is mentioned, is ascribed to *Ta Ped'n*, not to Karei' (Schebesta 1957: 32). It seems apparent from the evidence cited that the reason Schebesta would make Ta' Pedn superordinate to Karei, in spite of explicit denials by his informants when he suggested this (Schebesta 1928: 187, 218), is that Ta' Pedn better fits Schmidt's definition of the Supreme Being of the primitive culture. Postulating a change in their relationship is one way to make the facts fit the theory.

There is no independent historical evidence for a change of the sort Schebesta postulates, though I would not deny that changes in the Negrito religious conceptions have gone on in the past and undoubtedly still do. But what little external evidence there is seems to suggest that the change in the relative importance of Karei and Ta' Pedn has been in the opposite direction to that suggested by him. That 'Kayai' is the name of an important superhuman being among a Philippine Negrito group, a being who indicates his displeasure at human misbehaviour 'by speaking through the thunder' (Garvan 1964: 227), suggests that the association of that name with the thunder-maker is a very ancient feature of Negrito culture. It seems more likely, then, that the name Ta' Pedn has replaced Karei, rather than the reverse, among those groups who now call the thunder-god Ta' Pedn. The close association of Ta' Pedn with the *ćenoi* and the *ćenoi* language is not necessarily, as Schebesta claims (1957: 31), evidence that Ta' Pedn is connected with an older phase of Negrito religion. In fact the type of shamanism with which this *ćenoi* language is associated is quite similar to Senoi and Malay 'spirit-mediumship' in form (see Schebesta 1928: 223–8; 1957: 130–50; Evans 1937: 190–214), and I suspect that it is a relatively recent development under outside influence. Schebesta says young Jahai men 'spent months among the Senoi from whom they brought the popular *Ćenoi* songs and introduced them to their fellow tribesmen' (1957: 126; see also 129n.). The *ćenoi* or their equivalents (e.g. Batek Dè' *hala' tahun*) are found in the pantheons of most, if not all, of the Malaysian Negrito groups, but they generally appear only as the bringers of fruit blossoms. However, in the religion of the Kensiu and Kintaq they are also thought to come down to the shaman, in a ceremony called *pano'*, and take control of him (see e.g. Schebesta 1928: 226–8; 1957: 137, 145–6), as do the 'spirit-helpers' of Malay and Senoi shamans. The shaman speaks the '*lingua sacra*' of the *ćenoi* when he is possessed by them (Schebesta 1957: 138), and Schebesta says the name Karei does not occur in the *ćenoi* language even among the groups in which he is the thunder-god (1957: 14–15, 30). One could interpret this as showing that the *ćenoi*-shamanism started among the Kensiu, whose name for the thunder-god is Ta' Pedn, and then spread eastward taking that identification of the thunder-god with it. Schebesta says that during both his visits to the Jahai (1924 and 1939), the people referred to Ta' Pedn as a son of Karei in ordinary discourse (1957: 15), but in 1939 they sang a number of songs about the *ćenoi* in which only the name Ta' Pedn appeared, apparently in the role of the pre-eminent deity (1957: 14–15). Schebesta writes: 'I should like to state emphatically that on my first journey I never heard among the Jahay and Lanoh that *Karei* and *Ta Ped'n* are one and the same person; I learned this from the Kensiu and the Kenta', and not until my last journey from the Jahay themselves' (1957: 14). If anything, this suggests that the use of the name Ta' Pedn for the thunder-god was spreading at the expense of the name Karei during the period between his two visits, rather than the reverse. Schebesta often uses the terms 'intruder' and 'interloper' (*Intrusus, Eindringling*) with reference to Karei (e.g. 1957: 31, 32, 123), but he was actually only given this characterization by the Senoi-Ple (Temiar), and he simply generalizes in such a way as to include the Negritos as well (1957: 31, 118). Karei could well be considered an intruder in the pantheon of the Temiar simply because he is a Negrito deity, and this would imply nothing about the developmental history of the Negrito conception.

The differences between the conceptions of Karei and Ta' Pedn are not nearly as great as Schebesta contends, and where they do occur, they can be understood on quite different grounds from those he proposes. It is to his very great credit, however, that he provides the evidence necessary for an alternative interpretation. I think that the 'evilness' or 'wickedness' attributed to Karei is a natural consequence of his being the enforcer of rules: the wielder of the punitive thunderstorm and demander of the blood sacrifice (see Schebesta 1928: 186). Schebesta's Jahai and Lanoh informants 'qualified the wickedness of *Karei* by saying that he rumbles in the thunder only when human beings do evil' (1957: 13; see also Schmidt 1931: 271). The Batek Teh say Karei is neither good nor bad, and they only fear him when they have broken a rule. There is no indication in the literature or in my findings to the effect that Karei is considered unjust or gratuitously cruel. The relative benignity of Ta' Pedn is probably due to his being detached from this punitive role. This is true to a certain extent even among the Kensiu, where he is the ultimate authority, because, according to some accounts, the actual making of thunder is performed by one of his subordinates, while 'Pedn himself merely looks on' (Schebesta 1928: 252; see also 1957: 23). Among the groups in which both Karei and Ta' Pedn occur, the latter is subordinate to the former and thus escapes the responsibility for punishing man. Yet Ta' Pedn's close connection with Karei makes him a logical intermediary between men and the thunder-god (e.g. Schebesta 1928: 186; 1957: 12), which of course puts him in a sympathetic light. The description of Karei as a *siamang*, or gibbon, is, I shall argue, closely connected with his being the thunder-maker. All the other images of Karei—man-like, hairy, shining, etc.—are shared by Ta' Pedn, and, indeed, they are said by some informants to 'have the same appearance' (Schebesta 1957: 31). Similarly, the 'decisive factor' that Karei dwells below Ta' Pedn in a cave (Schebesta 1957: 32), must be balanced against the numerous statements in which Karei is given a place in the heavens. In fact Schebesta originally said 'once, and only once, I heard that Ta Pedn and his companions sit upon this beam, called *galogn*, while Karei lives below in a cave' (1928: 187). In any case, the cave in question may well be in Batu Ribm, whose top is above the clouds, rather than in the earth as Schebesta seems to think. Finally, although Ta' Pedn is associated with some, though not all, acts of creation, he is sometimes explicitly said to have done it under orders from Karei (e.g. Schebesta 1928: 187). As I mentioned above (Chapter 2), the actual work of creating things seems to be regarded as menial labour by the Negritos. In the position of creator, Ta' Pedn is in the company of such minor *hala'* as the dung beetle and the sandpiper bird.

In short, I consider Schebesta's attempt to portray Ta' Pedn as a displaced 'high god' to be rather strained, but nevertheless an intelligent and worthwhile effort to make sense of a highly complex set of data. The difficulty seems to be that he takes too literally Schmidt's description of the Supreme Being as benevolent and a creator, and thus feels compelled finally to reject Karei from that category. Even when he was with the Jahai in 1924 he said he considered it strange 'that Karei, the supreme being—for there was no doubt he was that,—was not the Creator; creation being ascribed to Ta Pedn, his son. Equally strange it was to hear Ta Pedn described as good, and Karei as evil' (1928: 186). Ironically, he applies the criteria of beneficence and creativity more uncompromisingly than Schmidt himself (Schmidt 1931: 268, 271, 272-3), who is willing to accept Karei as the Supreme Being of the Malaysian Negritos (Schmidt 1931: 258, 269, 271). But any undue emphasis on a single 'high god' produces a serious problem of what to make of the other superhuman beings in the pantheon who are often only slightly less prominent than the one chosen as 'supreme'. My own impression, which of course is unsubstantiated by any first-hand knowledge of the western Negritos, is that Ta' Pedn is basically a fruit-giving being similar to Jawéc of the Batek Nòng. The name

itself indicates the flower of some kind of tree (Evans 1937: 149).
Ta' Pedn is equated with the Temiar deity Ple by Schebesta (1957:
31, 88), and Vaughn-Stevens' Kintaq informants apparently always
used the name Ple for the being who was called Ta' Pedn by later
writers (see e.g. Skeat and Blagden 1906b: 178, 185, 213–15;
Schebesta 1957: 88, 111–16). *Ple* means 'fruit' in Temiar (Batek Dè'
pelò', 'ripe fruit'), and the being named Ple is said to be 'the fruit-
bringer, as is *Ta Ped'n*, who makes the *tahud'n* (fruit season)'
(Schebesta 1957: 112, 320). Also Vaughn-Stevens records that it is
Ple who puts the blood from the blood sacrifice into red fruit
(Schebesta 1957: 88). In explaining the beneficence of Ta' Pedn,
one of Schebesta's Jahai informants said it was he 'who cares for us,
it is he who gives us our food' (1928: 186). His close connection with
the *cenoi*, the fruit-bringers, also supports the proposed connection
of Ta' Pedn with fruit production. One could then explain the
dominant position of Ta' Pedn in the Kensiu pantheon as being
connected with the rise of *cenoi*-shamanism in that group.

Reinterpretation

The nature of Negrito deities

In order to gain a new perspective on the 'deities' of the Malaysian
Negritos, it is worth while looking at them as cultural conceptions
and to try to determine what kind of conceptions they are and how
they are used by the Negritos. I will begin to answer the second
question by considering the kinds of situations in which the Negritos
normally make reference to superhuman beings. Most of the time
the Negritos (here I am referring to the Batek and Mendriq whom
I know personally) go about their everyday activities without
prayers, offerings, or other rituals, and they explain events, when
called upon to do so, in predominantly naturalistic terms. Deities
and lesser superhumans are mentioned in only a few easily specifiable
situations. The most dramatic of these is the thunderstorm; the
thunder-god is often spontaneously mentioned when thunder is
heard and he, and the earth deity, may be invoked when a blood
offering is made, though the invocation is not obligatory. Supposedly
people also think of the deities when certain rules (*lawac*) are broken,
although the connection of the deity with the rules is seldom made
explicit except when adults are admonishing children, for the adults

need no reminding of the means by which the rule is enforced. The deities are also commonly mentioned in story-telling sessions and in explanations of the way the world is and came to be so. These occur in the instruction of children and, exceptionally, of outsiders such as myself. The names of deities may also appear in songs, though my impression from reading Schebesta is that this is far more frequent in the songs of the western Negritos than in those of the Batek. These few situations are the natural settings in which the deities are mentioned; they may be thought of more often, but there is no reason to suppose that people think of them in radically different ways and situations from those in which they speak of them.

The way the deity concepts are used suggests that their main importance is as part of the conventional description of how the world works. They are the concepts in terms of which certain 'natural' processes and events are described and explained. The deities and lesser *hala*' are the postulated causes of these processes and events. The processes so explained are mainly those that have a continuing practical importance to the Batek, either as a possible source of danger (e.g. thunderstorms and floods) or of well-being (e.g. the fruit season) but which are somewhat unpredictable and therefore are subject to speculation, not merely taken for granted. The deities are conceived in such a way that they can be used to explain not only how thunderstorms are produced, but why they occur at particular times and places; and not only how fruit is produced, but why it appears at particular times and in particular quantities. The interconnections between such things as weather and fruit production can also be understood in terms of deities as can the connections between human behaviour and these natural processes. The part a superhuman being plays in the working of the universe is what I will call its 'function' (cf. Horton 1967a: 52). This is normally conceived as the causation of some process. For example, one function of the Batek Dè' deity Gobar is the causation of thunderstorms.

What I am calling the deities of the Negritos are, I suggest, ideas built up out of imagined actions, corporeal images, and names. The action by which a being is supposed to carry out its function is what I call its 'role' (cf. Horton 1962: 206). Any process can conceivably be caused in a number of different ways. Therefore, a given function can be performed by beings acting out different roles. The role of a superhuman being is its characteristic behaviour, by which it is presumed to perform a certain function in the workings of the universe. The form the being is supposed to have is what I will call its 'image'. The Negritos typically picture animate beings, though not necessarily human-like beings, as the causative agents for the events they are explaining. These images are drawn mainly from the humans and animals found in the forest environment, though a few—such as the image of a Malay sultan—are known by hearsay only. The image of a superhuman being is not limited to those occurring naturally, however, for features of natural species can be exaggerated or combined in novel ways. The names of the superhuman beings are drawn from the stories of the Negritos or neighbouring peoples or are epithets appropriate to the role or image (e.g. Mąwąs, a name for the gibbon). Thus, the deity concepts of the Negritos, like many scientific constructs, give concrete form to the postulated causes of events and processes which are not directly observable and thus make them easier to think about. The picture of a deity causing thunder, like the image of electricity flowing through a wire as if it were water in a pipe, may be scientifically inaccurate, but it is adequate to interpret the experience of the ordinary observer.

Certain images and roles are particularly appropriate to each other, as I will show; they are often found together in relatively stable image-role sets. The names of the superhuman beings, however, are partially independent of the images and roles, especially the names given to minor figures. For example, the name Chemioi, which was once given to Schebesta by the Kintaq as the name of the wife of Begjag (1928: 219), was later said to be the name of a male *hala'* who is lord of the place of winds (1957: 18). The well-established names are fairly consistently linked with particular functions, for example, the name Karei with the making of thunder, but the way he is thought to make it (i.e. his role) and his image vary from group to group. This partial independence of names from images and roles has been a source of great confusion in attempts to explain the Negrito deities. It is important, I think, to regard names as just one component, of no more defining importance than images and roles, of the composite ideas which are the deities of the Malaysian Negritos.

The enormous variation in the attributes and position of named beings between different groups and even between different informants within a group can be partly explained by this partial independence of name from image and role. But what is more important is that the named deities normally consist of combinations of image-role sets, and there are more ways to combine components of a set of (more than two) elements than there are elements in the set. In fact, the natural phenomena for which the deities are held responsible by the Negritos are quite limited in number, as I shall show, but the number of possible ways of combining these phenomena, as the actions of deities, is fairly large. The greatest number of beings would be produced, of course, if each phenomenon to be explained were attributed to a specialized being, like the Malay *hantu* ('spirits'); the smallest number of beings would result from attributing all the phenomena to a single, multifaceted being. I think there are strains both toward differentiation of image-role sets and toward consolidation of them to be seen in all Negrito groups, but the opposing tendencies are realized in different proportions, so that some groups have fewer deities than others, though none of them reach what would normally be termed monotheism.

Functions of the superhuman beings

The functions attributed to superhuman beings, the parts they are supposed to play in the workings of the universe, are basically the same for all Malaysian Negrito groups, though the numbers and identities of the beings associated with each function vary. The *hala'* beings as a group are held responsible for creating the earth, mankind, and certain other components of the universe; holding the parts of the universe in their proper places; causing thunderstorms and up-welling floods; enforcing certain rules of human behaviour; teaching man how to live; producing fruit and tubers; and maintaining human life. It is impossible systematically to separate the functions that are performed by deities from those performed by the undifferentiated *hala'* because a function that is performed by a deity in one group may be performed by an anonymous *hala'* or group of *hala'* in another.

Some stories of the creation of the earth, human beings, plants, and animals have been given in previous chapters. Creation, in the Negrito view, is seldom, if ever, *ex nihilo*; rather, it consists of the manipulation of certain materials which, like the deities themselves, were already in existence before any given act of creation. As in the cosmogonic myths of many cultures, one basic feature of the creative process is the differentiation of relatively homogeneous

materials into heterogeneous parts. In one version of the creation of
the world, Schebesta says 'the *terhob'm*, dung beetle, lifted the earth
out of the ooze' (1957: 35), creation being the separation of 'ooze'
into its liquid and solid parts. In the Batek Dè' version, the matter
which became the earth was painstakingly extracted from the
water and stuck together bit by bit. The mound of earth first
produced was then shaped into hills and valleys by *hala'* birds or
bears, and divided by rivers (Schebesta 1957: 35: Evans 1937: 159).
In one story the creation of the world included the separation of the
sky from the earth. Schebesta records that after the earth was
formed, 'the *ćebreb* (bird?) [actually a flying insect] lifted up the
firmament, which was resting on the earth' (1957: 35). A common
story of the origin of the various plants and animals derives them
from the constituent parts of a giant bear-cat which was hacked to
pieces by two *hala'* heroes. In the creation of man, an additional
process is introduced—the endowment of the body with life in the
form of a life-soul (*ñawa'*). Yet the bodies of the first humans were
produced by a kind of differentiation in that both the male and
female were moulded out of homogeneous earth. Thus, the *hala'*
beings are creators mainly by virtue of being the active agents in
the successive differentiation of primordial matter into heterogeneous parts.

The deities and lesser *hala'* are also credited with preserving the
constituted order of the universe by exerting a continuous effort and
influence over it. They are not merely the creators, but also the
maintainers of an order which, the Negritos seem to believe, would
break down without active support. Schebesta records a Kensiu
notion that the sun is suspended on a vine which is held up by a
brother of Ta' Pedn. 'Pedn is afraid lest his younger brother should
let go of the liana, which would cause everything on earth to be
shattered and turned to water' (1928: 250-1). The Lebir Batek Dè'
say that the *hala'* *'asal* above the firmament must guard the ropes of
wind, rain, and thunder or they will break and cause an earth-
destroying storm. In part, the maintenance of order is effected by
keeping apart those things that have been separated in the act of
creation. For instance, the Batek Dè' describe Gobar and Ya' as
'holding back' the waters of the heavens and the underworld in
order to prevent them from crashing together on earth. Indirectly,
nearly all recurring phenomena attributed to the deities reinforce
the sense of order in the universe. The locations of the deities help

define the basic co-ordinates of space, and occasionally the very persistence of the natural order is said to depend on their staying in their proper positions. Evans was told by the Batek Nòng that 'if Bonsu [the deity of the fruit island] were to come down to earth, the whole world would dissolve and become a sea' (1927: 17). The deities represent temporal order as well, for they are held responsible for the repetitive processes, such as the fruit cycle, that give order to time. Thus, any events that are taken as evidence of the existence of the deities must also be evidence of the persistence of cosmic order.

Thunderstorms and up-welling floods are the exceptions that prove the rule. They are localized breakdowns in the separation of the elements of heaven, earth, and underworld. The destructive force of the storm derives from the sudden unleashing of high winds and torrential rains which together can undermine and topple trees. Thunder is sometimes said to carry the wind and rain down from Batu Keñam. The proper place of strong winds is high in the sky, sometimes even in a special 'place of the winds' (Schebesta 1957: 17), or locked up in a cave in a stone pillar. Similarly, celestial water is harmless when confined to the clouds or the stone pillar, and the waters of the underground sea are only dangerous when they rise up and dissolve the surface of the earth. The disastrous mixing of earth and water, from the heavens and the underworld, is a reversal of the process of creation in which the land was separated from the waters and the sky from the earth. Such storms and floods occur, according to the Batek Dè', when Gobar and Ya' can no longer 'hold back' the forces of their respective realms. But their loss of control is deliberate, it seems, for they can restore order when retribution (usually in the form of a blood offering) has been made. Thus, in the very breakdown of order, the deities demonstrate their control over it.

The enforcement by the deities of certain rules of human behaviour is merely a part of their general function of maintaining cosmic order. As I have suggested in a previous chapter, the *lawac* rules have mainly to do with preventing the mixing or confusion of things and behaviours which, in the proper order of things, are separated (see Needham 1967: 282-3) and with preventing ridicule of the *hala'* and the created order. These are not moral rules in the ordinary sense. They do not regulate the conduct of persons toward each other so much as they regulate the conduct of humans in relation to the environment. The Negritos, like most hunting and gathering peoples, see themselves as an integral part of the natural environment and as subject to natural forces which are more powerful than themselves. But they realize that human behaviour is to some extent independent: it can work against nature as well as in harmony with it. Proper behaviour should conform to the constituted divisions and distinctions within the world, and this is what the *lawac* rules tend to promote. It is especially appropriate, then, that actions which undermine those distinctions should be punished by the utter breakdown of cosmic order. The deities merely serve up a sample of what such disruptive behaviour leads to.

The establishment and enforcement of *lawac* rules is closely related to the *hala'* beings' function of teaching humans how to live. When human beings were first created, they did not know how to behave, not even how to reproduce. They learned this gradually from *hala'* who communicated with them through dreams or appeared among them as 'culture heroes'. Some of their instruction took the form of practical advice, such as how to make fire and what fruits are edible, but other instruction had the form of rules prohibiting certain kinds of behaviour, such as marrying siblings. The rules and the practical advice together serve to define the proper place and role of man in the natural order. Just as it is distinctively human to use fire, so is it human not to marry siblings. The rules and practical advice differ only in that the behaviours enjoined by the latter need no enforcement, as their value is self-evident. It is no less important for the survival of mankind, however, that behaviour contrary to the natural order of things be suppressed. But the danger of such behaviour is not always self-evident, and thus it must be prohibited.

The functions of producing fruit and tubers and maintaining human life are closely interconnected in Negrito ideology. Fruit and tubers are in fact the staples of the diet of the nomadic Negritos, and their fundamental importance is well-attested in numerous stories. Both have claims to being regarded as the primordial human food. It is said by some Negritos that seasonal fruit is the only food of *hala'* beings (see e.g. Schebesta 1957: 13), presumably because they have cool water life-souls and therefore must avoid cooked food. Some Aring Batek say that human beings would also have been able to live on fruit alone except that Allah unfortunately spilled the water life-soul he was bringing to the clay bodies of the first man and woman, and he had to substitute a wind life-soul instead. Because of this, man must eat cooked food as well as seasonal fruit.

On the other hand, several Batek Dè' stories describe early men as living on tubers alone and only beginning to eat fruit after a *hala'* (in the form of a bird) told them which fruits were not poisonous. The importance of tubers and fruit in the traditional Negrito economy is so great that they may be termed prerequisites for human existence. In the case of seasonal fruit at least, the deities are not only supposed to have created them, but also to play a continuing and crucial part in their production. The provision of life-souls to unborn babies is, in a still more direct way, necessary for human life, and this too is carried out by the *hala'* beings. Thus, the continuance of human life depends, in more than one way, upon the continuous efforts of the superhuman beings, and it is under their constant control.

Roles and images of the superhuman beings

Even though the basic functions of the *hala'* beings, the phenomena attributed to them, are nearly the same for all groups of Negritos, the exact means by which they are supposed to perform these functions vary. For example, thunder is said by different groups to be caused by a superhuman being roaring or growling, swinging vines against heavenly planks, rolling stones across the planks (cf. Radcliffe-Brown 1922: 145), spinning stone tops, making a fire in the clouds, and turning the wheel of a cart (Evans 1927: 13). These are all roles that might be attributed to a thunder-making being. The image of a being often fits a particular role: it is an appropriate form for the performer of such actions to have. Such images are not tied to particular named beings, I contend, but to the roles themselves. Thus, named beings with more than one role can be expected to have more than one image or a complex image which combines features of different images. Differences in the images of a named being from one group to another can often be traced to differences in roles. Not all images or components of images are bound to roles, but it is worth while looking at a few of the common images of *hala'* beings which can be interpreted in that light before considering the images that express more abstract properties and associations.

The image of the gibbon or *siamang* as applied to superhuman beings seems to be associated with the function of making thunder and specifically with the role of making thunder by roaring or growling. Schebesta's Mendriq informants described Karei as having 'the shape of a siamang', and they said that 'thunder is *Karei*'s voice

admonishing sinners to atone for their transgressions' (1957: 24).
Evans records that 'Chemam, who looks like a gibbon (*mawah*),
makes thunder with his mouth, . . . but when he gives sickness he
looks like a Malay' (1937: 184). This is a very revealing statement
in two respects. First, it shows that different images of the same
named being may be associated with different roles. Second, it
shows that the gibbon image is an attribute of the being whose voice
is thunder, whatever his name, rather than being specifically an
image of Karei, as Schebesta seems to think (1957: 31). Probably the
connection between the gibbon image and the making of thunder
by mouth is based on the booming, whooping cry of the gibbons and
siamang (see Medway 1969: 53-4). The racket produced by a troop
of gibbons, compounded by its echoes, is truly impressive, especially
in view of the small size of the animals. Gibbons and *siamang* also
appear in a set of stories (which are undoubtedly influenced by the
Ramayana tale of Hanuman, the monkey-god) found among the
western Negritos in which two 'tribes' of apes engage in a war.
These apes are not equated with any of the immortal beings, however, nor are they connected in any way with the making of thunder
(Schebesta 1957: 57-9). Thus, it seems unlikely that the image of
the thunder-maker as a gibbon or *siamang* is drawn from these stories
rather than from the animals themselves.

Of course the gibbon is not the only animal that can make a loud
noise with its mouth. Both the Batek Teh and the Lebir Batek Dè'
combine this method of making thunder with a human image. In
both cases, as I shall explain, there are other reasons why the human
image should dominate, and there are also good reasons why the
voices of these beings should be louder than those of ordinary men.
The thunder-god of the Batek Teh, though human-shaped, is a
giant. The loud voice of the thunder-god of the Lebir Batek Dè' is
attributed to his having been burned by bees, his having stolen the
loud voice of the tortoise, or to his voice being amplified by the rope
of lightning. The unusual image of Gobar as two water monitor
lizards, given me by one of my Aring Batek informants, is also
combined with the role of making thunder by mouth. It seems that
here the idea of Gobar's sitting at the edge of the sea, like a water
monitor sunning itself on a rock, dominates the image. But it is
notable that the water monitor has a more thunder-like growl than
any of the other animals in the Batek environment that habitually
sit on the banks of streams.

Occasionally certain *hala'* beings are pictured as looking like pig-tailed macaques (Batek Dè' *bawac*; Malay *beruk; Macaca hemestrina*). Usually these beings are the guardians of the afterworld or the fruit paradise (Skeat and Blagden 1906b: 190; 210–11, 223). One such 'monkey-monster' is said to protect the fruit heaven from would-be pilferers (human shamans) by pelting them with large, prickly jungle fruits (Skeat and Blagden 1906b: 211). Captive pig-tailed macaques are often trained by the Malays to climb coconut palms and throw down the fruit (Medway 1969: 51). I know from personal experience that they are as likely to throw the coconuts at a person as not, so it is no wonder that they are regarded as appropriate models for the guardians of fruit orchards. It is somewhat more surprising that one of my Batek Nòng informants pictured the thunder-maker (Jawac) as a pig-tailed macaque rather than as a gibbon. Perhaps this is because he is thought by them to make thunder by throwing down a stone on a string rather than with his mouth.

A number of superhuman beings are pictured as birds of various species. The *kawaw kedidi'* which appears as the creator of the land in one Batek Dè' story is a type of sandpiper or plover. Probably this image suggests itself for this role because the *kedidi'* is a shore-bird and is thus associated with the spatial transition between land and water. Its habit of feeding in the water but producing semi-solid droppings provides a vivid image for the building up of land in the primordial sea. Birds also appear as minor culture heroes, coming down to teach man such things as how to make fire and what fruits to eat. Here it seems to be their ability to fly which is focused upon. Such *hala'* are usually said to come down from the sky or the moon, and birds are obviously well-equipped for journeying between the heavens and earth. But the Negritos do not regard birds in general as *hala'*, and they do not practise bird-augury as do many of the native peoples of Borneo. It is merely that the image of the bird is applied to certain superhuman beings when the properties of birds happen to fit the role being played.

The role of supporting the earth in the underground sea is appropriately played by a semi-aquatic animal which habitually floats on the surface of the water. Both the turtle and snake images fit these requirements, and one or the other seems to be favoured depending on what other roles the being is supposed to play. The turtle image seems more prominent in connection with the creation of the world, perhaps because a turtle can be more easily pictured as building up a mound of mud than a snake can. But the snake image is more prominent later on, when the role of punishing man for breaking prohibitions is combined with that of supporting the earth, since a snake is more dangerous to man than a turtle.

Several types of human or semi-human images of *hala'* beings are found. Quite frequently *hala'* are pictured as looking like ordinary Negritos; this is especially common when the *hala'* are living on earth like humans and among humans, in culture hero roles. The true *hala'* shaman is thought to be superficially indistinguishable from ordinary Negritos, and in many stories only his superhuman feats reveal him for what he is. It is thought that the blood of a *hala'* is clear like water, but this distinguishing feature would seldom be evident in the ordinary course of events. Many of the heroes of stories about *hala'* living on earth are pictured as Negrito youths, both male and female, usually pairs of siblings. This fits the actual Negrito pattern of behaviour in which most of the long-distance travelling is done by young people searching for adventure and sometimes spouses. Nevertheless, older people appear as well when the role being taken is appropriate to someone older. For example, Gobar (or Mạwạs and Nạwạs) depended upon an aunt (named Ya') for tubers when he lived on earth, just as unmarried Negrito youths today are often supplied with tubers by older female relatives. Ya' retains the image of a human female later, after she has gone into the earth, when she is pictured merely as residing there or as digging holes in the ground to let through the underground sea. But generally the more frightening image of the *naga'* comes to the fore when the role of punisher is being played. Some Batek Nòng even describe the *naga'* as chasing the offender and catching him in its mouth. The Aring Batek Dè' also seem to picture Mạwạs and Nạwạs in human shape when they make thunder. Thunder is thought to be caused by the two deities spinning stone tops and competing to see who can make the loudest noise. This image is probably modelled after the top-spinning competitions that are sometimes staged by Kelantan Malays (Sheppard 1972: 180–9). The fruit-giving role is commonly associated with a human-like image, though the *hala'* who send fruit may also take the form of actual fruit.

Another human image of certain deities—a somewhat surprising one—is that of a Malay, often an authority figure of some sort. The Kensiu describe Ta' Pedn as looking like a 'Malay raja' (Skeat and

Blagden 1906b: 210), and Karei is said to look like a Malay head-man (*penghulu*) by the Lanoh (Schebesta 1957: 11) and a 'Malay chief or prince' by the Jahai (Schebesta 1928: 185). The Batek Teh description of Karei as dressed in golden clothing and wielding an iron and gold sword also suggests the appearance of a Malay of high rank. In these conceptions the great size and power of the being are often emphasized, as in the Batek Teh description of Karei as being the size of a mountain and able to cut down trees and kill *hantu* with a single stroke of his enormous sword (see also Skeat and Blagden 1906b: 177; Schebesta 1957: 11). According to Evans (1937: 184), the Malay image is associated with the role of sending disease as punishment. Apparently this is seen as being like the alleged power of Malay royalty to kill anyone who offends them 'by a quasi-electric discharge of the Divine Power which is called "Daulat" or "Royal Sanctity" ' (Skeat 1900: 23–4). This is not very different from Gobar's sending a spark of lightning to enter the foot of one who has committed incest. As the Negritos do not attribute such power to any of themselves, the model for this type of punishment has of necessity been borrowed from outside, and the Malay image has been retained in conjunction with this essentially Malay role.

An even more unusual human-like image is that of a person who is old above the waist, with a long beard, and young below the waist. This seems to express the immortality of the being. *Hala'* beings are often said to grow old and then become young again like the moon (e.g. Evans 1927: 21, 24; Schebesta 1957: 24), and the young–old image expresses statically this process of rejuvenation. The Lebir Batek Dè' image of Gobar as an extremely old man with no teeth is probably a variation on this theme. Similarly, the grass and trees on Tohan's back are said by the Lebir Batek to show his great age.

The colours of the *hala'* beings seem to be partially independent of the images and roles. Often the colours merely reinforce the meaning of a being which is expressed by his image and role, as in the case of the red-tinted skin of the fruit *hala'*, but they may also express additional associations and meanings. Both the gibbon image and the human image appear in black and in white versions. Karei is described as being black and looking like a *siamang* by certain Mendriq and Jahai informants (Schebesta 1957: 14, 24), and as a *siamang* with shiny white hair by some Lanoh (Evans 1937: 144). Similarly, the Mos Negritos of Thailand describe Kagei (or Kagi) as looking like a Semang (Negrito) (Schebesta 1957: 24) and as being black in colour (Evans 1927: 13; see also Evans 1937: 146), while the Kensiu describe Ta' Pedn as having the appearance of a man but being 'as white as cotton' (Skeat and Blagden 1906b: 210). Probably these two colours have different meanings for the different images, as they are connected with different roles. The connection of the gibbon image with the making of thunder suggests that the black colour represents the darkness of the sky and clouds during the storm, just as the name Gobar does. The white colour, which is often described as dazzling or fiery (e.g. Schebesta 1928: 188; 1957: 13), could represent the lightning. The representation of the gibbon image in black and white versions is not entirely unnatural, as two species of gibbons (though not the *siamang*) occur in black and buff or cream-coloured variants (Medway 1969: 53–4). The different colours of the human image may correlate partially with differences in role. As culture heroes, it is not unexpected that the *hala'* are black 'like Negritos' (Evans 1937: 146), while in some of the celestial roles, such as guarding the fruit island in the Batek Nòng cosmology, the bright colour of the being might well, as Schebesta argues (1957: 33), express an association with the sun, which is sometimes given as a dwelling place of certain celestial *hala'* (e.g. Evans 1937: 147).[2] The multicoloured image of the *naga'* expresses a connection between it and the rainbow, which is said by the Batek Dè' and other groups to be the shadow or reflection of the *naga'* (see e.g. Schebesta 1957: 30, 66–70).

These images and roles are the main conceptual components out of which the Malaysian Negrito *hala'* beings are constructed. Each *hala'* has (one might even say *is*) at least one image and one role, usually images and roles that fit together in a coherent set. Names are also components of the *hala'* beings, but they belong to a higher order of phenomena: they are labels applied to complexes of image-role sets which are attributed to single beings. Occasionally a simple being, composed of a single image-role set, may be given a name, but they are usually reserved for the more complex and important beings—the ones I am calling deities.

Consolidation and differentiation

The pantheons of the different Negrito groups may be described as showing varying degrees of consolidation and differentiation (or

[2] The Batek Dè', however, say *hala'* can no longer live on the sun because it is too hot.

separation) of image-role sets depending upon how many deities they contain. I would argue that in the realm of Negrito deity concepts, consolidation and differentiation are not merely descriptive devices, but are dynamic tendencies within the bodies of ideas. In other words, the people who hold these notions are under pressure both to consolidate and to differentiate the image-role sets that make up their deity concepts. These pressures are opposed and irreconcilable, which is one reason, I suggest, why there is so much variation from one informant to another, even within a single dialect group, and so much fluctuation over time in the reported numbers and attributes of the deities of particular groups. The pantheons of the Malaysian Negritos are always in a state of unstable equilibrium.

The tendency to consolidate several image-role sets into clusters, thus producing a limited number of multi-faceted beings, is present in all Negrito groups, though it is manifest in different degrees in different groups. It is most evident among the Mendriq and Batek Teh where a single being—Karei—is supposed to perform all the celestial functions, most importantly the production of fruit, punishment by storm, and the general maintenance of heavenly order. Although the Batek Dè' and Batek Nòng sometimes distinguish a pair of major celestial deities, their underlying unity is indicated by their being given rhyming names, and the Aring Batek Dè' explicitly say that Mặwặs and Nặwặs together are equivalent to Gobar, the name usually mentioned for the thunder-god. Yet even among the Mendriq there is no true monotheism, for a separate being, a *naga'*, reigns below the earth, and the tiger plays a punitive role on the earth itself. Normally the division between the sky and the underworld is maintained, and consolidation of roles takes place only within those separate realms. There are a few interesting exceptions, however. One of Evans's Lanoh informants explained punitive floods in the following way: Tapern (Ta' Pedn), who lives in a cave in the sky, is informed of human offences by a dragon-fly and 'he then throws down a huge quartz crystal which goes into the earth, and the waters well up from the hole which it makes and drown the offenders' (1927: 23–4; also 1937: 145). Thus a celestial deity takes over a role usually reserved for a subterranean one. Conversely, a Kintaq informant told Schebesta that thunder was the roaring of a dragon called Tanyogn who lives in the underground sea, and that lightning was water he spurts into the air (1928: 222). Here the underground being takes over a role which is normally performed by a celestial being. Yet even when consolidation overrides the division between upper and lower worlds, it stops short of a complete unification of all superhuman beings. Thus, even though the Lanoh sometimes attribute upwelling floods to Ta' Pedn, they nevertheless distinguish between Ta' Pedn and Karei who is said to cause the thunder (Schebesta 1957: 14).

The counter-tendency toward differentiation of image-role sets, attributing them to separate beings, is also present among all Negrito groups. Although this increases the number of beings, it decreases their complexity, thus removing some of the contradictions and incongruities in the characteristics of the more complex beings. For example, the moral ambiguity of the thunder-god is removed among the groups, such as the Lanoh and Kintaq, who separate the punitive and fruit-producing functions. But of course differentiation produces complications of its own, for, if separate beings are held responsible for different phenomena, there is a need for a theory of how these things are related and how the phenomena are co-ordinated. In general the tendency to differentiate seems most developed among the western Negrito groups where the pantheons are highly complex, though the Kensiu are somewhat exceptional in making Ta' Pedn the single major sky god.

The roots of this tendency toward differentiation are both external and internal to the individual dialect groups. The raw materials for deity conceptions—names, images, mythical episodes, etc.—are frequently introduced from other groups. It seems that mere knowledge of alternative beliefs creates a certain strain to take account of them, though whether they are accepted and how they may be reworked is determined by the cosmology of the receiving group. The fact that all Negrito groups differentiate space along up-down and east-west axes seems both to encourage the differentiation of existing beings and to facilitate the incorporation of introduced beings in order to fill the cosmos and to reproduce its symmetries in the medium of *hala'* beings. In addition, the splitting or pairing of superhuman beings is promoted by the Negrito tradition of having pairs of heroes in stories. Thus, both cosmological and mythological features exert some pressure in the direction of differentiation, and they work together to give a dualistic cast to the Negrito pantheons.

Although all Negrito pantheons show strains both toward consolidation and toward differentiation, the balance struck obviously differs from group to group. In general, the eastern groups have fewer beings and the western groups more, even though the functions performed by superhuman beings as a group are roughly the same. This difference is due more to the external relations of the dialect groups, I think, than to any internal dynamic of religious evolution. At any rate the social organization of the different groups is very similar, and there is no apparent correlation between economic differences and the different degrees of deity differentiation. The important variable seems to be the amount of exposure a group has to the religious ideas of other dialect groups, especially to alternative names for superhuman beings. Differences in names can arise from mere linguistic differences or from the use of different epithets, but the names used by a particular group would appear to outsiders to indicate distinct beings in so far as the names differed from their own. Prolonged contact between dialect groups usually leads to some attempt to reconcile their pantheons (see e.g. Schebesta 1928: 187–8, 250), and this is done in part by incorporating the named beings of other groups into one's own pantheon. If new beings are to be introduced without overlapping previously established ones, the roles played must be freshly subdivided to provide separate roles to attach to the incoming names. Thus, groups that are in close communication with other dialect groups would be expected to have more differentiated pantheons than groups that are relatively isolated.

The western Negrito groups are located close together, have frequent contact with each other, and have regularly formed mixed camps at least since the early years of this century (see Schebesta 1928). The eastern Negrito dialect groups, by contrast, are centred quite far from each other, and communication between groups is less frequent. The Batek Nòng, in fact, are completely cut off from other Negrito groups at present, so their religion has probably received little stimulation from other Negrito groups recently. Their religion shows some traces of influence from neighbouring non-Negrito aboriginal groups, however. The only mixed settlement of eastern Negritos I know of, the one at Post Lebir, is very recent, dating only from the middle 1960s. Even there the several dialect groups tend to keep to themselves, as is indicated by their practice of building their shelters in separate clusters. Thus, the western Negritos would be more exposed to the alien ideas and terms of other Negrito groups than would their eastern counterparts. It

appears that contact with non-Negrito groups has less effect on the
complexity of the Negrito pantheons, presumably because there are
more social barriers to the flow and acceptance of non-Negrito ideas.
Even so, there seems to be a strong Malay or Temiar influence in the
pantheons of the western Negritos in the proliferation of minor
named beings (*cenoi*) which can be summoned up by a shaman in
the manner of a Malay 'spirit-raising' seance (see Schebesta 1928:
224–8; Evans 1937: 193–201).

Batek Dè' Deities in Perspective

The comparison and analysis carried out makes it possible to place
the deity conceptions of the Batek Dè' in their proper perspective. It
can be seen that they have relatively few separate deities which are,
therefore, rather complex. Gobar is connected with the making of
thunderstorms, production of seasonal fruit, and maintenance of
cosmic order, though he performs the last two functions in conjunction with the undifferentiated *hala' 'asal* who live mainly on top
of the firmament. Because he is associated both with processes that
are dangerous to man and those that are necessary to man's well-
being, the Batek attitude toward him is ambivalent. Only where the
beneficial and detrimental processes are attached to separate beings
are those beings unequivocally loved or hated. The basic image of the
Batek thunder-god emphasizes his great age and immortality rather
than any particular role he plays. This image is compatible with
various roles and thus remains stable when the deity shifts from one
role to another. The intermittent division of Gobar into two beings
is a mild expression of a tendency that is carried much further by
some of the other Negrito groups. The Batek not only retain strong
indications of the underlying unity of the two beings (as in the
rhyming of their names), but they also make no division of labour
between them. The impetus for this partial division of the thunder-
god seems to be the knowledge that thunder comes from more than
one direction (with this knowledge being expressed in terms of the
dominant east-west orientation in space) and the connection of the
thunder-god with mythical figures who generally occur in pairs.
The earth deity of the Batek Dè' is credited with supporting and
maintaining the earth and also with withdrawing that support to
punish people who break *lawac* prohibitions. Comparison shows that
the difference between the *naga'* image emphasized by the Lebir

people, and the 'grandmother' image, emphasized by the Aring people, is a minor matter which does not reflect any radical difference in function. The image of the *naga*' seems merely to emphasize the making of floods (both punitive and seasonal), while the grandmother image emphasizes the provision of tubers and the tie of the earth deity with the thunder-god. The last major deity of the Batek Dè'—Tohan—has no obvious counterpart among most other Negrito groups. No doubt his main function—sending and retrieving human life-souls—is performed by other superhuman beings among other groups, but information on this is scarce. His image and location are rather uncertain. The deities of the Batek Dè', then, are unique and yet clearly related to the deities of all the other Negrito groups. They are merely one set of concepts of a type used by all the Malaysian Negritos to make sense of some of the major forces of nature.

8

CONCLUSIONS

Batek Religion and the Batek World

In this study I have argued that Batek religious ideas are the concepts with which they understand their world. But I do not mean to imply that this elaborate conceptual system is motivated solely by intellectual curiosity, by a pure 'thirst for knowledge', although this certainly plays a role. In part, as the description shows, Batek religious ideas cluster around practical problems of Batek life, such as averting thunderstorms and increasing the fruit crop. Understanding is sought in order to enable them to avoid disaster and to improve their lives. And even where their understanding of the forces impinging on them is scientifically erroneous, it still has the value of providing a focus for thought and action. While the concept may be no more benign than the force it gives shape to, as in the case of the Batek thunder-god, merely having a concept at all reduces the fear of the unknown.

Although the religious concepts of the Batek may seem exotic to westerners, they are formed and used very much like the explanatory concepts of more 'advanced' cultures, including the theoretical constructs of scientists. They explain by analogy between the known and the unknown (cf. Horton 1967a: 64). All such concepts use familiar, concrete, observable things and occurrences as images for distant, less concrete, less perceptible phenomena (cf. Barth 1975: 199). The images used by the Batek are drawn from their environment and from the animals and humans that inhabit it. These images may be exaggerated or combined in novel ways, to fit more closely the phenomena to be explained, but their inspiration clearly lies in the familiar world. Like most non-industrial peoples, the Batek draw many of their images from human society, and thus they often base their explanations on the activities of anthropomorphic beings. This gives the Batek world-view a strikingly different complexion from the commonplace world-view of westerners, who use predominantly mechanistic concepts in explaining the world. But the difference is superficial. It is due mainly to the lack of mechanical devices in the Batek environment which can serve as conceptual models, not to the way models are used to achieve understanding. In fact, the few mechanical devices used traditionally by the Batek, such as rattan 'ropes', are fully employed in their explanations. And, as we discovered, the Batek very quickly incorporated such things as tape-recorders and cameras into their explanations, even though most of them had never seen these things before we came. Another difference between the Batek world-view and the common-sense world-view of more 'civilized' peoples is that the Batek scheme contains alternative, even inconsistent, models of things and processes. The tolerance of inconsistency is, of course, an essential defining characteristic of 'prelogical thought', according to Lévy-Bruhl (see Evans-Pritchard 1965: 81–2). But western scientists are also willing to retain inconsistent models of phenomena (e.g. the 'wave' and 'particle' models of light) because they know that the model is only a representation which is intended to make some aspects of the phenomenon intelligible. Where a single, consistent representation cannot be produced, they are willing to maintain more than one model and to switch from one to another depending on the problem being examined. For similar, though far less sophisticated reasons, the Batek often retain more than one explanation of a given phenomenon. They know that opinions differ on many matters, but they do not attempt to discover and eliminate those that are 'incorrect'. They seem to believe that all notions have value as long as they shed some light on the phenomenon to be explained. In a sense, then, the Batek are more sophisticated than those who believe in the 'absolute truth' of some concepts and therefore feel compelled to sweep aside all concepts that are inconsistent with those that are 'true'.

The Batek understanding of their world is founded on two complementary and interdependent constructs: a mechanistic notion of a 'natural order' and an anthropomorphic notion of 'superhuman beings'. Neither of these constructs would be adequate by itself, but together they do the job. The idea of natural order applies mainly to the constant features of the world and to some of the more regular processes in it. The natural order is exemplified in the Batek cosmology. The concepts used in representing the cosmos are based on familiar things—such as sandbars, pools, and rock outcroppings. These concepts are woven together into a general picture of the whole universe. Regular occurrences, such as the passage of the sun through the heavens, are regarded as part of the natural order of things. The states and processes of the natural order seem to be regarded as the normal condition of the world, the cosmic *status quo*. In some areas this *status quo* takes on moral connotations, as the right and proper state of things. But the notion of the natural order is a sort of indigenous 'ideal-type' concept. The Batek well realize that the world is not always, in fact, stable and harmonious. The notion of superhuman beings is brought in to help explain deviations from what is assumed to be the normal run of events. The superhuman beings are pictured as maintaining the natural order as a whole and as performing specific functions in the processes of the natural order. Yet, although the nature of their actions is fairly narrowly circumscribed, they have some freedom regarding when and to what extent they carry out their assigned duties. For example, the fruit *hala'* may be more or less generous in sending fruit blossoms, and Gobar may be more or less strict in enforcing the *lawac* prohibitions. Thus the notion of superhuman beings plays a similar role to the notion of 'uncertainty' in western science. It allows for unpredictable variation within fixed limits. The superhuman beings account of the 'give' between ultimate causes and ultimate effects as postulated in the theory of natural order. Among the Batek, then, irregular and unpredictable processes are represented as being like human behaviour. By contrast, among the traditional societies of Africa, according to Horton, scientific-type concepts are modelled after 'the human scene [which] is the locus *par excellence* of order, predicability, regularity' (1967a: 65). This difference may be due in part to actual differences between Batek and African societies. Very probably Batek behaviour is less orderly than African behaviour because Batek society gives an unusual degree of freedom to the individual. But this comparison also shows that order and disorder are relative, not absolute, conditions. What is considered orderly in one scheme may be disorderly in another, depending upon what it is compared with. Human behaviour is not inherently orderly or disorderly, though it can be represented as either. The meanings of things are always imposed by cultures, and any of their properties may be focused upon and emphasized in creating explanatory analogies.

The use of anthropomorphic beings in explanations of the world opens up the possibility of ritually influencing those beings in order to manipulate the forces they are supposed to control. According to van Baal, people living under primitive conditions feel a need to reduce their sense of alienation from their environment by personifying aspects of it and then communicating with the environment through the created beings (1971: 223–37). He says 'communication can be realized by various means: by a dialogue, by a gift, i.e. an act of exchange, and by identification. The dialogue implies prayer and the use of sacred formulas, the gift [implies] sacrifice, the identification [implies] the staging of the vision in ritual' (1971: 237). The Batek attempts to communicate with the *hala'* by means of songs and invocations, blood sacrifice, and singing sessions fit quite well into these categories. Most Batek attempts to manipulate their environment, beyond what they can do by direct physical means, are aimed at influencing the *hala'*. Only some curing techniques appear to operate directly on nature, on the diseases themselves, without the intervention of the *hala'*.

In so far as Batek religious concepts represent some of the features of the world that impinge on them, the characteristics of those concepts reveal indirectly the attitude of the Batek toward their environment. In general, those things that are dangerous, such as thunderstorms and flash floods, are represented by appropriately fear-inspiring beings, such as the thunder-god and the earth-snake. But the great majority of *hala'* are portrayed as benevolent to man and as freely bestowing their bounties on him. Though the fruit *hala'* demand singing before they will send fruit blossoms, they always send them in abundance when the songs are forthcoming. The *hala'* who originally created tubers and game now demand nothing in return for them. The *hala'* are portrayed as coming to earth merely for the pleasure of sharing a good singing session with the Batek. They do not threaten to interfere in human affairs, nor do they demand sacrifices or offerings (except for Gobar and Ya' who demand the blood sacrifice). They are portrayed as fond of the Batek, and it is no exaggeration to say that the Batek 'love' (*sayèng*) the *hala'*, as they often claim in their songs. This suggests that the Batek see their forest world as basically a hospitable place to live, one in which they feel relatively safe and secure. This evidence is corroborated by the obvious pleasure they take in being in the forest, especially after spending time outside it at clearings or in towns. The positive attitude of the Batek toward the forest, which is reflected in the concept of the *hala'*, contrasts sharply with the attitude of the up-river Malay farmers toward the forest which surrounds their swiddens. To them the forest is thickly populated with 'evil spirits' (*hantu*), in which category some of them place the Negritos (see Annandale and Robinson 1903: 101). In a previous work, I argued that some of the Malay spirit beliefs were a way of giving shape to their fear of the forest (Endicott 1970: 64). The sources of this fear, in other words, are not the spirits, which merely rationalize the fear, but the danger implicit in an area that is largely unknown, is easy to get lost in, and which contains some real hazards for the inexperienced. This conjunction of evil spirit beliefs and fear of the forest is probably common among forest-dwelling agricultural peoples. There is a sense in which the forest is for them an enemy which must be pushed back in order for them to make a living. Such peoples often build symbolic boundaries between the forest and the area of human habitation and attempt magically to defend the socialized world from its imagined external enemy (see e.g. Benjamin 1967). The Batek, as the Malay farmers realize, are on the other side of that divide, an integral part of the forest environment.

Batek Religion and the Religion of Ancient Man

Some students of comparative religion maintain that the present-day hunting and gathering peoples of the world have preserved, to a greater extent than the more developed peoples, certain features of the religion of ancient man (see e.g. Schmidt 1931). It is worth asking whether this is true in the Batek case. There are, in fact, similarities between the religions of the Negritos of the Philippines, Malaysia, and the Andaman Islands that may go back thousands of years to the time when there was still contact between the ancestors of those populations (Cooper 1940; see also Benjamin 1974). Yet, as van Baal points out, 'the primitive religions of the present are not really primitive at all. They are as much the result of an age-long history as the so-called historic religions' (1971: 240). In fact, the conditions prevailing in Batek society make it likely that their religion has been highly susceptible to change, in the past as well as in the present. The Batek have no religious authorities who could establish an orthodox religious tradition, and they have no written records or enduring material symbols that could preserve it. At the same time, there is a contant flow of new ideas into the religion, both from the dreams and inspirations of group members and from outside sources. The Batek are always open to knowledge from outside, and they eagerly incorporate any new ideas that have practical or metaphysical value. As a result, few of the notions that compose Batek religion are distinctively Negrito and likely to have come down directly from their ancient ancestors, though the total configuration of ideas is uniquely their own. It is likely, then, that Batek religion has been less stable over time than the religions of those more 'advanced' peoples who fix, record, and defend their religious conceptions. Paradoxically, we can probably learn more about ancient religion from the modern religions with written traditions—such as Christianity, Judaism, and Islam—than from a hunting and gathering people like the Batek, who are foragers of ideas as well as foragers of food.

BIBLIOGRAPHY

ANNANDALE, NELSON, and ROBINSON, C. (1903). *Fasciculi Malayenses: Anthropological and Zoological Results of an Expedition to Perak and the Siamese Malay States, 1901–2; Anthropology, Part 1*. The University Press of Liverpool, London.

BAAL, Jan van (1971). *Symbols for Communication: an Introduction to the Study of Religion*. Van Gorcum, Assen.

BARNES, Robert (1974). *Kédang: a Study of the Collective Thought of an Eastern Indonesian People*. Clarendon Press, Oxford.

BARTH, Fredrik (1975). *Ritual and Knowledge among the Baktaman of New Guinea*. Universitetsforlaget, Oslo and Yale University Press, New Haven.

BENJAMIN, Geoffrey (1967), 'Temiar Religion'. Unpublished doctoral dissertation, Cambridge University, Cambridge.

—— (1973). 'Introduction'. In Paul Schebesta, *Among the Forest Dwarfs of Malaya* (trans. Arthur Chambers), pp. v–xiv. Oxford University Press, Kuala Lumpur. (Original impression 1928, Hutchinson, London.)

—— (1974). *Indigenous Religious Systems of the Malay Peninsula*. Working Paper No. 28, Department of Sociology, University of Singapore, Singapore.

—— (1976). 'Austroasiatic Subgroupings and Prehistory in the Malay Peninsula'. In *Austroasiatic Studies* (ed. Philip Jenner), pp. 37–128. University Press of Hawaii, Honolulu.

BOSCH, F. D. K. (1960). *The Golden Germ: an Introduction to Indian Symbolism*. (Indo-Iranian Monographs, vol. 2), Mouton, 's-Gravenhage.

BURKILL, I. H. (1966). *A Dictionary of the Economic Products of the Malay Peninsula*. Two volumes, Ministry of Agriculture and Co-operatives, Kuala Lumpur. (Original impression 1935.)

CAREY, Iskandar (1976). *Orang Asli: the Aboriginal Tribes of Peninsular Malaysia*. O.U.P., Kuala Lumpur.

CLIFFORD, Hugh (1897). *In Court and Kampong*. Grant Richards, London.

COLE, Sonia (1965). *Races of Man*. British Museum (Natural History), London.

COLLINGS, H. D. (1949). 'Aboriginal Notes'. *Bulletin of the Raffles Museum*, Series B, No. 4: 86–103.

COOPER, John M. (1940). 'Andamanese-Semang-Eta Cultural Relations'. *Primitive Man: Quarterly Bulletin of the Catholic Anthropological Conference* 13: 2: 29–47.

CUISINIER, Jeanne (1936). *Danses magiques de Kelantan*. Institut D'Ethnologie, Paris.

DAVIS, Richard (1974). 'Muang Metaphysics: a Study in Northern Thai Myth and Ritual'. Unpublished doctoral dissertation, Sydney University, Sydney.

DENTAN, Robert K. (1968). *The Semai: a Nonviolent People of Malaya*. Holt, Rinehart and Winston, New York.

DIFFLOTH, Gérard (1974). 'Austroasiatic Languages'. In *Encyclopedia Britannica, Macropedia* 2: 480–4. Encyclopedia Britannica, Chicago.

ENDICOTT, Kirk M. (1970). *An Analysis of Malay Magic*. Clarendon Press, Oxford.

EVANS, Ivor H. N. (1923). *Studies in Religion, Folk-lore, and Custom in British North Borneo and the Malay Peninsula*. C.U.P.

—— (1927). *Papers on the Ethnology and Archaeology of the Malay Peninsula*. C.U.P.

—— (1937). *The Negritos of Malaya*. C.U.P.

EVANS-PRITCHARD, Edward Evan (1965). *Theories of Primitive Religion*. Clarendon Press, Oxford.

FREEMAN, Derek (1968). 'Thunder, Blood, and the Nicknaming of God's Creatures'. *The Psychoanalytic Quarterly* 37: 353–99.

FÜRER-HAIMENDORF, Christoph von (1967). *Morals and Merit*. Weidenfeld and Nicolson, London.

GARVAN, John M. (1964). *The Negritos of the Philippines* (ed. Hermann Hochegger). Verlag Ferdinand Berger, Vienna.

GEDDES, W. R. (1961). *Nine Dayak Nights*. O.U.P., London.

GEERTZ, Clifford (1975). *The Interpretation of Cultures*. Hutchinson, London. (Original impression 1973, Basic Books, New York.)

HORTON, Robin (1962). 'The Kalabari World-view: an Outline and Interpretation'. *Africa* 32: 3: 197–220.

—— (1967a). 'African Traditional Thought and Western Science; Part I. From Tradition to Science'. *Africa* 37: 1: 50–71.

—— (1967b). 'African Traditional Thought and Western Science; Part II. The "Closed" and "Open" Predicaments'. *Africa* 37: 2: 153–87.

JENSEN, Erik (1974). *The Iban and their Religion*. Clarendon Press, Oxford.

LEE, Richard B. and DEVORE, Irven (eds.) (1968). *Man the Hunter*. Aldine-Atherton Press, Chicago.

LIENHARDT, Godfrey (1961). *Divinity and Experience: the Religion of the Dinka*. Clarendon Press, Oxford.

MEDWAY, Lord (1969). *The Wild Mammals of Malaya*. O.U.P., London.

MIJSBERG, W. A. (1940). 'On a Neolothic Palae-Melanesian Lower Jaw Found in a Kitchen-Midden at Guak Kepah, Province Wellesley, Straits Settlements'. In *Proceedings of the Congress of Prehistorians of the Far East, Singapore 1938* (eds. F. N. Chasen and M. W. F. Tweedie), pp. 100–18. Government Printing Office, Singapore.

MIKLUCHO-MACLAY, N. von (1878). 'Dialects of the Melanesian Tribes in the Malay Peninsula'. *Journal of the Straits Branch of the Royal Asiatic Society* 1: 38–44.

NEEDHAM, Rodney (1967). 'Blood, Thunder, and Mockery of Animals'. In *Myth and Cosmos* (ed. John Middleton), pp. 271–85. The Natural History Press, Garden City, New York. (Originally published in *Sociologus* 14 (1964): 136–49.)

—— (1972). *Belief, Language, and Experience*. Blackwell, Oxford.

—— (1975). 'Polythetic Classification: Convergence and Consequences'. *Man* N.S. 10: 3: 349–69.

POORE, M. E. D. (1964). 'Vegetation and Flora'. In *Malaysia: a Survey* (ed. Wang Gungwu), pp. 44–54. Donald Moore Press, Singapore.

PORÉE-MASPERO, Eveline (1961). 'Kron Pali et Rites de la Maison'. *Anthropos* 56: 179–251, 548–628, 883–929.

RADCLIFFE-BROWN, A. R. (1922). *The Andaman Islanders*. C.U.P.

RAJAH, Nirmala (1974). 'The "Indianised" Culture of North-west Malaya'. Unpublished M.A. thesis, The Australian National University, Canberra.

RENTSE, Anker (1933). 'Notes on Malay Beliefs'. *Journal of the Malayan Branch of the Royal Asiatic Society* 11: 2: 245–51.

—— (1937). 'Panganerne: Malayas Jungledvaerge'. *Geografisk Tidsskrift* 40: 110–36.

RICHARDS, P. W. (1952). *The Tropical Rain Forest: an Ecological Study*. C.U.P.

ROSS, Gillian (1971). 'Neo-Tylorianism: a Reassessment'. *Man* N.S. 6: 1: 105–16.

SCHEBESTA, Paul (1928). *Among the Forest Dwarfs of Malaya* (trans. Arthur Chambers). Hutchinson, London.

—— (1952). *Die Negrito Asiens: Geschichte, Geographie, Umwelt, Demographie und Anthropologie der Negrito*. Studia Instituti Anthropos, Vol. 6. St. Gabriel-Verlag, Vienna-Mödling.

—— (1954). *Die Negrito Asiens: Wirtschaft und Soziologie*. Studia Instituti Anthropos, Vol. 12. St. Gabriel-Verlag, Vienna-Mödling. Partially translated by Frieda Schütze, Human Relations Area Files, 1962.

—— (1957). *Die Negrito Asiens: Religion und Mythologie.* Studia Instituti Anthropos, Vol. 13. St. Gabriel-Verlag, Vienna-Mödling. Partially translated by Frieda Schütze, Human Relations Area Files, 1962.

—— (1961). *Ursprung der Religion: Ergebnisse der Vorgeschichtlichen und Völkerkundlichen Forschungen.* Morus-Verlag, Berlin.

SCHMIDT, Wilhelm (1910). *Die Stellung der Pygmäenvölker in der Entwicklungsgeschichte der Menschen.* Stuttgart.

—— (1931). *The Origin and Growth of Religion: Facts and Theories* (trans. H. J. Rose). Methuen, London.

SCHNEIDER, David M. (1976). 'Notes Toward a Theory of Culture'. In *Meaning in Anthropology* (eds. Keith H. Basso and Henry A. Selby), pp. 197–220. University of New Mexico Press, Albuquerque.

SHEPPARD, Mubin (1972). *Taman Indera: Malay Decorative Arts and Pastimes.* O.U.P., Kuala Lumpur.

SKEAT, Walter William (1900). *Malay Magic.* Macmillan, London.

—— (1901). *Fables and Folk-tales from an Eastern Forest.* C.U.P.

—— and BLAGDEN, C. O. (1906a). *Pagan Races of the Malay Peninsula*, Vol. 1. Macmillan, London.

—— (1906b). *Pagan Races of the Malay Peninsula*, Vol. 2. Macmillan, London.

SKORUPSKI, John (1976). *Symbol and Theory: a Philosophical Study of Theories of Religion in Social Anthropology.* C.U.P.

SNELL, C. A. R. D. (1949). 'Human Skeletal Remains from Gol Ba'it, Perak, Malay Peninsula'. *Acta Neerlandica Morphologiae Normalis et Pathologicae* 6: 1–25.

SPERBER, Dan (1975). *Rethinking Symbolism* (trans. Alice L. Morton). C.U.P.

SPIRO, Melford E. (1969). 'Discussion'. In *Forms of Symbolic Action* (ed. Robert F. Spencer), pp. 208–14. American Ethnological Society, University of Washington Press, Seattle.

STARGARDT, Janice (1973). 'The Extent and Limitations of Indian Influences on the Protohistoric Civilizations of the Malay Peninsula'. In *South Asian Archaeology* (ed. N. Hammond), pp. 279–303. Duckworth, London.

THOMAS, David and HEADLEY, Robert K., Jr. (1970). 'More on Mon-Khmer Subgroupings'. *Lingua* 25: 398–418.

TOBING, Philip Lumban (1956). *The Structure of the Toba-Batak Belief in the High God.* J. van Campen, Amsterdam.

TREVOR, J. C. and BROTHWELL, D. R. (1962). 'The Human Remains of Mesolithic and Neolithic Date from Gua Cha, Kelantan'. *Federation Museums Journal* N.S. 7: 6–22.

TURNBULL, Colin M. (1961). *The Forest People.* Chatto and Windus, London.

—— (1965). *Wayward Servants: the Two Worlds of the African Pygmies.* The Natural History Press, Garden City, New York.

TWEEDIE, M. W. F. (1970). *Common Birds of the Malay Peninsula.* Longman Malaysia, Kuala Lumpur.

WILKINSON, R. J. (1932). 'Some Malay Studies'. *Journal of the Malayan Branch of the Royal Asiatic Society* 10: 1: 67–137.

—— (1959a). *A Malay-English Dictionary*, Part 1. Macmillan, London.

—— (1959b). *A Malay-English Dictionary*, Part 2. Macmillan, London.

INDEX

Abdullah bin Sepien, Encik, 146n
Aboriginal Malays, 37n, 38n, 68n, 87.
  See also Jakun
Africa, 1, 218
afterworld, 49–50, 102n, 138n, 207;
  characteristics of, 48, 50, 110, 111,
  112, 113; gaining entry to, 115, 117,
  118, 119, 122, 127; location of, 49–50,
  51; state of shadow-souls in, 93, 96,
  97, 137. *See also cemampeng*
agriculture, 13–14, 15, 40, 61–2, 131;
  beliefs about crops, 61–2; magic in,
  22
Allah, 83, 84, 88, 98, 108, 142, 170, 172,
  173, 204
Andaman Islands, 1, 2, 220
animals, classification of, 74–6
animism, 22, 23
Aring River, 3, 5, 9, 27, 42, 119, 140

Baal, Jan van, 219, 220
babies, 99; burial of, 120–2; magical
  protection of, 91, 100–1. *See also*
  foetuses
Baling, 3
banana plant, 83, 85, 89, 90, 93
bark platforms, 34, 57, 112, 137, 147n,
  148, 151–2, 153
Batek 'Iga', 3, 5, 22, 71, 135
Batek Nòng, 3–5, 27, 36n, 38, 40n, 47,
  48, 49, 50, 67n, 68n, 71, 86, 87, 92,
  102n, 115, 118, 119, 145n, 155, 161,
  168, 173–4, 184, 185, 188, 189, 197,
  203, 207, 208, 210, 211, 213
Batek Tè', 5
Batek Teh, 5, 27, 41, 43n, 49, 64, 71, 76,
  80, 90, 94, 100, 104n, 118, 119, 120,
  152, 153n, 163, 174–5, 176, 186–8,
  189, 196, 206, 209, 211
Batu Balok, 43–5, 51; as home of *hala'*-
  tigers, 132, 136–7, 138, 140, 154; as
  home of thunder-god, 150, 164, 172,
  175; as source of fruit blossoms, 47,
  167, 170, 171
Batu Hala', 43n, 175, 188. *See also* Batu
  Balok
Batu Keñam, 41, 42–3, 171, 203; as
  home of thunder-god, 44, 45, 142,

164, 165, 168, 172; as source of fruit
  blossoms, 47, 150, 167; origin of,
  42–3, 56, 126, 164
Batu Rib'm, 46–7, 48, 50, 180, 183,
  197
bearcat, 62–3, 71, 76, 202
bees, 42, 44, 59–61, 67, 80, 163, 165,
  167, 206
Begjeg, Begjag, 179, 180, 181, 183, 190,
  191, 200
Benjamin, Geoffrey, 28
Berlin Ethnographical Museum, 189
Bertram, 96
Besisi, 120n
birth, 22, 88, 90, 98–102, 106, 120, 121
birth-hut, 98–9, 100, 101
Blagden, C. O., 2, 36n, 38n
blood, 63, 80, 89–90, 96, 97, 114, 122;
  as medicine, 93, 106, 107, 109. 110;
  in blood sacrifice, 77, 93, 156, 157,
  158, 159, 160, 179, 198; menstrual,
  76, 90, 98, 100, 159; of superhuman
  beings, 62, 112, 124–5, 129, 132, 134,
  136, 208; role in development of
  foetus, 88, 89, 96, 98
blood *lawac*. *See lawac* prohibitions,
  'blood *lawac*'
blood sacrifice, 23, 68, 69, 77, 89, 93,
  106, 142, 155–60, 169, 179, 182, 183,
  186, 196, 198, 203, 219. *See also*
  thunderstorms, rituals to deter
blowpipes. *See* equipment, hunting
bodies: of dead, 111–12, 113, 114, 115,
  117, 129, 137, 139; of humans, 88–91,
  107, 128, 133, 149, 155, 202, 204; of
  superhumans, 124, 125, 126, 128, 169.
  See also corpses; tiger-form bodies
body decorations, 152–3, 154
bomoh (healer), 130
bones, 88, 112, 114, 117, 168n
Bonsu, 174, 203
Borneo, 28, 62, 65n, 207
breath, 89, 90, 92, 97, 109, 110, 122
Buddha, Buddhism, 185, 186
burial, 110, 113, 114–19, 120, 137–8,
  143; earth, 111, 114, 115, 119, 120,
  122, 138n. *See also* tree-burial
burial platform, 116, 138n

Burma, 1

Cambodia, 188
camps, 10–11, 15–21 *passim*, 53, 98–9
cane. *See* trade, rattan
cemam: prohibited sexual behaviour, 77, 94, 102–3, 156, 166, 181; disease, 77, 103, 108, 166, 181
cemampeng, cepeg'n, Cepèng (land of the dead), 49, 96, 113. *See also* afterworld
cemròy, cenoi, Ćenoi, 38, 47, 130, 133, 138n, 139, 161, 173, 181, 183n, 189, 194, 195, 198, 214. *See also* superhuman beings, seasonal fruit (*hala' tahun*)
centre of world, 36, 43, 45, 46, 48, 51, 168, 179
Cheka River, 5
Chemam (superhuman being), 181, 206. *See also* cemam
Chemioi, Ćimioi, 180, 200
Chiku River, 3, 5
children, 15, 17, 18, 20–1, 79, 83, 91, 112, 121, 122, 156, 198, 199
Chinese, 87
Christianity, 221
clouds, 39, 40, 68, 77, 125, 163, 165, 197, 203, 210; as solid layer in sky, 36–7, 38, 51, 173, 175, 188, 205
Cole, Sonia, 1
coolness, 41, 50, 53, 55, 153, 175; in curing, 106, 107, 108, 109, 110, 133, 151; of superhuman beings, 124, 125, 137
copulation, beliefs about, 98, 101
corpses, 38–9, 111, 112, 113, 114, 115, 116, 117, 118, 119, 120, 122, 127, 137
cosmology, 33–52, 176, 217
creator beings, 83–4, 126, 193, 194, 197, 202
Cuisinier, Jeanne, 133n
curing, 89, 93, 131, 133; techniques for, 102, 104n, 105–9, 127, 129, 130, 219; shaman's role in, 109, 134, 139, 150–51, 155, 170

dancing, 130, 149, 151, 153, 154
darts, poison. *See* equipment, hunting
death, 22, 82, 85, 88, 91, 92, 96, 97, 109–23 *passim*, 125, 126, 133, 137–9, 140, 166, 170
deities, 22, 26, 38, 51, 76, 79, 85, 97, 133, 143, 156, 158, 159, 160, 161–

215; ancestor, 191–3. *See also* earth deity; Ta' Ped'n; thunder-god; Tohan
Dentan, Robert K., 28, 80n
Department of Orang Asli Affairs. *See* J.O.A.
dew (*mun*), 59, 112, 116, 124–5, 127, 132, 133, 136, 150, 151, 153
Dharaṇī, 185
Diffloth, Gérard, 188
directions, cardinal, 39, 45, 50–1, 52, 172
diseases, 55, 67, 88, 89, 95, 97, 100, 105–10, 114, 125, 128, 129, 133, 150, 219; as punishment, 77, 80–2, 94, 166, 182, 209; causes of, 41, 53, 93, 102–5, 187; prevention of, 91, 100, 101
divorce, 10, 86
dragon. *See naga', naga*; earth deity, *naga'*
dreams, 93, 94–5, 96, 97, 113, 123, 128, 129, 145, 220; as source of information from superhuman beings, 61, 105, 106, 108, 127, 130, 134–5, 136, 143, 144, 149, 166, 171, 204
dung-beetle, 34n, 35, 179, 197, 202

earth: destruction of, 35, 36, 45, 53, 65, 72, 79, 127, 169, 202–3; layers of, 36, 147n; origin of, 33–6, 126, 184, 192, 201, 202, 203, 207; (soil), 6, 7, 33n, 34, 35, 83, 88, 89, 104, 164, 167, 175, 193, 202. *See also* floods, up-welling
earth deity, 70, 164, 165, 168–9, 170, 172, 174, 184–8, 198, 214, 215; Manoij, Manoid, 177, 179, 180, 182, 183, 184, 185, 186, 193; *naga'*, 63, 69, 72, 74, 76, 77, 80, 164, 168, 169, 173, 175, 176, 186, 188, 208, 210, 211, 214, 215; Takel, 176, 177, 179, 180, 182, 183, 184, 185, 186; Ya', 157, 164, 165, 168, 169, 173, 184, 186, 187, 192, 202, 203, 208, 219. *See also naga', naga*; earth-snake
earth-snake, 63, 69, 70, 127, 143, 155, 156, 157, 158, 159, 219. *See also naga', naga*; earth deity, *naga'*
east-west axis, 50, 51, 52, 164n, 174, 180, 184, 185, 212, 214
eclipses, 39n, 40
economy, 11–21, 213
Emergency (communist insurrection), 9

environment: natural, 6–9, 53–82 *passim*, 103–4, 203–4, 219; social, 9
equipment: domestic, 10, 17, 20, 21; fishing, 21; gathering, 16–17, 87; hunting, 12, 16–17, 19, 20, 21, 66, 74, 87, 116, 164
Evans, I. H. N., 23, 39n, 46, 50n, 65n, 71n, 118, 161, 162, 174, 177, 181, 182, 185, 186, 191–2, 203, 205, 209, 211

family, conjugal, 9, 10
fire, 93, 100, 104, 120, 175, 176, 188, 205; aversion of superhumans and dead to, 111, 113, 116, 122, 125, 129, 137, 153; origin of, 126, 184, 207
firmament, 33, 34, 36–8, 39, 41, 42, 43, 51, 52, 66, 113, 147, 148, 155, 180, 182, 183, 202; as home of super-human beings, 45, 54, 58n, 59, 124, 128, 167, 170, 171, 179, 214; as location of afterworld, 49, 111, 112, 128; as source of fruit blossoms, 47, 48, 56
first fruits ceremony, 59, 61, 67, 175
fishing, 12, 13, 21, 182–3; lack of magic for, 22
floods, 14, 36, 56, 57, 59, 68, 69, 87, 95, 150, 151, 175, 185, 186, 187, 188, 189, 199, 214, 219; up-welling, 65, 69, 70, 72, 79, 155, 165–6, 169, 174, 175, 182, 185, 187, 188, 201, 203, 211, 212
flowers, 64, 105, 113, 115, 124, 127, 128, 143, 152, 198. *See also* fruit blossoms
foetuses: acquisition of souls, 92, 93, 96, 98, 111, 170, 189, 205; development of body, 88, 89, 90, 93, 94n, 96, 98
folk-tales, 24, 40, 176, 179
food avoidances, 95, 103
forest: as source of danger, 67–82; as source of food, 54–67; Batek attitudes toward, 53–4, 67, 82, 86, 219
Freeman, Derek, 159
fruit, 7, 8, 9, 12, 14, 50, 55–9, 80, 106, 150, 159, 216; connections with superhuman beings, 43n, 113, 125, 126, 161, 165, 171, 174, 198, 204, 205, 207, 209; origin of, 55, 56, 163
fruit blossoms, 34, 38, 42, 44, 46, 47, 48, 50, 56, 57, 59, 60, 61, 67, 69, 113, 125, 127, 131, 150, 159, 167, 168, 170, 171, 173, 174, 175, 176, 189, 195, 218, 219

fruit island, 38, 47, 48, 173, 174, 203, 210
fruit production, Negrito theories of, 38, 46, 48, 56–7, 127, 170–1, 173, 174, 184, 186, 198, 199, 201, 204, 205, 208; role of thunder-god in, 56–7, 158–9, 160, 167, 175, 176, 179, 181, 189, 211, 214
fruit seasons, 11, 12, 14, 38, 44, 56–7, 150, 160, 167, 168, 175, 198, 199, 203
'functions' of superhuman beings, 199, 200, 201–5, 212, 213, 218
Fürer-Haimendorf, Christoph von, 72

game, 12–13, 19–20, 62–6, 116, 219
gathering, 11–12, 16–18
gelong, galogn, 39, 40, 180, 182, 194, 197
gening (shaman's assistant), 130–1, 138, 145, 154, 155
ghosts, 22, 23, 44, 81, 113–14, 118–23, 129, 191; ritual to deter, 114. *See also* stone-ghosts
gibbons, 12, 64, 65–6, 75, 76, 114; as images of deities, 165, 175, 176, 181, 182, 183, 194, 196, 205–6, 207, 209, 210
Gobar. *See* thunder-god, Gobar
graves, 112, 116, 117, 118, 119, 120, 121, 135, 136, 137; fear of, 116, 117, 118–19, 135
Gunung Kenderong (Mount Kender-ong), 183
Gunung Kerunai (Mount Kerunai), 183
Gunung Tahan (Mount Tahan), 45n, 147n, 187

hair, 87, 90, 173, 181, 182, 186, 209; amulets of, 91, 101; origin of human, 88; ritual burning of, 143–4, 155
hala'-tigers, 44, 45n, 47, 59, 61, 132, 135, 136, 137, 138, 139, 140, 141. *See also* tiger-form bodies
Hanei, 176
Hanuman (the monkey-god), 206
haya' tebew (large shelters used in singing sessions), 34, 57, 151, 152
headmen (*penghulu*), 11, 131
hearts, 83, 85, 89, 90, 92, 96, 97, 109, 110, 122, 125, 132, 136
heat, 41, 53, 87, 93, 104, 109, 110, 116, 124, 137, 153, 163, 210n

honey, 8, 12, 44, 55, 59–61, 163
Horton, Robin, 218
hot/cold distinction, 40–1, 50, 53, 93, 128
human beings, 83–123; components of, 88–97, 111; origin of, 83–6, 92, 93, 192, 193, 201. *See also* life-soul (*ñawa'*); shadow-souls (*bayang*)
hunting, 12–13, 16, 19–20, 21; magic in, 22, 66–7

image-role sets, 200, 201, 210, 211; consolidation of, 201, 210, 211–12; differentiation of, 201, 210, 212–13
images, 24, 57, 177, 199, 200, 201, 205–10, 212, 216; of earth deity, 168, 184, 185, 186, 214–15; of thunder-god, 165, 173, 174–5, 179, 181, 182, 183, 194, 196–7, 214; of other deities, 169, 170, 182, 183, 215
incense, use of, 59, 61, 135, 136, 138, 143, 145, 149, 153, 155, 175; at grave, 111, 116, 117, 126, 137; in curing, 65, 107, 127, 130; to attract superhuman beings, 129, 144, 154
Indianized settlements, 40, 48
Indo-China, 87
Indonesia, 48, 52, 184, 187, 188
internal organs, 88–9, 114. *See also* hearts
invocations, 143, 157, 158, 159, 198, 219
Islam, 22, 30, 52, 86, 221

Jahai, 29, 35, 46, 47, 48, 50, 177, 181, 182, 183–4, 185, 189, 195, 196, 197, 198, 209
Jah Hut, 102n
Jakun, 37n, 85, 149
Jalan, 179, 180, 182, 183n
Jamoi, 179, 180, 182
Japanese army, 5
Java, 113n
Jawac (Batek Nòng deity), 155, 156, 173, 184, 207
Jawéc (Batek Nòng deity), 38, 173, 174, 184, 189, 197
Jeho' Mahang (Mahang Tree), 47
J.O.A. (Jabatan Hal Ehwal Orang Asli; Department of Orang Asli (Aboriginal) Affairs), 3, 9, 11, 14, 45n, 62n, 131
Johore, 68n, 149

Judaism, 221

Kalchegn, 179, 184
Kapig'n, Karpeg'n, 182, 183, 184
Karei. *See* thunder-god, Karei
Kechau River, 3
Kedah, 3, 38n, 40, 46, 47, 48, 109n, 179
Kédang of Lambata, 187
Kelantan, 1n, 3, 5, 6, 27, 42, 46, 56, 65, 67n, 68, 86, 122, 133n, 183
Kelantan River, 114
Keniyam River, 42
Kensiu, 38n, 85, 109n, 177, 179, 183n, 184, 185, 189, 195, 196, 202, 208, 210, 212
ke'òy disease, 107, 109–10
keramat (sacred places), 46
kinship, 9, 177; of deities, 177–9
Kintaq, 47, 138n, 177, 179–81, 182, 183, 184, 185, 189, 190, 191, 193, 195, 196, 198, 200, 211, 212
Kuala Krai, 5, 46n, 114
Kuala Lumpur, 45n
Kuala Pahang, 47
Kuala Perak, 34
Kuala Tahan, 22, 135
Kuala Tembeling, 22
Kuala Trengganu, 34

Lah River, 5, 96
Land Dayaks of Sarawak, 188
languages: Aslian, 2–3, 46n; Austroasiatic, 2–3; Austronesian (Malayo-Polynesian), 2; Kintaq, 50n; Lanoh, 2; Malay, 2, 108, 122, 125n, 143, 144, 145, 146n; Mon-Khmer, 2; Negrito, 2–3, 6, 27, 50n; Senoi, 2, 3, 6, 50n
Lanoh, 2, 39n, 108n, 177, 181, 182–3, 185, 189, 196, 209, 211, 212
lawac animals, 63, 64, 65, 71–3
lawac prohibitions, 63, 65, 70–8, 79, 141, 155, 156, 158, 198, 203, 204; 'blood *lawac*', 73n, 76–7, 157; 'body *lawac*', 77, 81–2, 83, 94, 97, 126; enforcement of, 69, 80, 94, 160, 165, 166, 172, 173, 175, 176, 185, 214, 218; 'fire *lawac*', 73–6, 80, 157; 'laughing *lawac*', 63, 64, 65, 70–3, 157, 165–6
Lebir River, 3, 5, 9, 42, 50
leeches, 7, 63, 70–1, 73, 74, 157, 166
Lepah River, 5
life-soul (*ñawa'*), 85, 91–3, 96, 97, 114,

119, 122, 123, 127, 129, 137, 202, 205; fate of after death, 111, 169, 170; in blood, 90, 106, 110, 159; Tohan source of, 81, 83, 84, 170, 215. *See also* water life-soul (*ñawa' tòm*); wind life-soul (*ñawa' 'angin*)

lightning, 45, 68, 70, 78, 144n, 158, 182, 183, 186, 206, 210; as cause of disease, 77, 103, 166–7, 209; Negrito explanations of, 69, 164–5, 173, 175, 179, 181, 211. *See also* thunderstorms

Ligoi (the place of the winds), 180, 190, 200, 203

lime paste, 107, 109, 116

locations of Negrito dialect groups, 3–5, 6, 178 (map); Batek Dè', 3, 5, 6, 10; Batek 'Iga', 3, 5; Batek Nòng, 3–5; Batek Tè', 5; Batek Teh, 5; Jahai, 183; Kensiu, 177; Kintaq, 179; Lanoh, 182; Mendriq, 5, 177

log-drums, 34, 147, 148, 149, 152, 154

magic, 22, 55, 80, 135n, 140, 141, 161, 183, 220

magical stones, 133

Maherani Mohd. Ishak, Puan, 121n

Mah Meri, 120n, 121n

Malacca, 87

Malays, 6, 9, 22, 40, 47, 65, 104, 107, 111, 112, 115, 133n, 135, 140, 179, 187, 207; as images of deities, 181, 182, 200, 206, 208, 209; as source of food, 13, 55, 61, 62; religious influence of, 28, 30, 52, 214; rituals of, 61, 99n, 108, 139, 149, 195; separation of Negritos and, 86–8; spirit beliefs of, 23, 97n, 105, 219–20. *See also* traders, Malay

male-female distinction, 83, 84, 90

Mantra, 85, 87

Māra, 185

marriage, 9–10, 22

mats, 20, 62, 115, 137, 147n, 148, 153, 156, 180

Mạwạs, 163, 164, 165, 167n, 173, 174, 208, 211

medicines, 80, 98, 100, 102, 106, 107, 108, 114, 133, 134, 150, 168; plant, 19, 99, 100, 105–6, 134

Melanesia, 1

Mendriq, 5, 49n, 55, 56, 63, 71, 76n, 77, 80, 94, 95, 96–7, 104n, 126, 139, 143, 149, 157, 162, 174, 175–6, 177,

179, 185, 186, 188, 189, 198, 205, 209, 211

menstruation, 76, 90, 98, 100, 101. *See also* blood, menstrual

midwives, 99, 101

millipedes, 71, 73

monkeys, 12, 16, 19–20, 64, 65, 66, 71, 72, 73, 75, 76, 86, 87, 89n, 90, 173, 207

moon, 33, 36n, 39–41, 51, 80, 93, 166, 207; phases of, 40, 209

Mos Negritos, 209

musical instruments, 144, 154

myth, 22, 24, 39n, 78, 84, 86, 89, 126, 172, 174, 201, 212, 214

Nabi Adam, 84, 86, 111, 172

Nabi Noah, 87

naga', naga, 33, 35, 36n, 39, 168, 184, 186–8, 211. *See also* earth deity, *naga'*; earth-snake

naga'-people, 188

names, 63, 73, 79, 80, 81, 83; of deities, 162, 168, 172, 177, 180, 181, 193, 195, 199, 200, 201, 210, 212, 213; of humans, 101, 117–18, 152n; prohibitions concerning, 117–18

natural order, 70, 78, 81, 127, 160, 184, 202, 203, 204, 214, 217–18

Nạwạs, 163, 164, 165, 167n, 173, 174, 208, 211

Needham, Rodney, 28, 30n, 159

Nenggiri River, 5, 96

north-south axis, 50, 51, 84

odours, 39, 40, 59, 66, 73, 80, 119, 149, 156, 159; danger of mixing, 74–6, 77, 94n, 103, 166; for communication with superhuman beings, 66, 143, 144, 153, 154; of medicines, 106, 107, 108. *See also pel'èng* (raw meat smell)

offerings to dead, 118–19

Orang Asli (Malaysian aborigines), 2, 27, 70n, 87, 104, 118, 121n, 135n, 138n, 139, 141, 149

Orang Dusun of Borneo, 65n

orang hidop, 26, 161, 162, 183n, 191, 194

Orang Hulu, 149

Pangan, *pangan*, 1n, 64, 79, 86

Pa' 'Angkòl, 55

Pahang, 3, 5, 6, 9, 22, 41, 42, 118, 138n, 155

Pahang River, 47
Palah River, 43
pel'èng (raw meat smell), 38, 76, 79, 80,
     106, 158, 159
Penan of Borneo, 28
Penghulu Selé', 27, 83, 84, 176n
Perak, 47, 138n, 140, 179, 182, 183
Perak River, 46, 183
Philippines, 1, 2, 195, 220
Philippines, 1, 2, 195, 220
placenta, 99, 100
Ple, 189, 198
political system, 10, 11, 77–8
populations of Negrito dialect groups,
     3–5
Post Lebir, 3, 5, 213
potew, puteu, Putéu, 161, 176
pregnancy, 92, 98
prohibitions, 23, 28, 55, 59, 66, 67, 82,
     110, 142, 143, 167, 169, 173, 174;
     food, 61, 90, 100–1, 103, 168; to deter
     tigers, 79–80; to prevent diseases and
     accidents, 80–2; to prevent thunder-
     storms and flash-floods, 68–80
prohibitions, *lawac. See lawac* prohibi-
     tions
prohibitions, social. *See tolah*: prohibi-
     tions
prohibitions, sexual. *See cemam*: pro-
     hibited sexual behaviour; *lawac* pro-
     hibitions, 'body *lawac*'
Pygmies, 1

race, Negrito, 1–2
races, story of separation of, 86–8
rain, 36, 37, 45, 104, 112, 151, 152, 157,
     173, 190; 'hot', 187; Negrito explana-
     tions of, 25, 68–9, 70, 166, 171, 203
rainbow, 175, 186–7, 210
rain personified (Ujan), 45, 68–9, 171,
     172
rainy season, 187, 188
Raja Yạh (king of tigers), 43, 137, 138,
     139
Ramayana, 206
rankel, 46, 47, 180, 181
rattan collecting. *See* trade, rattan
Redam, 146, 147
Relai River, 3, 5, 43, 164, 175
reway: type of disease, 80–1; term for
     soul, 96
Rinjén, 176
rites of passage, 22, 23, 101–2, 117

'roles' of superhuman beings, 199, 200,
     201, 205–10, 213, 214
ropes supporting cosmos, 37, 45, 69,
     127, 130, 164, 171, 202, 212

sacred books, 22, 86, 87, 88
Sam River, 114
sandpiper bird (*kawaw kedidi'*), 34, 35,
     43, 84, 86, 172, 197, 207
Sang Kelmai, 47
Schebesta, Fr. Paul, 1, 3, 23, 26, 28, 29,
     36n, 38n, 39n, 46, 47, 48, 49, 71n,
     72, 108n, 126, 130, 140, 161, 173,
     175, 176, 177, 179, 180, 182, 183n,
     186, 191, 193–8, 199, 202, 205, 206,
     210, 211
Schmidt, Fr. Wilhelm, 1, 192, 194, 197
sea, 33, 34, 36, 39, 42, 51, 68n, 112,
     147, 148, 206; underground, 34, 36,
     51, 124, 127, 147, 166, 168, 169, 187,
     188, 203, 207, 208, 211
Selangor, 120n
Semai, 6, 28, 65n, 80n, 125n, 138n,
     144n, 153n, 188
Semang, 1n, 85, 109n, 194, 209
semangat, 96–7, 99n
Semaq Beri, 145, 149, 168n
semen, 96n, 98
Senoi, 2, 3, 6, 65n, 102n, 118, 120n,
     125n, 188, 195, 196
shadows, 38, 77, 93, 94, 97, 103, 115,
     149, 152, 156, 158, 159, 166, 175,
     186, 210
shadow-souls (*bayang*): of humans,
     93–7, 98, 105, 151; of humans after
     death, 81, 111, 112, 113, 114, 115,
     116, 117, 118, 119, 122, 123, 128;
     of shamans, 58, 59, 127, 130, 132,
     134, 136, 139, 140, 145, 147, 148,
     149, 150, 152, 154, 155, 156, 167; of
     shamans after death, 44, 137, 138; of
     superhuman beings, 54, 56, 57, 124,
     125, 126, 166, 169, 170. *See also* souls
     of the dead
shamans (*hala' té'*), 37, 76, 95, 108n,
     128–41, 153n, 161, 170, 207; activities
     of, 41, 58–9, 61, 65, 81, 127, 133–4, 144,
     145–51, 154–5, 156, 167, 168, 189,
     195, 214; after death, 44, 49, 114–15,
     137–9; becoming, 134–7; character-
     istics of, 93, 104, 113, 126, 131–3;
     147n; connection with tigers, 139–41
shaman-tigers, 132, 138, 139, 140

sharing, 10, 11, 21
Siamese, 87
singing, 21, 35, 108, 137; by super-
    humans and the dead, 66, 113, 126,
    127, 128, 153; to superhumans, 57,
    60, 67, 124, 129, 144, 154, 219; with
    trancing, 111, 130, 145, 149, 155
singing sessions, 23, 57, 109, 119, 130,
    132, 134, 139, 144, 150–5, 167, 219;
    equipment for, 34, 115, 143, 151–3;
    trancing at, 131, 145, 154–5
Skeat, W. W., 22, 23, 24, 36n, 37n, 38n,
    43, 50n, 52, 68n, 85, 87, 114, 120n,
    140, 179n
sky (ketò'), 36, 37, 39, 51, 80, 111, 155,
    157, 158, 173, 202, 210, 211; as home
    of superhuman beings, 175, 182, 183,
    191, 193, 207; layers of, 37, 147n,
    174. See also firmament
smells. See odours
snakes, 7, 64, 71, 72, 73, 124, 137, 168,
    175, 184, 186, 187, 188, 207, 208
social organization, 9–11
soil. See earth (soil)
songs, 35n, 59, 66, 139, 144–9, 187n,
    199; examples of Batek, 57–8, 60–1,
    146–8; learned from superhuman
    beings, 95, 112, 113, 127, 128, 129,
    130, 134, 136; of shamans, 76, 81,
    132, 134, 136, 150, 155; sung to
    superhuman beings, 108, 151, 154,
    219
souls. See life-souls (ñawa'); shadow-
    souls (bayang); souls of the dead
souls of the dead, 37, 47, 48, 49, 95,
    110–23 passim, 127, 128, 129, 155
South-East Asia, 1, 2, 48, 49, 184, 186
speech, as method of communication
    with superhuman beings, 141–2, 155
spells (jampi'), 59, 99, 102, 116, 117,
    117, 120, 121, 122, 138, 143, 155,
    175; examples of, 121–2, 142; learned
    from superhuman beings, 95, 127,
    128, 129, 135–6; use in curing, 80, 81,
    100, 101, 106, 107, 108, 109, 114,
    134, 139, 150
spider-hunter bird, 42, 43, 56, 164
spirit-mediumship, 139, 149, 150, 195,
    198, 214
spirits (hantu), 8, 55, 114, 187; Malay
    beliefs about, 23, 44, 61, 97n, 171,
    201, 220; Orang Asli beliefs about,
    102n, 105, 109n, 118, 139, 153n, 174,

189, 209. See also spirit-mediumship
Spiro, Melford E., 29n
stars, 40, 41, 42, 43, 51, 80
stone-ghosts, 119–23; defences against,
    121–2
stone pillars, 41, 42–8, 51, 52, 56, 59,
    69, 70, 124, 150, 164, 165, 167, 203.
    See also Batu Balok; Batu Hala'; Batu
    Keñam
sun, 37, 38–9, 51, 80, 93, 173, 184, 202;
    characteristics of, 33, 34, 40, 41, 49,
    112, 124, 183, 210; movement of,
    36n, 50, 168, 169, 179, 180, 218
superhuman beings (hala'), 23, 33–122
    passim, 124–60, 161–219 passim;
    communication with, 131, 132, 133,
    141–60; original (hala' 'asal), 49, 54,
    112, 113, 124–8, 129, 130, 132, 133,
    134, 135, 136, 141, 145, 150, 151,
    152, 153, 154, 155, 169, 184, 202,
    214; seasonal fruit (hala' tahun), 56,
    171, 189, 195; transformed (hala'
    senalin), 111–12, 125. See also cemròy,
    cenoi, Cenoi
Supreme Being, 193, 194, 197
symbolism, 24, 29, 65, 84, 95, 102, 117,
    141, 147n, 151, 159, 167, 220

Ta' Allah, 83, 84, 88, 172, 173
Tadoh River, 46
Tahan River, 3, 5, 140
Tahun (fruit deity), 56, 170–1, 189.
    See also superhuman beings, seasonal
    fruit (hala' tahun)
Taku River, 5
tangkal (talismans), 116, 117, 119, 120
Ta' Ped'n, 133, 189, 192, 195, 196, 197,
    198, 212; as Supreme Being, 161,
    162, 194; Jahai beliefs about, 183,
    184; Kensiu beliefs about, 177, 179,
    195, 202, 208, 210; Kintaq beliefs
    about, 180, 181, 191; Lanoh beliefs
    about, 182, 211
tattooing, 106–7
Tekam River, 168n
Temiar, 1, 6, 28, 46n, 115, 120n, 189,
    196, 198, 214
Temoq, 149
Teng, 174
Thailand, 1, 49, 185, 188, 209
thunder, 18, 56, 69, 78, 163, 164, 167,
    171, 172, 173, 181, 183, 186, 188,
    193, 195, 203; Negrito explanations

of, 164, 167, 173, 174, 175, 179, 181,
    183, 184, 205–6, 208, 210, 211, 212.
thunder-god, 3, 22, 51, 57, 63, 76, 78,
    90, 94, 100, 143, 155, 156, 157, 165,
    185, 190, 198, 212, 215, 216, 219;
    Gobar, 43, 44, 45, 56, 59, 61, 68, 69,
    74, 77, 78, 80, 103, 130, 150, 157,
    158, 159, 160, 163–8, 169, 170, 171,
    172, 186, 199, 202, 203, 206, 208,
    209, 210, 211, 214, 218, 219; Karei,
    3, 77, 163, 174, 175, 176, 177, 179,
    180, 181, 182, 183, 184, 186, 188,
    189, 193, 194, 195, 196, 197, 200,
    205, 206, 209, 211, 212
thunderstorms, 50, 68, 163, 188, 210,
    216; as punishment, 59, 61, 69, 70,
    72, 77, 78, 79, 94, 115, 155, 165, 166,
    167, 169, 174, 176, 179, 181, 182,
    196, 211; danger from, 8, 41, 67, 68,
    159, 199, 219; Negrito explanations
    of, 25, 43, 44, 45, 56, 68–9, 70, 143,
    171, 198, 199, 200, 201, 203, 214;
    rituals to deter, 9, 141–3, 155–60.
    See also blood sacrifice.
tiger-form bodies: of dead, 112, 113,
    115, 135; of dead shamans, 137, 138,
    140; of living shamans, 130, 131, 132,
    133, 134, 136, 139, 141, 145; of
    superhuman beings, 124, 126, 135,
    150, 154
tigers, 7, 43–4, 78n, 119, 132–3, 141,
    175, 176, 211; danger from, 8, 64,
    67, 79–80, 95, 132, 141, 159, 182;
    fear of, 23, 64, 67, 73, 118, 119, 135,
    141; guardian, 138, 161; means of
    deterring, 8, 79–80, 115, 116; sacred,
    44; spirit, 43–4, 139
tiger's fold, 43–4
tigers, superhuman. See hala'-tigers
Timor, 187
Tingring, 146, 147, 148, 187n
Tohan, Tuhan, 47, 55, 98, 130, 169–70,
    172, 189, 209, 215; as controller of
    life-soul, 83, 85, 92, 93, 110, 111, 125,
    137; as enforcer of tolah prohibitions,
    81, 103, 110, 113; role in creation of
    human beings, 81, 83, 84, 89, 90
tolah: prohibitions, 81–2, 103; disease,
    81–2, 103, 110, 113, 170
tops, spinning, 164–5, 167, 181, 205,
    208
trade: rattan, 13, 15, 16, 18–19; other
    products, 15

traders: Malay, 9, 12, 13, 53, 61, 106;
    Mon-Khmer, 2
trancing, 23, 93, 105, 111, 129, 130,
    132, 145–9, 156; in singing, 58, 109,
    131, 134, 139, 144, 150, 152, 154–5
tree-burial, 49, 64, 114–19, 120n, 122,
    137
trees: danger from, 8–9, 156; original,
    34–5, 37, 47
Trengganu, 5, 43, 86
tubers (wild yams), 11, 12, 15, 16,
    17–18, 21, 103, 106; beliefs about,
    54–5, 61, 62n, 141, 163, 184, 186,
    201, 204, 205, 208, 215, 219
Turner, Victor, 29
turtle-snake, 33, 34, 35, 36, 45, 168.
    See also naga', naga

umbilical cord, 91, 99, 101
underworld, 35, 39, 48, 51, 76, 147, 148,
    155, 165, 168n, 202, 203, 211
up-down axis, 50, 51, 172, 174, 176,
    180, 184, 212
upper world, 35, 37–8, 48, 51, 57, 155

variation in beliefs, 26–8, 30–1, 35, 37,
    48, 56–7, 83, 84, 125, 128, 158–9,
    165, 184, 211
Vaughn-Stevens, Hrolf, 189, 198

water life-soul (ñawa' tòm), 83, 84, 85,
    86, 92, 93, 103, 104, 112, 113, 124,
    125, 128, 137, 138, 170, 192, 204
were-tigers, 140
western Negritos, 3, 9, 24, 28, 34n, 38n,
    39n, 40, 41, 46, 48, 87, 130, 131, 133,
    139, 145n, 149, 161, 162, 163, 176–84,
    186, 188, 189, 195, 199, 206, 212,
    213, 214
wind, 36, 38, 60, 92, 96, 104, 109, 110,
    145, 170, 173, 175; danger from, 8,
    68, 141, 203; Negrito explanations 69,
    166, 171, 203; ropes, 45, 77, 164
wind life-soul (ñawa' 'angin), 83–5,
    91–3, 96, 97, 104, 107, 111, 125, 137,
    170, 204
wind personified (Angin), 45, 141, 171,
    172, 175
world-tree, Indian concept of, 48

Ya' Kedat, 55
ye'yò (irreverent rhyming), 80–1